超越概念——高等院校英语专业系列教材
Beyond Concept

总主编　何其莘　[美] 杨孝明

U0095468

美国文学史

A History of American Literature

（下）

主编　陈世丹　屈晓丽

编者　（以姓名拼音首字母为序）

陈世丹　李金云　屈晓丽　史岩林　苏　凤

王阿芳　王桃花　吴银燕　吴泽庆　尹　宇

张东芹　张丽秀　赵　丽

中国人民大学出版社
·北京·

CONTENTS

PART V

AMERICAN LITERATURE IN THE MODERN PERIOD

(1900—1945)

Historical Introduction

The modern period in American literature refers to the period between the two World Wars, WWⅠ (1914—1918) and WWⅡ (1939—1945). It was a period that witnessed economical boom and recession and a period that underwent great social changes. It was a period of spiritual crisis, a time of turmoil and a time characterized by artistic experimentation and a time of literary prosperity. It was a period when America established its leadership in world politics, military as well as literature. In short, it was a period of great importance with lasting influence.

The First World War (1914—1918) The First World War, also called the "Great War," broke out in 1914. It was fought between the Entente Countries/Allies: Britain, France, Italy, and Tsarist Russia, and the Allied Nations: Germany and Austro-Hungary. America did not enter the war until the day when the US Congress formally declared war on Germany. It was April 6, 1917. While the war thrust Europe into a world of killing, blood, death, and chaos, it served as an important stimulating factor to American economic development. Between 1914 and 1916, the American industrial production increased gradually. By the end of the war, the United States had emerged as a new world leader with an expanding economy and the unmatched prosperity. In spite of that, with the ending of the war there was a prevailing new disillusionment, especially among writers. Americans were confident and optimistic when they initially participated in the war. But that cheerful mood was soon taken over by the brutality, savagery, cruelty, and horror of the war. Many Americans took to the battle field for the sake of patriotism, heroism, and the devotion to a great cause, "saving" civilization. To their disappointment, the war didn't change the world for the better. It caused heavy toll/loss of lives, and Europe was still plagued by turmoil and economic crisis which made the sacrifices meaningless. The victors, while made great sacrifices, also committed killing. The ending of the war brought with it a sense of failure and disillusionment. In America, the shift from patriotism to disillusionment was also intensified by the fact that the social problems existent before the war, such as racial discrimination, inequality between men and women, and so on, remained the same.

The Roaring Twenties (1919—1929) American economy suffered from an acute recession in 1920—1921, which is known as the post-World War I recession. But it soon recovered as soldiers returning from the battlefields re-entered the labor force and factories shifted back to produce consumer goods. The economy of the country successfully transitioned from a wartime economy to a peacetime economy. Mass production made it possible for the middle class to gain access to technological products like radios and cars. As the first mass broadcasting medium, radio enjoyed a "golden age," together with movies and advertising, it played a very important role in giving rise to the mass culture. With the expansion of the automobile industry, cars, no longer a luxury as they used to be before the war, now mass-produced, became a commonplace throughout the country. Its popularity not only led to the development of such industries as highway building, motels, service stations, and so on, but also enhanced mobility, which in a way contributed to urbanization. The period from 1923 to 1929 was the "thriving" stage of American economy marked by the enormous economic growth, such as the rapid rise of auto, electric, architectural, and iron and steel industries, and widespread prosperity. Now the USA became one of the richest countries in the world, with its culture becoming consumer-orientated.

The 1920s was an age of affluence. It was also an age of swift social changes and a decade of deep cultural conflicts, a time full of disturbing noises. Industrialization and urbanization generated excitement but also shock and chaos. The rise of a consumer-oriented economy and of mass entertainment became impetus of and helped to bring about a "revolution in morals and manners." The decade witnessed a huge conflict between the old and the new. Immigration, race, alcohol, evolution, gender politics, and sexual morality, etc. all became major cultural issues.

Prohibition Among the events that dramatically affected the American society was the issuing of Prohibition. On January 16, 1919, Prohibition was instituted with ratification of *The Eighteenth Amendment to the United States Constitution*. It was actually a major reform movement from the 1840s into the 1920s. The law prohibited the "…manufacture, sale, or transportation of intoxicating liquors within, the importation thereof into, or the exportation thereof from the United States…" On October 28, 1919, the American Congress passed the *Volstead Act* to enforce the law. But the law was not strictly implemented in most large cities. As a result, it led to an increase in organized crime, although alcohol consumption declined. Many became millionaires by bootlegging. During the "thriving" years of the 1920s, people were partying everywhere and indulging in a life of dissipation.

After years of endeavor, women finally won the struggle for suffrage. *The Nineteenth Amendment to the United States Constitution* passed in 1920 granted women the right to vote. The passage of the law was the major victory of the movement known as the First-wave Feminism Movement. The passage of the law also marked the end of this movement. The 1920s saw significant changes in the lives of women. The old mentality about the role of women was challenged and replaced by the new ideas that women could pursue both a career and a family successfully. Women began to receive higher education. Women, especially, young women, took part in a sexual liberation of their generation. Ideas like equality and free sexuality were very popular. These young, rebellious, middle-class women, labeled "flappers" by older generations, did a breaking-off from the rigid Victorian way of life. Unlike the older generation, these "new women" were less interested in politics but they were more concerned about personal fulfillment. They wore short dresses, raccoon coats, had short hair, a chin-length bob. They smoked and drank in public, celebrated the sexual revolution, and embraced consumer culture. Opposing to these new ideas and changes, the notion of the "feminine mystique" was produced, which re-stressed the women's role as housewives, causing frustration and dissatisfaction among many well-educated women.

In the 1920s, the American government tightened its law on immigration. Racial discrimination still existed. The Ku Klux Klan executed persecution on the blacks. The "Red Hunt" after the war, the Prohibition led to the contempt on and the widespread violation of law. Despite the soaring of economy, there was a prevailing mood of discontentment with the society. The justice of the war was questioned. The war did nothing to the world's problems. Serious social problems such as racial and gender discrimination existent before the war remained unsolved. Disillusion with the war prevailed. Darwin's theory of evolution and Nietzsche's statement that "God is dead" broke the myth of God. God was no longer the center of the universe. Men were left alone helplessly at the mercy of natural forces, obsessed by the loss of faith and the sense of dislocation. The development of modern science on the one hand enriched and facilitated human life, but on the other hand, it impelled men to be skeptical about everything, generating a strong sense that life was fragmented and chaotic and hence meaningless and futile. Industrialization and mass production intensified this feeling. The sense of spiritual disorientation and nihilism became the mood of the time. In summary, the 1920s was a period in which the economic boom was accompanied by the pursuit of pleasure and material comfort and simultaneously the prevailing pessimism.

The Jazz Age The 1920s is also nicknamed the Jazz Age. Jazz was introduced into the mainstream of American culture and became the most popular form of music for young people, but to older generations, it was immoral and threatening to old cultural values. Jazz played a significant part in promoting cultural changes during the period, and had a lasting influence on pop culture. Jazz was originally played by black Americans. It has a strong beat, with the characteristic of improvising, full of changes, free of control and spontaneous. It expresses an open, free, casual, and even bold and wild mood. It was seen to well represent the rebellious spirit of the time. The desire to break with the old tradition, to welcome changes, to follow the vogue of the day found its expression in the music. Hence the name, it was called the Jazz Age.

The Great Depression of the 1930s The "frenetic," "glittering," and "feverish" time was brought to an end by the sudden collapse of stock prices on Wall Street. The Wall Street crash occurred on October 29, 1929, also known as Black Tuesday, throwing America into what is later called the Great Depression, which also added to a worldwide depression throughout the 1930s. During this time, the American economy was stuck in severe recession. By the winter of 1932—1933, the country was caught in the deepest crisis since the Civil War, with women, the urban poor and all people of color suffering the most. People began to doubt and question the social system and the nation's way of life. President Franklin Delano Roosevelt issued the New Deal as anti-crises measures. The New Deal took effect and helped the country out of crisis.

The economic crisis between 1929 and 1933 intensified the contradictions already existent in the capitalist system and led to wars in the imperialist countries, which finally triggered the outbreak of the Second World War on a full scale. In America, after the economic crisis, the American monopoly capital was further concentrated. In 1941, the US entered the war. The Second World War greatly stimulated the American industrial production. By the time the war ended in 1945, the whole productive forces of the country had increased by 40 per cent compared with 1939.

The Development of Literature

The Influence of New Theories and New Ideas From the mid-19th to the early 20th centuries, the developments in natural sciences and the social sciences, and innovations in industry as well as in the field of art in Europe functioned as impetus for the rise of modernism in the United States. Darwinism and Marxism still influenced the writers, artists, and intellectuals of this period. Besides, German philosopher Arthur Schopenhauer (1788—1860), French philosopher of positivism Hippolyte Adolphe Taine (1828—1893), and German philosopher Friedrich Nietzsche (1844—1900) also exerted influence on the writers, artists, and intellectuals of this time. But more direct and more important influence came from French philosopher Henri Bergson (1859—1941) and French existentialism. Bergson put forward the theories of intuitionism and psychological time, viewing the interior "duration" and "*élan* vital" as the real existence, which could be perceived through intuition rather than experience. Existentialism held a negative view on life, believing that man's life is full of suffering, loneliness, and pain. These philosophies became the sources of the post-war pessimism, skepticism, nihilism, and anarchism. The keynote of literary writing in this period is "tragic sense of life." The development of psychology also contributed to the birth of modernism. Austrian neurologist Sigmund Freud (1856—1939) developed what was known as psychoanalysis, which put great importance on the unconscious or the irrational in the human psyche. Freud's interpretation of dreams was another influence on the development of modernism. In addition, American psychologist, William James' theory of "stream of consciousness," and Swiss psychiatrist, Carl Jung's theory "collective unconscious" and "archetypal symbol" were also contributing factors. Their theories, plus that of Freud, prompted the modernist writers to shift their attention from the external world to the inner world and to probe into the inner world of human reality.

The Historical and Socio-Cultural Background The First World War (1914—1918) serves as a dividing line between the 19th-century American literature and the modern American literature. The war and its aftermath had enormous impact on the postwar America. The war consumed countless property, took millions of lives, and traumatized the survivals. War means violence, devastation, blood and death, helpless in solving the existent problems, instead, leaving the world fragmented and chaotic. Traditional ideas and values and the "American dream" collapsed. After a short-time economic boom, a severe economic crisis broke out. The whole country was stuck in the ten-year depression. The world was disintegrated and turbulent, with a sense of unease and restlessness underneath, and spiritual and moral decline, which resulted in the feelings of fear, loss, disorientation, and disillusionment. New ideas and new approaches and techniques were needed to define and present the postwar life and the society. It was under these circumstances that modernism emerged.

The Impact of European Avant-Garde Art Prior to WWI, the modernist movement, labeled as the avant-garde movement, in painting, photography, sculpture, music, and so on exerted a great impact on American literature, catalytic to its reform and innovation. This influence was evident in the works of American modernist writers. For example, in 1909, Gertrude Stein (1874—1946), by then an expatriate in Paris, published her innovative fiction *Three Lives* (1909), which was a result of the influence of cubism, jazz, and other contemporary movements in art and music. In painting, both the French impressionist and the German expressionist artists tended to represent the human reality from subjective perspective, offering a highly personal vision of the world. This approach was employed in literature as a revolt against realism and naturalism, with the attempt to depict psychological or spiritual reality instead of reflecting external reality. The employment of impressionism and expressionism was apparent in the works of F. Scott Fitzgerald, William Faulkner, Eugene O'Neill, etc. Eugene O'Neill's plays like *Emperor Jones* (1920), *The Hairy Ape* (1922), etc. are typical plays written in the mode of expressionism. In America, cubism, a popular school of modern painting in the early 20th century also found its way into the works of American writers of the modern period. It emphasized the formal structure of a work of art and the multiple-perspective viewpoints, which gave the American writers the idea to depict the reality from multiple perspectives.

The Lost Generation The catastrophes of the war and traumatic experience it brought to people shattered people's belief in the former ideals and values and gave them a strong feeling of uncertainty and disillusionment. There was a prevailing new disillusionment, especially among writers. They rebelled against former ideals and values, but replaced them only by despair or a cynical hedonism. Disillusioned and disgusted by the frivolous, greedy, and heedless way of life in America, many writers and poets left America for European countries, esp. Paris France. They formed a community of writers and artists there experimenting with new modes of writing with other European counterparts. These "expatriates" who lived in Paris in the 1920s and 1930s were called the "Lost Generation," a label given by Gertrude Stein. Included in this group were distinguished artists such as T. S. Eliot (1888—1965), F. Scott Fitzgerald (1896—1940), Ernest Hemingway (1899—1961), and John Dos Passos (1896—1970). Writers of this group were disillusioned with former ideals and values and even with the so-called civilization of the capitalist society. In literary creation, they sought to break with the traditional and the obsolete and experiment with new approaches and techniques to capture the essence of the postwar life. In addition, many of them had war experiences and they used them as the basis for their writings.

The Waste Land Image American literature of the 1920s was characterized by a prevailing disillusionment, pessimism, and nihilism. T. S. Eliot's poem "The Waste Land" (1922) presents a picture of the sterility and chaos of the postwar western world, the decline of western culture and expresses the despair and depression of the postwar era. This waste land image is recurrent in the works of Eliot's contemporaries. F. Scott Fitzgerald, the representative of the Jazz Age, portrays a spiritual waste land of the age in his books. The theme of disillusionment and spiritual decadence is expressed poignantly in his novel *The Great Gatsby* (1925). Beneath the restlessness, pleasure seeking, there was only meaninglessness and emptiness, a kind of spiritual and moral deterioration and the collapse of ideals. As the spokesman of the Lost Generation, Ernest Hemingway gives a portrait of the expatriate group, the Lost Generation with his novel *The Sun Also Rises* (1926). His novels convey the sense of loss and despair among the postwar generation both physically and psychologically. William Faulkner illustrates the modern society as a wasteland through his own fictional world, the Yoknapatawpha County, which is not only the mirror of the decline of the southern society but also the spiritual decadence of the modern American society devoid of essential human values.

Literary Achievements in the 1920s The decade of the 1920s witnessed a flowering of literature so that it can be termed the second renaissance in the history of American literature. Heavyweight writers in great number emerged, many of whom gained international recognition and helped to promote the popularity of American literature in the world. In 1920, Sinclair Lewis published *Main Street* and in 1922, *Babbitt*. The year 1922 saw the appearance of a monumental modernist innovative work of art, T. S. Eliot's "The Waste Land." In 1925, Theodore Dreiser's masterpiece of naturalism, *An American Tragedy* came out. In 1926, F. Scott Fitzgerald's novel *The Great Gatsby* caught the attention of the public. In 1926, Ernest Hemingway brought out his novel *The Sun Also Rises*. The 1929 was signalized by two important modern novels, *A Farwell to Arms* by Hemingway and *The Sound and the Fury* by William Faulkner. American playwright, Eugene O'Neill, published three important plays successively in 1920, 1921, and 1922. These plays, *The Emperor Jones* (1920), *Anna Christie* (1921), and *The Hairy Ape* (1922), established him as an international playwright. Of the writers of this decade, Sinclair Lewis, T. S. Eliot, Ernest Hemingway, William Faulkner, and Eugene O'Neill were winners of the Nobel Prize in literature.

The literary thrive of this decade was also indebted to some other important writers who wrote and published their works then. Sherwood Anderson (1876—1941) published *Poor White* (1920) and *The Triumph of the Egg* (1921). Willa Cather (1873—1947), who continued to write in the realistic tradition, published *Professor's House* (1925) and *Death Comes for the Archbishop* (1927). Thomas Wolfe (1900—1938) published his first book *Looking Homeward, Angel* (1929).

Literary Development in the 1930s   America of the Depression era was shrouded in a prevailing despair and panic. The economic crisis and the rise of fascism in Europe set the keynote for American literature during this period. Writers were greatly concerned with social problems and the living conditions of the lower class. Literature at this time was characterized by its blunt and direct social criticism. The "social conscience" novels became prosperous again. The then proletarian writers, Marxists and their follow travelers, exposed and criticized the capitalist system, the cause of the Depression, and also spread their revolutionary ideas by means of fiction. Among them were John Dos Passos and John Steinbeck (1902—1968). John Dos Passos was best known for his *USA* trilogy composed of *The 42nd Parallel* (1930), *1919* (1932), and *The Big Money* (1936). The trilogy is a record of the history of America beginning with the Gilded Age through the First World War to the booming twenties. It shows how America as an industrial giant dominates and depersonalizes the individuals. John Steinbeck was preoccupied with the poor, working-class people and wrote about their struggle for a decent and honest life. His masterpiece *The Grapes of Wrath* (1939), a "social conscience" novel tells the story of the Joads, a poor family from Oklahoma. In search of a better life, the family embarked on a journey to California, which turned out to be a journey accompanied by pain, suffering, and death. With their journey, the author presents a landscape of decay and desolation. The author also expresses his sympathy with the poor and wretched and more importantly his belief in humanity and the future, and that's where he is different from other writers of his time. Another popular novel of his published in the same decade was *Of Mice and Men* (1937). He was awarded the Nobel Prize in literature in 1962.

The Second American Literary Renaissance   The 1920s and the 1930s were considered as the second American literary renaissance due to the emergence of the large number of great writers and the enormous quantities of books they created and the huge influence both national and international they produced, which enhanced American literature to a new height.

The Southern Renaissance The 1920s and 1930s also witnessed the revival of American southern culture and literature known as the Southern Renaissance. It is considered as the most striking literary development of the thirties. Important writers in this period included William Faulkner, Caroline Gordon, Elizabeth Madox Roberts, Katherine Anne Porter, Allen Tate, Tennessee Williams, Robert Penn Warren, and others, among whom William Faulkner was the most influential and famous. Different from the writers before the Southern Renaissance, writers in this period tended to deal with such major themes as the burden of history, the southern history being a history burden with slavery and military defeat, the existence of individuals in the conservative culture of the South where one's personal value was not important as compared to those of family, religion, community, and racial issues. Writers also experimented with modernistic techniques, such as stream of consciousness and complex narrative techniques in their artistic activity. The southern literature shares some distinctive features of modern literature. For example, it also expressed the sense of dislocation and alienation. It was central to the southern writing in the 1930s, which stemmed partly from the South's ambivalence about America's advance toward secularism, progress, prosperity, and power. The predicament, the desire to honor its past and the desire to desert it, led to a tension involved in the southern fiction of the 1930s. It dealt with the issues of class, caste, race, and gender, and produced "stories about being other." Faulkner gave voices to the poor, female, and the black. His fiction bears features of modern fiction, pessimistic, violent, brutal, and despairing. Welty wrote in the formalist tradition common with world modernism. Other southern writers of this time include Thomas Wolfe and Anne Porter.

The Harlem Renaissance In addition, the 1920s and the 1930s saw the thrive of Afro-American literature—The Harlem Renaissance. The Harlem Renaissance was a cultural movement between the 1920s and 1930s. At the time, it was known as the "New Negro Movement." The concept of "New Negro" was first introduced in the 19th century and became popular during the Harlem Renaissance. The term stressed African American assertiveness and self-confidence during the years following World War Ⅰ and the Great Migration, achieving a new image of pride and dignity, a striving after "spiritual emancipation," as a contrast to the "Old Negro." Its headquarter was in northern Manhattan, Harlem, where gathered African American writers, mostly newcomers from the South. The publication of Countee Cullen's "I Have a Rendezvous with Life (with apologies to Alan Seeger)" and Langston Hughes' poem "The Negro Speaks of Rivers" in 1921 marked the beginning of the movement. The peak of this "flowering of Negro literature" was between 1924 and 1929. The movement dated back to the late 1910s. The Harlem Renaissance was a burst of creative activity by African American writers and artists. African-American literature and art developed rapidly during this period. There emerged many important African American writers including Langston Hughes, Countee Cullen, Claude McKay, Zora Neale Hurston, and others, most of whom moved to Harlem during the renaissance. Through literature and art, they expressed their racial pride, challenged the pervading racism and stereotypes against the blacks, and promoted progressive politics, and racial and social integration and equality. The art that emerged in this period involved a wide variety of cultural elements and styles. The renaissance was more than a literary or artistic movement and it did a lot in promoting social development through proclaiming a new racial consciousness and advocating racial integration. It made it clear that the black experience was part of American cultural history in terms of culture and sociology. It redefined how America, and the world, viewed the African-American population. It encouraged the new appreciation of folk roots and culture. It contributed a lot to the rise of jazz. But in its attempt to create a new culture and art, the Harlem Renaissance could not sufficiently be immune to white, European culture. African American writers and artists were consciously or unconsciously drawn to the social norms and values created by the whites. The Harlem Renaissance continued throughout the 1920s and into the 1930s. It ended abruptly due to the Great Depression.

High Modernism   American literary modernist movement experienced three phases: early modernism, high modernism, and late modernism. The modernist movement between the end of the First World War and the beginning of the Second is referred to as high modernism. The term is specially used to describe literary modernism of this time. American modernist writers of this time include Ezra Pound, T.S. Eliot, William Faulkner, Ernest Hemingway and others. The American modernist movement reflected American life in the 20th century. The prevailing sense of disillusionment found its way into American literary works, which were becoming more and more cynical and more tended to explore the darker aspects of human nature. Artistically, American modernists abandoned traditional literary modes, doubting if they were adequate in depicting the harsh realities of the time. They experimented with all kinds of new approaches and techniques to capture the essence of modern life. They broke up the narrative continuity and coherence by omitting the transitions, expositions, explanations, and resolutions common in traditional literature so that their works were full of fragments which were well suited for presenting a picture of the modern world, a world that was fragmented. Instead of directly stating their themes, they endeavored to have them implied so as to create a sense of uncertainty, the kind of sense the modern world evoked. The works of American modernist writers covered a wide variety of themes concerning race relations, gender roles, sexuality, and so on. Affected by the trauma of the First World War or disillusioned with their war experience, many American modernist writers explored the psychological and spiritual wounds caused by the war. The economic crisis in America at the beginning of the 1930s was also the theme of their works. Another theme is the loss of self and need for self-definition.

Modernism

Modernism is a general term used to describe the widespread movement or a trend of thought concerning art, literature, architecture, music, and so on, which took place around 1850 and lasted for about a century. In a narrow sense, this term is specially used to refer to the modernist movement in literature and the other arts in the early decades of the twentieth century, especially after World War I (1914—1918). Modernism is characterized by its revolt against some of the traditional bases constituting the western society, culture, religion, and art. Modernists deliberately and radically sought to break with conventional notions and the established norms and experimented with new and even "shocking" modes and means of expression to reflect the reality of their time. The spiritual sources of modernism are from the thinkers who had questioned the plausibility of the traditional social systems, religion, morality as well as the traditional conception about human self. The catalytic factors of modernism include the development of natural sciences and social sciences, industrialization and urbanization, rapid social changes and the outbreak of WW I and its aftermaths, as well.

The origins of this movement can be traced back to the early 19th century. Two ideas originating in France had particular impact on modernist movement. The first was impressionism, a school of painting. The second was symbolism, whose beginning was marked by Fleur du mal, (1857), a poem by the French poet Charles Baudelaire (1861—1867). There were two thinkers who exerted major influences on the development of modernism in this period. They were biologist Charles Darwin (1809—1882), author of *On Origin of Species by Means of Natural Selection* (1859), and political scientist Karl Marx (1818—1883). From the late 19th to the early 20th centuries, the influential intellectuals and thinkers were Sigmund Freud (1856—1939), Carl Jung (1875—1961), Friedrich Nietzsche, and Henri Bergson (1859—1941). Important literary precursors of modernism at this time included Fyodor Dostoevsky (1821—1881), Walt Whitman (1819—1892), and others. From 1910—1930, the development of modernism entered a new phrase. Pablo Picasso shocked the world with his radical painting practice. In 1907, the first expressionist play came out. In 1909, futurism came into being. The year 1911 saw the first abstract painting. In 1913, Ezra Pound founded imagism. Modernism in this period assumed new characteristics. It preferred discontinuity to smooth change. It favored disruption, rejecting simple realism. All this showed that modernists were more radical, seeking to overthrow traditional norms and traditional social structure, as they were hindering progress. Two events, the First World War (1914—1918) and the Russian Revolution of 1917, further pushed modernism forward. Modernism which used to be a minority pursuit before the war came to permeate into the public life. It appeared in various forms and in various fields. For example, in painting, it appeared as Dada and in literature, it appeared as surrealism. Each of them sought to break with the traditional and the obsolete and experiment with new approaches and techniques, just as the poet Ezra Pound appealed to "Make it new" in 1934. The modernist movement between the end of the First World War and the beginning of the Second is referred to as high modernism. The term is specially used to describe literary modernism of this time. Modernist writers of this time include Ezra Pound, T. S. Eliot, Virginia Woolf, Yeats, Joyce, and others. By 1930, modernism had become part of the mainstream, either politically and artistically and had entered popular culture.

The core of modernism is its self-conscious break with tradition and desire for innovation. Many modernists believed that tradition should be abandoned so that new modes of artistic creation could be found. They stressed the freedom of expression, experimentation, the use of radically new and even primitive means. In literature this often meant the rejection of plots or characterization easy to understand in novels, or the defying of clear interpretation in composing poetry. Literary modernists were keen on disjunctive narratives, surreal images, and incoherence.

American literary modernist movement experienced three phases: early modernism, high modernism, and late modernism. In America, modernism as a literary movement reached its peak in the 1920s and ended by 1939. The American modernist movement reflected American life in the 20th century. In a quickly industrializing world, the pace of life was hastened, social norms, boundaries and structure were all being challenged and were dissolving and the individual was left alone, wandering, purposeless, with no identity. Loss of identity led to a feeling of isolation and alienation. In addition, the catastrophe of the First World War shook faith in western civilization and idealism about the country. The world was falling apart and violence, vagueness, and spiritual emptiness were all what were left. The Great Depression at the end of the 1920s and during the 1930s intensified the sense of disillusionment and crashed the optimism about the economic prosperity and stability of the country.

This prevailing sense of disillusionment found its way into American literary works, which were becoming more and more cynical and more tended to explore the darker aspects of human nature. Artistically, American modernists abandoned traditional literary modes, doubting if they were adequate in depicting the harsh realities of the time. They experimented with all kinds of new approaches and techniques to capture the essence of modern life. They broke up the narrative continuity and coherence by omitting the transitions, expositions, explanations, and resolutions common in traditional literature so that their works were full of fragments which well suited/reflected/vividly presented a picture of the modern world, a world that was fragmented. Instead of directly stating their themes, they endeavored to have them implied so as to create a sense of uncertainty, the kind of sense the modern world evoked. In this aspect, two American modernist writers are worth special mentioning. They are T. S. Eliot (1888—1965) and Gertrude Stein. T. S. Eliot's "The Waste Land" (1922) is considered to be a monument of modernist innovation. It is composed with a fragmented structure without an obvious central, unifying narrative, a reflection of the western culture, decayed and fragmented, a spiritual waste land. Gertrude Stein, a trail-blazing modernist, experimented with automatic writing and other modes of sentence structure as a means of rebellion. Her abstract writings have been compared to her friend Pablo Picasso's Cubist paintings, fragmentary and multi-perspective. William Faulkner's *The Sound and the Fury* (1929) is another good example of modernist novel.

The works of American modernist writers covered a wide variety of themes concerning race relations, gender roles, sexuality, and so on. Affected by the trauma of the First World War or disillusioned with their war experience, many American modernist writers explored the psychological and spiritual wounds caused by the war. The economic crisis in America at the beginning of the 1930s was also the theme of their works. Another theme was the loss of self and need for self-definition.

Other important American modernist writers include Ezra Pound (1885—1972), Eugene O'Neill (1888—1953), William Carlos Williams (1883—1963), Wallace Stevens (1879—1955), F. Scott Fitzgerald (1896—1940), Ernest Hemingway (1899—1961), and William Faulkner (1897—1962). Though largely a romantic poet, Walt Whitman is sometimes regarded as a pioneer of American modernist movement. Black writers also made a breakthrough in literature in American modernist movement.

Terms of Modernist Literature

Imagism Imagism was a poetic movement launched in England and America in the early 20th-century, lasting from 1909 to 1917. It was the first organized modernist English language literary movement and the prelude to the American literary modernist movement. It was a revolt against the sentimentality and discursiveness typical of much romantic and Victorian poetry. Short-lived as it was, it marked, in T. S. Eliot's words, "the starting-point of modern poetry."

The founder of the theory of imagism was T. E. Hulme (1883—1917), an English critic and poet. The most important influences on his thought were Bergson and, later, Wilhelm Worringer (1881—1965), German art historian and critic. Hulme founded the Poets' Club in London and had his two poems published in 1909 by the Club. They were known as the first imagist poems. Hulme advocated the use of free verse with an attempt to reform the contemporary poetry through it. In 1908, Hulme delivered his paper "A Lecture on Modern Poetry" to the club, in which he stated his ideas about modern poetry. In 1909, Hulme left the Poets' Club and started meeting with other poets in a new group. One prominent member of this imagist group was F. S.

Flint (1885—1960), an English poet and critic, and a champion of free verse and modern French poetry. In April 1909, the American poet Ezra Pound was introduced to the group. Later, Flint became a leading spokesman for imagism. Theoretically, he contributed a lot to the later imagist movement.

The March 1913 issue of *Poetry* carried an essay entitled "Imagism" written by Pound but attributed to Flint. This essay contained the statement about the poetic principles of the imagist group. And imagism as a movement was launched.

The principles are:

1. Direct treatment of the "thing," whether subjective or objective.
2. To use absolutely no word that does not contribute to the presentation.
3. As regarding rhythm: to compose in sequence of the musical phrase, not in sequence of the metronome.

The first principle indicates that the expression should be made as concrete as the "object" and abstractions should be avoided. Poets should resort to an image "which presents an intellectual and emotional complex in an instant of time." "Direct treatment" means avoiding the use of unnecessary words, particularly adjectives. This is a revolt against the overuse of rhetoric like the inversion of word order and overuse of adjectives. The second emphasizes brevity, the economy of words. That is, in Hulme's words, "absolutely accurate presentation and no verbiage." This can be seen as a reaction to the sentimentality and discursiveness typical of much romantic and Victorian poetry. The third suggests the rejection of conventional versification, pointing out the similarity between music and poetry.

To promote the work of the imagists, in 1914, Pound published an anthology with the title *Des Imagistes*. The book contained thirty-seven poems, including those by Richard Aldington, H.D. (Hilda Doolittle), Ezra Pound, F. S. Flint, Amy Lowell, William Carlos Williams, and James Joyce. It became one of the most important and influential English-language collections of modernist poetry.

Later, Pound left the group and went on to co-found the vorticists with his friend, the name of which was given by him in 1913. Around this time, the American imagist Amy Lawrence Lowell (1874—1925) moved to London. She replaced Pound as the leading figure of the movement. The imagist movement gradually declined after Pound abandoned it. During her leadership of the movement, Amy Lowell and other imagists expanded imagist principles into six:

1. Direct treatment of the "thing," whether subjective or objective.
2. To use absolutely no word that does not contribute to the presentation.
3. As regarding rhythm: to compose in sequence of the musical phrase, not in sequence of the metronome.
4. Complete freedom of subject matter.
5. Free verse was encouraged along with other new rhythms.

6. Common speech language was used, and the exact word was always to be used, as opposed to the almost exact word.

The additional three principles put emphasis on the freedom in subject matter, versification, and language.

Three anthologies edited by Amy Lowell, with the title *Some Imagist Poets*, were published respectively in 1915, 1916, and 1917. The 1917 anthology marked the end of imagism as a movement.

Although the movement didn't last for a long time, it played an important role in the history of 20th-century poetry. It was to have a lasting influence on later poets and poetic movements to come, such as the objectivist poets, the Beat Generation, the Black Mountain poets.

Symbolism   The term "symbolism" refers to the use of symbols as means of representation or the practice of endowing a symbolic meaning or character to something. A symbol is what that represents, something that is often of a more abstract nature.

One distinctive literary feature of romanticism is the employment of symbols as an effective mode of representation. Many writers and poets in this period favored the technique of symbolism, such as the England poets Percy Bysshe Shelley and William Blake, American novelists Nathaniel Hawthorne and Herman Melville, and American transcendentalist writers Emerson and Henry David Thoreau, and American novelist, poet, and literary theorist Edgar Allan Poe, to name only a few. As the key figures of the romantic movement, they either used recurrent or dominating symbols, or invested symbolic meanings to objects, or systematically made use of symbolic elements in their works. This artistic practice was rooted in the Puritan tradition of typology and the theory of "correspondences" of Emanuel Swedenborg (1688—1772), a Swedish theologian. American Puritan's mode of perception was chiefly responsible for the development of American literary symbolism.

In historical criticism, symbolism denotes a loosely organized literary and artistic movement in the late 19th century. It was initiated by a group of French poets, and later, it spread to other areas like painting and theatre. In literature, the beginning of symbolism was marked by the publication of *Les Fleurs du mal* (*The Flowers of Evil*, 1857) by Charles Baudelaire (1821—1867), a French poet, essayist, and art critic. Baudelaire was a follower of the American poet Edgar Allan Poe. He saw in him a precursor. His translation of Poe's works provided an initial impetus for the symbolist movement. Another important influence Baudelaire received came from the ancient theory of correspondences holding that the human mind is correspondent with the outer world, so is the material world with the spiritual world. Other three influential French poets are Stéphane Mallarmé (1842—1898), Paul Verlaine (1844—1896), and Arthur Rimbaud (1854—1891). They contributed a lot to the development of French symbolism in terms of its aesthetics, its goal, and so on.

Symbolism was largely a reaction against naturalism and realism, which were anti-idealistic styles seeking to represent reality with particularity, and to celebrate the humble and the ordinary instead of the ideal. In contrast, symbolism was in favor of spirituality and the ideal. The symbolist poets upheld the doctrine of "art for art's sake" inherited from Parnassianism, a French literary style between romanticism and symbolism. They believed in the supremacy of art over all other means of expression or knowledge. They held that art should represent absolute truths and the best way to do that was through indirect, suggestive, and metaphorical means, endowing particular images or objects with symbolic meaning. They also believed that there was another reality underlying the physical world. The best way to have a glimpse of the essence of this reality was through the subjective emotional responses. Thus, symbolists sought to represent individual emotional experience or describe the fleeting, immediate sensations of man's inner life and experience by using private metaphors or symbols, uniquely identifiable with the individual poet, so as to convey the state of the poet's mind and give some hint to the reality.

In technique, the symbolist poets were inclined to the use of free verse as a resort to escape rigid metrical patterns governing the traditional poetry. Another important technique is the use of symbolic imagery. Unlike the romantic poets whose symbols were unique and privileged objects, the symbolist poets were more extreme, investing all things with symbolic meanings. Besides, symbolist symbols were intended to evoke particular states of mind rather than primarily to describe. In terms of thematic matter, symbolists favored the themes of mysticism, mortality, and sexuality, as a revolt against the conventional poetic themes.

The French symbolist movement in poetry reached its peak around 1890 and began to decline rapidly in popularity about 1900.

As a vital part of the development of literary modernism, symbolism exerted a significant influence on European, England, and American literatures in the twentieth century. This influence was specially noticeable in the modern period, the decades after World War I. Many of the major writers of the period had strong affinities with symbolism, including T. S. Eliot, Wallace Stevens, W. B. Yeats, Hart Crane, James Joyce, Virginia Woolf, Gertrude Stein, and William Faulkner. Symbols or patterns of images, an integral component, often play a preeminent role in their works. For example, the persistent use of symbols is evident in such works as T. S. Eliot's poem "The Waste Land", James Joyce's novel *Finnegans Wake* (1939), and William Faulkner's novel *The Sound and the Fury* (1929).

Psychological Analysis Psychological analysis refers to literary criticism or literary theory based on the theory of psychoanalysis developed by Austrian neurologist Sigmund Freud (1856—1939) in the late 19th and early 20th centuries.

In the early decades of the nineteenth century, there emerged a literary critical approach which stressed the correlation between a work of literature and the psychology of its author.

The theoretical basis of this psychological criticism was the assumption that a work of literature, including its details and form, was inextricable with its author's personality. So during the romantic period, literary criticism was conducted to explain and interpret a literary work by referring to the author's personality, to establish the personality of the author by referring to literary works, or to experience the subjectivity or consciousness of the author through reading his/her literary work.

Since the 1920s, a form of psychological literary criticism known as psychoanalytic criticism has been widely employed in literary criticism. The basis of this literary critical approach is the theory of psychoanalysis developed by Austrian neurologist Sigmund Freud in the late 19th and early 20th centuries. Freud used the theory for the treatment of neuroses but soon he applied it to many other fields including literature.

The core of Freud's theory is the unconsciousness. In his view, the unconscious is where the socially unacceptable ideas, wishes or desires, traumatic memories, and painful emotions are repressed. The unconscious is a force that can only be recognized through the symptom with which it expresses itself. Freud proposes that the mind is made up of the conscious mind, the ego, and the unconscious mind composing the id and the superego. The id involves the instinct, libidinal, and other desires; the superego means the conscience, the internalization of social norms, and moral standards; and the ego functions to negotiate the conflicts between the id and the superego. Another important concept of Freud's theory is Oedipus complex. It denotes a boy's desire to sexually possess his mother, and kill his father, which is repressed in the adult's unconscious.

Freud compares artistic creation to dreams and neurotic symptoms. In his view, the creation of literature and the other arts is the vehicle of the fulfillment of wishes in the manner of imagination and fantasy because they are either denied or prohibited in reality by social norms or moral standards. The forbidden wishes are mainly sexual, that is "libidinal." They are repressed into the unconsciousness of the artist's mind by the "censor," the "internalized representative" of moral standards and social norms within each individual. They can only be fulfilled through fantasy in distorted forms which help to disguise their real motives. According to Freud, the Oedipus complex is the foundational source of all art, myth, religion, philosophy, therapy—indeed of all human culture and civilization.

Influenced by Freud, early psychoanalytic literary criticism would often treat the text as if it were a kind of dream, that is, the real or latent content of the text is repressed behind its obvious or manifest content. Critics analyze the language and symbolism, etc. of the text so as to arrive at the underlying latent content. The criticism of the author is very similar to psychoanalysis itself. Critics would treat the fictional characters as a psychological case study by referring to such Freudian concepts as id, ego and superego, Oedipus complex, penis envy, etc. Psychoanalytic criticism provides a new perspective for reading and analyzing a literary work of art and can throw light on the sometime baffling symbols, actions, and settings in it. However, it is not without limits. A great literary work is rich in significance and it also provides aesthetic experience. It should not be primarily treated as a psychological case study.

Stream of Consciousness   The term was first used by the American philosopher and psychologist William James (1842—1910) in his book *The Principles of Psychology* (1890) to describe the continuous flow of conscious and sub-conscious thoughts, feelings, and impressions in the mind. It was later applied to the world of literature. With the rise of modernism in the 20th century, it became an important literary technique. Besides William James, other theoretical precursors for the birth of it were Sigmund Freud and Henri Bergson. Freud laid emphasis on the play of basic drives and instincts, which were the basis of all subjective reality and through which the outside world was perceived. Bergson's idea on psychological time and consciousness had special influence on modernist novelists who adopted the stream of consciousness technique.

As a literary technique, stream of consciousness was the product of the time. It was innovated and used as a revolt against the traditional norms regarding artistic creativity, esp. realism. The stream-of-consciousness writers, Virginia Woolf in particular, attacked the realistic writers for their over emphasis on the external world, calling them materialists. To capture the essence of the time and to present the inner state and chaos, the inner reality of the modern people, they turned to explore and expose the complex and chaotic psyche of the modern people.

Stream of consciousness is primarily a technique used in fiction. As a mode of narration, it undertakes to present the natural flow of the character's thoughts, memories, feelings, sense impressions, and random associations. Stream-of-consciousness writing is usually considered as a special form of interior monologue. As a matter of fact, interior monologue and the term stream of consciousness are used interchangeably by some critics. The stream-of-consciousness novel commonly uses the narrative technique of interior monologue to present a character's thoughts directly, precisely as it occurs in his/ her mind. The author does not intervene, as describer, guide, or commentator, and does not put the mental process into grammatical sentences or into a logical or coherent order. In form, a stream-of-consciousness passage appears without punctuation so that the flowing thoughts continue without being interrupted. To represent the richness, speed, and subtlety of the mind working, the writer incorporates fragments of incoherent thought, ungrammatical constructions, and free association of ideas, images, and so on.

Probably the most famous example is James Joyce's *Ulysses* (1922), a complex representation of the inner states of the characters. William Faulkner's *The Sound and the Fury* (1929), a record of the characters' fragmentary and impressionistic mental responses to events; and Virginia Woolf's *The Waves* (1931), a complex novel presenting the psychological development of the six characters and their common conscious.

Bibliography

常耀信 . 美国文学简史 . 天津：南开大学出版社，1995.

胡荫桐 . 美国文学教程 . 天津：南开大学出版社，1995.

李维屏 . 英美现代主义文学概观 . 上海外语教育出版社，1998.

虞建华 . 美国文学的第二次繁荣 . 上海外语教育出版社，2007.

Abrams, M. H. *A Glossary of Literary Terms*, *9th Edition*. Beijing: Foreign Language Teaching and Research Press, 2010.

Bercovitch, Sacvan. *The Cambridge History of American Literature*, *Vol. 6*. Cambridge U.K. and New York: Cambridge University Press, 2002.

Levenson, Michael. *The Cambridge Companion to Modernism*. Shanghai: Shanghai Foreign Language Education Press, 2000.

http://www.britannica.com/EBchecked/topic/290310/interior-monologue 2012-08-12

Wikipedia, thefreeencyclopedia. http://en.wikipedia.org/wiki/Slaughterhouse-Five 2012, 7, 3; 2012-08-14

Ezra Pound

His Life and Writing Career

His Life

Ezra Pound (1885—1972) was born in Harley, Idaho Territory, the only child of Homer Loomis Pound (1858—1942) and Isabel Weston (1860—1948). Both parents' ancestors emigrated from England in the 17th century. From 1898 until 1900 he attended the Cheltenham Military Academy, where the boys wore uniforms and were taught to submit to authority. Pound thought independently and wanted to be a poet. Later he entered Hamilton College and the University of Pennsylvania, in which he studied Romance languages and literature. He received a master degree for arts in the University of Pennsylvania in 1905. In the following year, he won a fellowship for travel to Spain and Italy to prepare for his doctoral dissertation. He returned soon from Europe.

In the fall of 1907 he took a job as a teacher of Romance languages at Wabash College in Crawfordsville, Indiana. But his unconservative actions were unaccepted there. After teaching at Wabash College for two years, he was dismissed and arrived in London in August 1908, where he stayed almost continuously for 12 years. He met W. B. Yeats whom he thought the greatest living poet. They became close friends though Yeats was senior to Pound by 28 years. Their friendship is often treated as an example of friendship between generations.

Pound was convinced that London was to be the centre of a new renaissance. But his hopes were damaged in the waste of the First World War, and the consequent disappointment was to color the rest of his life's work. Pound married Dorothy Shakespeare in April 1914, who was introduced to him in February 1909. In 1924, he moved to Italy, during this period of voluntary exile, Pound became involved in fascist politics, and did not return to the United States until 1945. Pound came to believe that the cause of the First World War was finance capitalism, "usury" in his word. Usury usually refers to the taking of unnecessarily high interest in loans. Anti-Semitism often used this word for the economic illness of modern society. Pound's interest in anti-Semitism was based on this monetary theory. He gave a series of lectures on economics, and made contact with politicians in the United States about education, interstate commerce, and international affairs. It seemed that he was more interested in social reform than literature. Although Hemingway advised against it, on 30 January 1933 Pound met Mussolini, the notorious figure in fascism. During the meeting he tried to present Mussolini with a digest of his economic ideas and *The Cantos*. Mussolini looked through *The Cantos* and said it was entertaining. Later Pound told his friend that he had never met anyone who seemed to get his ideas so quickly. He broadcasted fascist propaganda by radio and recorded hundreds of broadcasts criticizing the United States, Roosevelt, and Roosevelt's family, and sometimes he talked about his idea about literature, economics, and Chinese philosophy.

In 1945, the death of Mussolini and Adolf Hitler marked the collapse of fascist world. Pound was interrogated by FBI and arrested on charges of treason. On 24 May he was transferred to the United States and was put in a steel cage without bed or communication. After several weeks, he began to break down under the strain. Medical staff moved him out of the cage and one of the psychiatrists examined him and declared Pound had symptoms of a mental breakdown. He was transferred to another place, being allowed to read. His imprisonment brought about an artistic recovery. He began to write *The Pisan Cantos*. In 1946, he was acquitted, but declared mentally ill which saved him from life imprisonment. He was moved to St. Elizabeths Hospital in Washington, D. C., where he spent the next 12 years. During his confinement, his friends, some literary figures tried to get him released. The jury of the Bollingen Prize—Library of Congress Award decided to recognize his poetic achievements rather than focus on his political interest. He was awarded the prize for Cantos 74—84 under the title *The Pisan Cantos* in 1948. But the award aroused a heated discussion in America and as a result it was the last time the prize was administered by the

Library of Congress. After continuous appeals from his friends, such as Robert Frost and Ernest Hemingway, Pound finally won his release. Pound returned to Italy and settled in Venice, where he died a semi-recluse, in 1972.

His Writing Career

In 1911, Pound, Doolittle, and Aldington lived in Church Walk and worked daily in British Museum Reading Room, where he was introduced to the East Asian artistic and literary concepts that would become so essential to the imagism. Under the influence of the scholar Ernest Fenollosa's unpublished notes, Pound became interested in Japanese and Chinese poetry. Beginning in 1912, Pound was exploring a new way of making poetry in an effort to break free from the mimetic. He named this new form imagism, which derived its technique from classical Chinese poems and Japanese Haiku. The movement got rid of poetry of excessive rhetoric, overly stated images or inessential details through the direct treatment of the "thing."

On the eve of the First World War Pound found the limitation of imagist movement, which in his understanding was sentimentalized by Amy Lowell. Pound extended the definition of imagism to art, which began another modernist movement named vorticism. It was an intensive art in an attempt to seek the most intense means of expression. The vorticists published two issues of the literary magazine *Blast*, in June 1914 and July 1915. Ezra Pound and T. S. Eliot published their works in it, but it was even shorter lived and vanished soon.

In 1915 Pound published *Cathay*, which was an alternative name for China in English. In Pound's own words, the book for the most part was from the Chinese Rihaku, from the notes of the late Ernest Fenollosa, and the decipherings of the professors Mori and Ariga. The book consists of 19 Chinese poems and the words are largely indebted to Chinese verses. Pound assured that West could meet East as long as human beings shared the common ground. Some people pointed out that the translated poems had mistakes and distorted meanings since his translation was not based on original versions, but Pound's translation of Chinese poems were highly praised by a lot of people. It was a good practice of translation of poems between two different cultures, which was originally thought untranslatable.

After the publication of *Cathay*, Pound began to work on his long poems. A year later, Pound had the form of his desired poems and the first draft of the first three cantos was published in 1917. It occupied Pound's attention and energy in the next sixty years. *The Cantos* (1917—1959) has always been a controversial work because of the experimental nature of the writing and his idea of anti-Semitism and Confucian ideals of government. However, there is no argument that *The Cantos* is Ezra Pound's most significant contribution to world literature, in which his enduring concerns and artistic innovations are presented.

In the short term it provoked his poems, "Homage to Sextus Propertius" (1919) and "Hugh

Selwyn Mauberley" (1920). Sextus Aurelius Propertius is widely considered to be the finest Latin elegiac poet, because he wrote in a formulated couplet. A large number of readers apparently thought that the work was intended to be a literal translation of classical Roman poetry though Pound was paying tribute to Sextus Propertius and attempting to capture the spirit of his verse, the beauty of his cadence, the quality of his irony, and the playfulness of his language. The free-verse Homage, an ironic persona poem based on this Roman poet, is a defense against the imperialism promoted by war. The name and personality of the subject is also reminiscent of T. S. Eliot's main character in "The Love Song of J. Alfred Prufrock." (1915)

All his life Pound had made a lot of contributions. He was a pioneer in launching a famous movement of imagism and he was famous for *The Cantos* which shows brilliant literary value as well as thought inspiration. Although he did not make a bestseller as "The Waste Land" (1922), *Ulysses* or *The Old Man and the Sea* (1952), works that appeal to both common people and criticism, he did help the young poets and novelists to reach their summit.

As an editor of several American literary magazines, Pound helped to discover and shape the work of contemporaries such as T. S. Eliot, James Joyce, Robert Frost, and Ernest Hemingway. Pound had blue-penciled a few of Hemingway's adjectives, and eliminated a great deal of Eliot's superfluous words in "The Waste Land," thus T. S. Eliot dedicated his poem to Pound and called him "a better craftsman," Pound even cut a large of W. B. Yeat's vague general terms and influenced the prestigious old poet's process of modernity. Because of his help, he was jokingly called the mid-wife for new literary talent.

Analyses of and Comments on His Representative Poems

 Ezra Pound's Poems

He was the creator of imagism and vorticism and launched the imagist and vorticist movement. His masterpiece "In a Station of the Metro" embodies his example about creating an ideal poem and is held as a milestone in the history of American literature. In his *Cathay* he tried to make use of ancient Chinese poems from Li Po to bring freshness to western language and literature as well. *The Cantos* (1917—1969) is a long, incomplete poem in 120 sections, each of which is a canto. Among them *The Pisan Cantos* was awarded the first Bollingen Prize in 1948. *The Cantos* is somewhat an encyclopedic epic poem and is generally considered one of the most significant works of modernist poetry in the 20th century. It is a book-length work and presents formidable difficulties to readers. It explores western civilization from the classical past through the medieval period and the renaissance to the modern age, and prescribes remedies for its cultural ills. It has been called Ezra Pound's intellectual diary. Pound's *The Cantos* addresses the profound human issues in history and in our time, and it is an encyclopedic masterpiece concerning themes of economics, governance, culture and so on.

Hugh Selwyn Mauberley is a long poem by Ezra Pound. It has been regarded as a turning point in Pound's career and after its completion Pound left from England for Italy. *Hugh Selwyn Mauberley* comprises eighteen short poems which are grouped into two sections. The first section is a biography of Ezra Pound himself. The second introduces the struggling minor poet Mauberley. Hugh Selwyn Mauberley expresses Pound's self-claimed failure as a poet. Speaking of himself in the third person, Pound criticized his earlier works to pursue aesthetic goals and art for art's sake. It can also be read as a wider attack upon the attitudes of society in the post-war period.

Ezra Pound's Imagist Poetry

Ezra Pound was an American expatriate and critic and an important figure in the early modernist movement in poetry. His life as well as his career was very controversial as some people said he was a genius in poetry and an honest man in heart, but some people argued that his works deserved nothing at all and he was a nation betrayer. Anyway, he was central to the development of modernist poetry. Pound is the mountain there, which you can dislike but cannot ignore.

Pound and his followers even made principles for imagism in an effort to make it clearer and easier to follow:

1. Direct treatment of the "thing," whether subjective or objective.
2. To use absolutely no word that does not contribute to the presentation.
3. As regarding rhythm: to compose in the sequence of the musical phrase, not in sequence of a metronome.

The point of imagism is that it does not use images as ornaments; the image itself is the speech. In Pound's mind, the image presents an intellectual and emotional complex in an instant of time, conveying these momentary impressions. As for language, he proposed using no superfluous word, no adjective which does not reveal something. But at the same time, he also warned people of abstractions.

The boundary of imagism and symbolism can be easily blurred, in fact, they have different points. Symbolism deals with association and allusion, while image is immediate and direct. Symbols have a fixed value but imagists' images have a variable significance. As a literary movement, imagism lasted only a few years (1909—1917). A single dominate image is hardly capable of sustaining long poems. The coverage area is narrow, which is not suitable for representing the significant society and the life subject. But imagism was widely discussed and influenced the poems to come.

In a Station of the Metro (1913)

Contents Summary

This short poem consists of only two lines:

The apparition of these faces in the crowd;
Petals on a wet, black bough.

The original can be paraphrased like this: "Several beautiful faces showing up in the crowd; / Petals on a wet, black branch." Pound's masterpiece of "In a Station of the Metro" is the embodiment of the imagism method. The process began in 1911 when he emerged from a Metro in Paris and saw suddenly a beautiful face, and then another, and then a beautiful child's face, and then another beautiful woman, which build a sharp contrast to the dark subway. The sudden emotion came out not in words but in colors. He tried all the day to find words for what this had meant to him. That evening, almost unconsciously, the single-image poem was his way out. He originally wrote a thirty-two-line metro poem, but six months later, he shortened the poem half that length, a year later he made it in two lines. Such a poem, he explained, was an attempt to record the precise instant when a thing outward and objective transformed itself into something inward and subjective in imagination.

Themes

As a typical imagist poem, it is written in free verse and approaches the things as precisely and tersely as possible without any comment or generalization. The scene of the metro viewed at that moment by Pound juxtaposes with the natural scene with beautiful petals and black, wet bough. Though short and alone, it presents every keen feeling of the poet and enables readers to experience the same feeling many years ago. He only felt that someone else understood what he understood. Poetry transcends time and place.

One word stands out: apparition. The word "apparition" alone means a ghostly figure, something strange or unusual that suddenly comes into view. Pound may have seen different faces in a Paris subway in the dark and noisy surroundings, but a few faces with pure and flawless beauty suddenly catch his eyes. With the word "apparition," it enables Pound to convey the expression of shock and awe once he steps into the metro station. More importantly, he might have not seen the faces clearly but only a blur. He imagined more than saw the real vision.

In the second line of the poem, one word overshadows all the rest: retals. Petals are one part of the blossomed flower, which are various in shape, size, color and so on. Pound identified petals with the "faces in the crowd" which are diverse and beautiful. The humid and dark subway station is vividly described through the comparison to a wet, black bough. The realistic view changes into an envisioned imagination, but the portrayal of nature is more impressive and colorful. You can have a colorful picture, and also you can feel the beauty of music through its repetition of different vowels and consonants, such as /au/ and /p/.

The apparition of these faces in the crowd;
Petals on a wet, black bough.

Literary Techniques

Obviously, it is a typical masterpiece that embodies Pound's way of interpreting on how to make a poem. The boiled down language and the intensive information reveal Pound's talent. Pound also compared his experience in Paris to a painting. The scene came into his consciousness just like an artist presented his memory or imagination into a picture in mind and marked it on a piece of paper to let it last forever.

The poem is incredibly short but meaningful. It is worth noting that the number of words in the poem (fourteen) is the same as the number of lines in a sonnet. Eight words in the first and six words in the second may as well suggest an Italian sonnet. Fourteen words expressed one dominant image of petals in a wet and black bough, which brings out the impression Pound experienced at that time and place. In this sense, the poem gives the equation of the same feeling. In Pound's words, image is not an ornament but a speech.

A Pact (1913)

Contents Summary

The following is the paraphrase of the original:

I make an agreement with Walt Whitman—
I dislike you for a long time.
I am a child growing up.
Who has a stubborn father;
I am old enough to be independent.
You are the person that get the new wood,
Now is a time for carving.
We have one sap and one root—

Let there be commerce between us.

A pact is "something agreed upon." In this poem, the ambivalence of Pound's response to Walt Whitman reflects his complicated feeling towards his American literary heritage. On the one hand, Pound expressed his respect to Whitman and he decided to follow Whitman to continue the American way. Pound's confrontation with Walt Whitman allows him to come to terms with a debt to his American forebear Whitman, the father of free verse expressionism. Pound recognized the authentic Whitman's "barbaric yawp," the self-conscious craftsman in him personally. Pound also used Whitman's open and spontaneous style. But he disliked Whitman for his crudeness and exaggeration, which is somewhat not in accordance with Pound's subtle and elaborate way. In his 1909 essay "What I Feel about Walt Whitman," he expressed his distaste for Whitman's expansive self-singing struggles. He distrusted Whitman's nakedness and crudity. He considered Whitman something of an artistic barbarian.

Themes

The result of this mixed acceptance was a curious hybrid form in the poem "A Pact." On the whole, it registers Pound's reconciliation with Whitman in 1913. Whitman is to America "what Dante is to Italy," Whitman's democracy of the spirit with Daniel's aristocracy of craftsmanship. Although he disliked Whitman, he admitted that Whitman was the forefather of American literature who broke the traditional rules and made the new way. He acknowledged the development of modernism from its foundations. "A grown child" now is "old enough to make friends." He was mature enough to make his own way of writing. He declared independence and gave freer rein to his own imagination. He gave freer rein to the Whitman in himself. "Now is a time for carving." Pound demanded for greater conscious techniques implied by "carving." Whitman broke the "new wood" of free verse, but the works were crude and Pound sought to refine the style, carving a finer product. At the end of the poem, Pound suggested "We have one sap and one root—" Pound intended to continue Whitman's new way of expression, and carve the future of poetry in a more precise and concrete way, thus achieving a contract between himself and his predecessor.

The River-Merchant's Wife: A Letter (1917)

Contents Summary

The speaker is a young wife about sixteen years old who married at fourteen. And about their relationship we know only that they were childhood playmates in a small Chinese village. The speaker communicates indirectly to her absent husband. First, she remembers their friendly play as children "without dislike or suspicion." From the beginning of her monologue we detect nostalgia feeling not only for the time when she first met her husband, but for innocence once when her hair was still cut straight across her forehead. Their marriage originally was not a matter of personal choice. Though married, she is unhappy about the marriage for the first year. "At fifteen," she begins to love him. Through various images, she expresses her loneliness and isolation she feels when separated from her husband, who went out for a five-month business trip.

Stanza One Lines 1—6 This opening stanza of 6 lines is organized around a central image of two children. The image goes like this: the picture of a little girl with her hair cut before her forehead playing games with a boy playmate. According to the ancient Chinese culture, the mark of an unmarried woman is hair cut straight across the forehead. By saying that the two children are on bamboo stilts playing with blue plums, it means that the man and the woman grow up together from childhood to adulthood. Each line contributes to a clearer understanding of the central image of a girl and a boy growing up without thinking of love. The repetition in three separate lines of the verb "playing" is to describe the happy time they spent together. The two images emphasize the natural, contented, and innocent activity of children. This stanza introduces the two characters: the "I" and the "you" in the world of the poem.

Stanza Two Lines 7—10 The central image of this stanza is the newly marriage between the young husband and wife. "Never laughed, being bashful." In ancient China, the marriage is usually not a personal choice but a deal made by a match' maker. Being young, the wife knows nothing about love and she is only timid to meet her man. She follows the role of being an obedient wife, lowering her head and looking at the wall.

Stanza Three Lines 11—14 The central image of this stanza is the growth of love between the young husband and wife. One year after their marriage, she starts to love her husband and be deeply involved in this relationship. The vows of the marriage ceremony, "till death us do part," are seen in Lines 12 and 13: "desired my dust to be mingled with yours" and strengthened by the triple repetition of "forever" in Line 13.

Stanza Four Lines 15—18 An image of separation is expressed in these lines as the husband takes on his role as a river-merchant and travels the waters, doing his business on a distant island. The 16-year-old wife's statement of the length of his absence for already five months is expressed in Line 18. Thinking of it in terms of its perilous "river of swirling eddies," she worries about the dangers of the far-away place where her husband is, and she is eager to be reunited with him. She feels worried as well as lonely. The effect of this long absence is affected by the use of the natural image of the sounds of the monkeys. Nobody answers her call of her husband but only the monkeys respond.

Stanza Five Lines 19—29 In Line 20 the phrase "by the gate" maybe is the same gate they played about as children, and in her memory she sees him reluctantly leaving month ago. For her it is the scene of the beginning of his absence. How moss has grown up over the unused gate; she has been counting the days, the slow passage of time and also she is afraid her husband may leave her for another woman. She has her own fugitive feelings of betrayal. And she knows this scene well: not only is there moss growing , but she is aware that there are different kinds of mosses, which she has not cleared away since his departure. The mosses and the worries are now too deep to clear away.

In Lines 22—23 the sadness of the river-merchant's wife is again reflected back to her by the natural world, by the falling leaves and wind of autumn. The leaves, full of greenness and energy, are now falling, which conveys the feeling of loneliness and depression. The leaves are becoming "yellow" changing with the season. She grows older as the winter is coming and another year is not far away. The image of autumn leaves becomes more defined with her observation of the butterflies in the garden, for they are "paired" but she now is single. The yellow butterflies "hurt" her because they emphasize the pain of her realization that she is growing older, but alone, not with her husband.

Themes

In these closing lines of the poem and the "letter" the river-merchant's wife composes, she gets out of her lonely world of sorrow to address her husband in a direct request: Please let me know when and by what route you are returning, so that I can come to meet you. Her village is a suburb of Nanking and she is willing to walk to a beach several hundred miles upstream to meet her husband; so deep is the love that she is willing to close the distance between them.

Literary Techniques

Allusion This is one of the most delicate poems in *Cathay*. For the most part of the book, it is from the Chinese book *Rihaku*. The poem "The River-Merchant's Wife: A Letter" was originally composed by ancient Chinese poet Li Po. Pound got the notes from the late Ernest Fenollosa, who studied Chinese poems. Even when he was given only the barest details, he was able to get into the central consciousness of the original author. But obviously some translators including Arthur Waley were apparently very unhappy with Pound's translation. They argued Pound did not translate for the literal meaning. For the very first line Waley translated as: Soon after I wore my hair covering my forehead. Pound: While my hair was still cut straight across my forehead. But Pound's piece is a masterpiece for those who hold dynamic translation. They think Pound's is the very example that exemplifies the translation of exerting the same feeling in both the original readers and the target language readers, for the same effect has been achieved. Pound's translation creates exactly this picture in the mind of a Chinese reader. Pound crossed the border of textual translation into cultural translation rather than being close to the original. Pound developed a method and a style in free verse, coupling with the Whitmanic principle of the syntactic and rhythmic integrity.

The translation of Pound's version of ancient Chinese poem serves also as an example of Pound's idea about imagism. The poem resorts to a series of images to convey the heroine's feeling towards a long left husband. The effect of an intense, repressed emotion is conveyed through carefully selected images. Rather than directly say love towards the husband, she memorizes in pictures of their play at young and their marriage later as well as the days he is gone. Accidentally, the emotion of the woman coincidences with the aim of imagists: a precise, objective rendering.

Unlike western women who directly express love for their husbands, the river-merchant's wife, an ancient Chinese woman conveys her love in a very subtle and repressed way. Only oneever direct statement about her love is her statement that she desires her dust be mingled with his "Forever and forever and forever." Between lines, one can sense her sincere and deep love. Some critics argue exploitation of the western projection of sexual oppression onto the "orient." The exotic Chinese setting of "The River-Merchant's Wife: A letter" calls the modern English reader's attention to the patriarchal obedience structure which has shaped and constrained the wife's voice.

Pound got his inspiration from Fenollosa's notes, the "ideogrammic method." It is the Chinese principle of poetic and metaphysical parallelism at work. The exotic way of composing poems inspires the practitioners in the modern and contemporary periods and imports a tender, melancholic tone into English.

Bibliography

Erkkila, Betsy. *Ezra Pound: the Contemporary Reviews*. Cambridge: Cambridge University Press, 2011.

Nadel, I. B. *The Cambridge Introduction to Ezra Pound*. Shanghai: Shanghai Foreign Language Education Press, 2008.

Wilson, Peter. *A Preface to Ezra Pound*. Beijing: Peking University Press, 2005.

http://en.wikipedia.org/wiki/Ezra_Pound 2012-01-10

http://www.english.illinois.edu/maps/poets/m_r/pound/pound.htm 2012-03-20

Robert Frost

His Life and Writing Career

His Life

Robert Frost (1874—1963) was born in San Francisco, California. His mother was of Scottish descent, and his father descended from England. Although known for his later association with rural life, Frost grew up in the city, and published his first poem in his high school's magazine. He attended Dartmouth College for two months. Frost returned home to teach and to work at various jobs—including helping his mother teach her class of unruly boys, delivering newspapers. He did not enjoy these jobs, feeling his true calling was poetry. In 1894 he proposed marriage to Elinor Miriam White, but she wanted to finish college before they married. Frost then went on an excursion and asked for her hand again upon his return. Having graduated, she agreed, and they were married at Harvard University, where he attended liberal arts studies for two years. He did well at Harvard, but left to support his growing family. Robert's grandfather purchased a farm for Robert in Derry, New Hampshire. Robert worked the farm for nine years, writing early in the mornings and producing many of the poems that would later become famous. However, his farming proved unsuccessful and he returned to the field of education as an English teacher at New Hampshire's Pinkerton Academy from 1906 to 1911, then at the New Hampshire Normal School in Plymouth, New Hampshire. In 1912 Frost sailed with his family to Great Britain. In England he made some important acquaintances, including T. E. Hulme and Ezra Pound. Surrounded by his peers, Frost wrote some of his best works while in England. WWI brought Frost's work to general public's notice.

As World War I began, Frost returned to America in 1915 and returned to New Hampshire, where he launched a career of writing, teaching, and lecturing. During the years 1916—1938, Frost taught English at Amherst College, in Massachusetts. His works were generally praised, but his short of concerning about social and economic problems of the 1930s depression, and his hostility toward the policies of the New Deal annoyed some more socially orientated critics. In 1940 he bought a 5-acre plot in South Miami, Florida, naming it Pencil Pines. He spent his winters there for the rest of his life. In the five decades following the publication of *North of Boston*, Frost reaped every possible reward and honor an American poet can get. Although Frost enjoyed a great honor in his public life, his private life was shrouded with gloomy atmosphere. His wife Elinor and Robert Frost had six children, but only Lesley and Irma outlived their father. Frost's wife who had heart problems throughout her life developed breast cancer in 1937 and died of heart failure in 1938. Frost was 86 when he spoke and performed a reading of his poetry at the inauguration of President John F. Kennedy on January 20, 1961. He died in Boston two years later, on January 29, 1963, of complications from prostate surgery. At the time of his death, Frost was considered a kind of unofficial poet laureate of the US. He was buried at the Old Bennington Cemetery in Bennington, Vermont. His epitaph quotes a line from one of his poems: "I had a lover's quarrel with the world."

His Writing Career

In 1894, Frost sold his first poem, "My Butterfly: An Elegy" for $15. Later, he published nine books of poems. *A Boy's Will* (1913) was his first poetry book, and *North of Boston* (1914) the second volume was published a year later. When he was forty, he marked his talent in poetry. His masterful poems include "The Witch of Coös," "Home Burial," "A Servant to Servants," "Directive," "Neither Out Too Far Nor in Too Deep," "Acquainted with the Night," "After Apple Picking," "Mending Wall," "The Most of It," "An Old Man's Winter Night," "Departmental," "A Considerable Speck," "Stopping by the Woods on a Snowy Evening," and "The Road Not Taken."

A popular and often-quoted poet, Frost received more than forty honorary degrees from different colleges and universities including Harvard, Oxford, and Cambridge. He also was a recipient of four Pulitzer Prizes for Poetry and a poet that read his poem at the presidential Inauguration ceremony. He was the unofficial poet laureate of America. Robert Frost was generally regarded as the poet of the countryside with philosophic understanding of life and the surroundings. He was more like an old gentleman farmer concerned about folksy rural settings. Warmly received during his lifetime, Robert Frost still enchants readers today.

Analyses of and Comments on His Representative Poems

Robert Frost's Poems

Frost's poems can be sorted into four kinds. The first is dramatic poetry, such as "A Servant to Servants," "The Death of a Hired Man," and "Home Burial." The poetry that simply expresses emotions is actually lyric poetry. Dramatic poetry also involves emotion but it is more of a narrative poem telling a story of a person in a specific situation. Frost's dramatic poetry is based on the background of New England farms, fields, and forests; the language is everyday spoken language, and the poem's characters are the people around normal life. The second class of poetry is meditative poetry. He had such poems as "The Road Not Taken," "Mending Wall," "Birches," and "Stopping by Woods on a Snowy Evening." They describe a scene of nature or an event in people's lives at the beginning, and then the scene of nature or event in the life becomes symbols, which draw out the philosophic thinking about the significance of life. The third type is satirical poetry such as "Departmental" and "A Considerable Speck." He borrowed some nature scenes, especially in certain animals or insects to comment on things, and ultimately pointed out problems in human life. His criticism of some of the shortcomings in the social life and people's behavior is not direct, but hidden between the lines with ironically spicy sense of humor. His forth type of poetry is philosophical poetry such as "Design", "Fire and Ice," "Nothing Gold Can Stay", and "Once by the Pacific." There are many similarities with his meditation poems. They describe the scene or event, and then deduce from the scene to thinking. But there exit differences. Philosophy poems generally are shorter and they involve more abstract concepts. The tone of philosophy poems is both caustic and pessimistic.

Frost's Natural and Pastoral Poetry

Robert Frost was highly regarded for his realistic depictions of rural life in New England in the early twentieth century. His images are often woods, stars, houses, and brooks which are usually taken from everyday life. He looks very positively predisposed toward his surroundings—particularly toward nature. By using seemingly simple direct and natural symbols, he actually suggested complex social and philosophical themes. His poems resist easy interpretation, as if they are to fool the innocent readers. He was likely to choose traditional forms for his poems, but the themes of his poems are mostly modern. In fact, he didn't try to create anything new to reform poetic forms, but he combined new contents with old forms of expression in his own ways. His fluency and creative thinking on the everyday things or phenomena leave us with great impression.

His poetry concerns New England's nature. He saw nature as a collection of analogy and symbols, so his concern with nature reflected deep moral uncertainties. His choice at normal life may reveal a deep philosophic thinking. However, there is a difference between the way a European perceives nature and the way Frost does. Europeans think of the civilization of nature by human's working. The poems are tinged with history and allusions and the poets are only the witnesses, whereas Frost treats nature as his equal, free from references, neither past nor future. It is the present. Nature in his poems is neither a friend nor a enemy.

The Road Not Taken (1916)

 ## Contents Summary

"The Road Not Taken" was published in 1916 in the collection *Mountain Interval*. The following is the paraphrase of the original:

One road split into two in a yellow wood,
I'm sorry I could not travel both at the same time.
As a traveler, I stood there for a long time
And looked down as far as I could
But I just saw the road bent in the bush.

It seemed the second choice was as good as the first one,
Maybe it had better scene
Because it was grassy and it invited people to walk on.
Even though both tracks seemed to have had about the same number of people
Passing there and had been worn about the same.

Both of the roads had not been used in the morning
Because no steps had trodden in the leaves.
I might keep the first one another day!
But I know one road may lead to another road,
I doubt whether I could ever come back to where I started.

Recalls the road taken and not taken, I sighed,
Many, many years later:
One road split into two and I took the one less traveled by,
And that has made all the difference to my life, to make the person I am today.

It is the first poem in the volume and is printed in italics. The title is often mistakenly given as "The Road Less Traveled," from the line "I took the one less traveled by." It has been one of the most analyzed, quoted, and anthologized poems in American poetry. The poem has two recognized interpretations: one is a more literal interpretation, while the other is more ironic. Frost himself warned readers to be careful of the tricky poem.

Themes

The poem begins when the poet is walking in a wood in late autumn at a fork in the road. And he stands looking as far down each one as he can see. He would like to try out both, but doubts he can do that, and therefore he continues to look down the roads for a long time trying to make his decision about which road to take. He is deciding which road he should follow. Actually, it is concerned with the important decisions people must make in life. He must give up one desirable thing in order to possess the other. Stanza Two: After the judgment and hesitation, the traveler makes up his mind to take the road which looks grassy and wants wear. This is often believed to be the symbol of the poet's choice of a solitary life—taking poetry writing as his life profession. But then he goes on to say that they actually are very similarly worn. The second one that he takes seems less traveled, but as he thinks about it, he realizes that they are "really about the same." Not exactly that same but only "about the same." Stanza Three: The third stanza continues with the cogitation about the possible differences between the two roads. The two roads are equally pretty, so as soon as he makes the choice of the one, the poet feels painful for abandoning the other. He has noticed that the leaves have freshly fallen on them and has not been walked on. Then again he claims that maybe he would come back and also walk the first one sometime, but he doubts he would be able to. He is quite aware that his intention of "next choice" will be nothing than an empty promise. Because in life one thing leads to another and time is short. Stanza Four: the poet is imagining many years later when he will be recalling the choice he made today, he would respond with nothing else but a sigh, for it would be too hard for anyone, after many more experiences in life, to make any comment on the choice made early in life.

The literal meaning goes like this: a traveler comes to a fork in the road and needs to decide which way to continue his journey. After much mental debate, the traveler picks the road "less traveled by." But the figurative meaning suggests that the poem describes the tough choices people stand for when traveling the road of life. It shows the difficulty of having to make choices in life. It calls for courage to make the untraditional choice. To some extent, it is an ode of individualism and nonconformism.

As a more traditional interpretation, it goes like this. In a situation of nature, the poet actually reveals a significant and philosophic contemplation of dilemma in making choices. It somewhat embodies the existentialism proposed by Paul Sartre (1905—1980). One has the choices in life and he is free to choose, but he has to be responsible for what he has chosen. He has options, but when he takes one, he will have to give up others. The result will be different. Life is a one-way journey; thus, you cannot go back.

The second interpretation: Frost intended the poem as a gentle jab at his great friend and fellow poet Edward Thomas. Frost used to take walks with him through the forest while Thomas always complained at the end that they should have taken a different path and seemed amused at this certain interpretation of the poem as inspirational. The lines "I took the one less traveled by / And that has made all the difference." are ironic: the choice made little or no difference at all, which is on the contrary with the interpretation we previously view. The speaker admits in the second and third stanzas that both paths may be equally worn and equally leaf-covered, and it is only in his future recollection that he will call one road "less traveled by." It is the road that one chooses that makes him the man who he is. The road that will be chosen leads to the unknown. As much he may extend his eyes to see as far the road stretches, eventually it surpasses his vision and he can never see where it is going to lead. It is the way that he chooses that sets him off on his journey and decides where he is going. It may be a kind of regret or self-satisfaction. In either case, the irony lies in the distance between what the speaker has just told us about the roads' similarity and what his later claims will be.

But a close reading of the poem does not moralize about choice; it simply says that choice is inevitable, but you never know what your choices will mean until you have lived it.

Literary Techniques

This is a narrative poem consisting of four stanzas of iambic tetrameter and is one of Frost's most popular works. It is written in classic five-line stanzas, with the rhyme scheme a-b-a-a-b and conversational rhythm.

Metaphor Frost compares one thing to another when the two have similarities. A fork in the road refers to choices we have in life; which road to take means making decisions in life; the well-trodden road implies common life. The grassy and wanted wear road refers to rare and different life; a traveler, a living person.

Symbolism Frost uses concrete image to represent abstract meanings: "Yellow"—the yellow coloring of the woods representing the light, hope, and harvest; "Woods"—a quiet, deserted place with no signs or people to stop and ask for directions; Similarly, people are left alone in making choices in life; "Roads"—the roads are symbol of the life we choose; "Morning" —the morning represents a new beginning and the endless possibilities the day ahead has to offer.

Stopping by Woods on a Snowy Evening (1922)

Contents Summary

It is a poem written in 1922 by Robert Frost, and published in 1923 in his *New Hampshire* volume. The following is the paraphrase of the original:

Whose are these woods?
I think they belong to a man in the village,
But he won't see me stop here to watch
The snow fall in the woods.

The horse that I am with must be thinking
It is odd to stop where there is no stable.
I stopped in-between the woods and the frozen lake,
On the night with no moon.

The horse shakes the bells,
As if he were to ask if I had made a mistake.
There is no other sound in the woods
Except the eerie whistle of the wind.

The woods are beautiful and dark,
But I have a commitment to keep,
And I have to travel a long time,
A long way before I have time to rest.

Stanza One: The speaker stops by woods which are far from the village. In other words, the woods are removed from the village—a world of human order. The poet is alone except for his horse. He stops by the woods of a neighbor, a man who lives in the village. The woods are filling with snow, and he simply wants to watch the scene. Stanza Two: The introduction of the foil—the little horse. Unlike the speaker, the horse, an animal that cannot reason or think, does not know why they stop here. "Queer" leads to an even lonelier scene, a kind of northern nowhere connected with the strangeness of the winter. In this second stanza the pattern is catching on to the readers, pulling them into the drowsy current. Stanza Three is heightened by the "shake" of bells and "to ask," humorously taking the horse's point of view, telling us that the driver is awake and sane. In the second and third stanzas the poet conjectures that his horse must think him crazy to stop in a deserted spot on such a cold night. Stanza Four: The speaker wishes to go on the journey before he finally ceases to be. The last stanza is the closing lines with the repetitions. It contains the poet's statement on the beauty of the scene, but he does not linger any longer— he has a long way to go home, and things to do when he gets there. The settling down on one sleepy rhyme running against what is being said, and with the speaker's echoing his sensible self in "I have promises" and "miles to go," he almost seems to be nodding off.

Apparently, the poem is descriptive. It is dark and cold. The poet stops his sleigh by the lovely, dark woods and lingers on to watch the snow filling up the woods,. He, however, realizes that he cannot stay there for long because he has miles to go before he sleeps. He acknowledges the pull of obligations and the considerable distance yet to be traveled before he can rest for the night.

Some critic suggests the poem is about the temptation of death, even suicide, symbolized by the woods that are filling up with snow on the darkest evening of the year. The speaker is powerfully drawn to these woods, which are "lovely, dark, and deep," and they are much more seductive to speaker than a field is. He wants to lie down and let the snow cover and bury him. The third stanza, the line "Of easy wind and downy flake" is drowsy, dream-like. The recognition of the power of nature, especially of snow, obliterates the limits and boundaries of things and of himself in the real world. It is a furtive impulse toward extinction. The horse's instinctive urge for home opposes to the man's subconscious desire for death in the dark, snowy woods. The speaker says, "The woods are lovely, dark, and deep," but he resists the attraction at the end in order to return to the mundane duties of daily life. Life in the sophisticated world is full of duties and tasks. Pressed by living pressure and challenged by the ambition, people are living so intensely and tiredly that the thought of rest—death is somewhat a resort from the demanding journey. Death is an attraction to many poets.

Another interpretation is that Robert Frost was writing about Santa Claus. The evidence supporting this is as follows: 1) In the second stanza, the first two lines say, "My little horse must think it queer/ To stop without a farmhouse near." It means that the horse is accustomed to stopping beside houses, so Santa could deliver his presents. 2) In the last stanza, the second and third lines say, "But I have promises to keep/ And miles to go before I sleep." The speaker says that because he knows all the little children are waiting for him and he cannot disappoint them by being late.

Themes

The poem is a figurative and metaphorical summary of life. The horseman is every man of the world; the horse stands for the resources of life. Woods are sometimes a symbol for wildness, madness, and the looming irrationality. But the owner of the woods lives in it. The woods stand for society and civilization, responsibility and sensibility. The end of the journey is the end of life; the owner of the forest is God who is never completely known to man though man thinks that he is unknown to his God. Every man is tired but he is to continue his voyage. The important aspect to his journey is that there is no end to it. After one milestone or station of rest or activity another milestone appears and thus even at the time of death, one cannot cover the whole part of this journey.

Literary Techniques

The poem is written in iambic tetrameter, each verse (save the last) follows a rhyming scheme of a-a-b-a with the following verse's a's rhyming with that verse's b, which is a chain rhyme. Overall, the rhyme scheme is a-a-b-a, b-b-c-b, c-c-d-c, d-d-d-d. The poet employs the drawing back rhyme, i.e. in the first stanza the third line is b, while in the second stanza the poem draws back to continue the rhyme b; it gives the poem a tone of hesitation, which shows the poet's deliberate consideration.

Imagery and personification are vividly represented in the work. Like his other poems, this poem is also associated with nature. Nature here is full of mystery, darkness, and irrationality while man is put in the bleak and chaotic landscapes of an indifferent universe.

Contrasts are formed: 1) The impractical poet and the practical owner of the woods. 2) The poet and his horse. The horse cannot imagine why his driver should want to stop in this inhospitable place. 3) The present natural world and the future world the speaker is heading for. 4) Life's responsibilities and the "lovely, dark, and deep" attraction that death offers.

Mending Wall (1914)

Contents Summary

The poem was published in 1914, setting in the countryside. This is Frost's typical poem: what begins in folksy straightforwardness and ends in complex ambiguity. A traditional form tinges with modern theme. The poem is telling a story about the speaker and his neighbor repairing the wall that collapses in parts due to interference of nature annually. The speaker starts to question why he and his neighbor must rebuild the stone wall dividing their farms each spring. As a matter of fact, the speaker just wants to communicate with his neighbor by spending time with him and repairing the wall. They work together to repair the wall, but they don't talk to each other as they do so. The speaker tries to convince his neighbor that there is no need for the wall. The neighbor rebuilds the wall without question, quoting "Good fences make good neighbors." But Frost's narrator questions the proverb, observing that neither his apple trees nor his neighbor's pine trees are likely to disturb each other.

Themes

The poem is a description of an ordinary and simple thing—repairing wall. However, behind this wall repairing, it contains the profound philosophy of life: communication between people. These implications inspire numerous interpretations and make definitive readings suspect.

The first interpretation is a political one: throughout the poem, it tells us that the United States in the twentieth century is abundance in industrial prosperity, and material, but people feel loneliness, longing for free and relaxed life. Frost thinks that the stone wall is the barrier between countries because of tradition, culture, and conservative thinking. The wall doesn't need to exist. The stone wall in real life might be just an excuse not to communicate with other people, to hide the embarrassment and estrangement between people. It is the one and only way to ignore other people in a "polite way."

But also, some people have different opinion about "the wall." The title "Mending Wall" is an ironic one. From the beginning to the end, the speaker tries to confirm that fences aren't necessary. The fence can be used for some reasons, and might be needed for some conditions, but in this poem, Frost asks and answers, "Where there are cows? But here there are no cows," stating that although fences may be necessary, there is no use of mending wall.

Some argue walls are necessary. The neighbors have different interests, different background, and different opinions about life. There wouldn't be interested in each other's topic. While coming out to walk, they save themselves from the embarrassing silence. They just pretend they don't see each other because of the wall. This wall doesn't only exist in reality; it exists in people's minds. The collapse of the wall is not going to solve the problem. The barrier can not be removed; there is an invisible wall between the neighbors. What's more, the wall serves as a shield to protect privacy. Some sort of mystery and space sometimes is not that bad. Too much intimacy is not as good as we think. The saying "A hedge between keeps friendship green" coincides with the saying "Good fences make good neighbors."

Others suggest the old form of Frost, that is, the description of nature in this poem. "Something there is that doesn't love a wall, / That sends the frozen-ground-swell under it, And spills the upper boulders in the sun." "Something" is hunters, sprites, and frost and thaw of nature's invisible or supernatural power that spill the upper boulders in the sun. Still, the neighbors persist. Every spring they are going to make it out of habit or tradition. The whole task reminds us of Sisyphus, who is a figure in Greek mythology. He is condemned perpetually to push a boulder up a hill, only to have the boulder roll down again. It may lead to the understanding of Sartre's existentialism. The individual's starting point is characterized by what has been called "the existential attitude" or a sense of disorientation and confusion in the face of an apparently meaningless or absurd world. These men push boulders back on top of the wall; just as inevitably Sisyphus pushes a boulder up a hill again and again. Hence, it may tell us the condition of modern human in the modern world. Seemingly endless choices actually give you no space to choose and the result may end as the same.

The wall is a metaphor that refers to a barrier between people. The wall could be any other walls in the world: the Berlin Wall and the forbidding array of defenses between North and South Korea, which cause the originally united countries to separate. The borders or walls segregate rather than unify. In today's modern world, there is still a hidden wall between all of us. We have little tolerance because of social and religious differences. We use walls to keep enemies out, mostly for political, economic, or social reasons. Walls are used to claim power, suppress people, or perhaps just to mask insecurities, flaws or weakness.

Literary Techniques

"Mending Wall" is a metaphorical poem written in blank verse, with little rhythm from line to line.

Bibliography

Frost, Robert. *The Poetry of Robert Frost: The Collected Poems, Complete and Unabridged.* New York: Henry Holt and Company, 1975.

Huang, Zongying. *A Road Less Traveled By: On the Deceptive Simplicity in the Poetry of Robert Frost.* Beijing: Peking University Press, 2000.

Poirier, Richard. *Robert Frost: The Work of Knowing.* Oxford: Oxford University Press, 1977.

http://en.wikipedia.org/wiki/Robert_Frost 2012-01-23

http://www.english.illinois.edu/maps/poets/a_f/frost/frost.htm 2012-01-10

Wallace Stevens

His Life and Writing Career

His Life

Wallace Stevens (1879—1955) was an American modernist poet. He was born in Reading, Pennsylvania, on October 2, 1879, and died at the age of seventy-six in Hartford, Connecticut on August 2, 1955. He was writing the poetry of modernism and recognized as a father figure in contemporary literature. At the same time he was a successful businessman, even reaching the position of vice-president of an insurance company. The seemingly two incompatible fields both witnessed his success.

Stevens' father was a prosperous lawyer who contributed a lot to the son's early education by providing their home with an extensive library and by encouraging reading. At the age of 12 Stevens began studying classics in Greek and Latin. He showed some early talents as a man of letters by reporting for the school's newspaper. Stevens attended Harvard as a special student from 1897 to 1900 but did not graduate, while he had received all of the school's honors for writing and published his poems at both the magazines of Harvard: *The Harvard Advocate* and *The Harvard Monthly*. He moved to New York City and briefly worked as a journalist. He then attended New York Law School, graduated in 1903 and was admitted to the New York bar in 1904. In the same year he met Elsie Kachel, a young woman from Reading, whom he married in 1909 over the objections of his parents. They considered her lower-class. After working for several New York law firms from 1904 to 1907, he was hired on January 13, 1908, as a lawyer for the American Bonding Company. By 1914 he had become the vice-president of the New York office of the Equitable Surety Company of St. Louis, Missouri. In 1914, under the pseudonym "Peter Parasol," he sent a group of poems under the title "Phases" to Harriet Monroe for a war poem competition for *Poetry* magazine. Stevens did not win the prize, but the poems were published by Monroe in November of that year. In 1916, his job as the vice-president was abolished as a result of mergers, and he left New York City to live in Hartford to join the home office of the Hartford Accident and Indemnity, of which he became vice-president in 1934. Amazingly, Stevens managed to maintain his career in an insurance company and at the same time he presented his special talent in his poems for over twenty years. He spent his last days suffering from stomach cancer and died on August 2, 1955, at the age of 75. He was buried in Hartford's Cedar Hill Cemetery.

 ## His Writing Career

As young, Stevens had began to establish an identity for himself outside the world of law and business, however, his first book of poems, *Harmonium*, published in 1923 by the distinguished firm of Alfred A. Knopf when he was already forty-four. Stevens felt that the reviews of this book were not as good as he expected, and was discouraged. He wrote nothing through the 1920s, but his business career achieved steadily during the 1920s. Like Frost, Stevens was relatively late in reaching his poetic maturity. His works exhibited the influence of both the English romantics and the French symbolists, infused with the light and color of an impressionist painting. For the next several years, Stevens focused on his business life. He began to publish new poems in 1930, however, and in the following year, Knopf published a second edition of *Harmonium*, which included fourteen new poems and left out three of the decidedly weaker ones. His major works include "Ideas of Order" "(1935)" "The Man with the Blue Guitar" (1937). In 1939, Stevens was sixty—an age when most poets are ready to retrospect on what they have achieved. But Stevens'

best writing still lay before him. In the loosely connected stanzas of these sequences: *Parts of a World* (1942), *Notes Toward a Supreme Fiction* (1943), *Transport to Summer* (1947), *The Auroras of Autumn* (1950). At the same time, he began to grow interested in putting his thoughts on aesthetics together in prose sentences, and his collection of essays on poetry was published as *The Necessary Angel* in 1951. *Collected Poems* (1954) and *Opus Posthumous* (1957) include his uncollected works. His reputation grew slowly, and his work was less generally known than that of Frost, or Pound. Stevens' status as a major American modernist was not clearly established until near the end of his life. After he won the Pulitzer Prize in 1955, he was offered a faculty position at Harvard but he refused.

Although he made great achievement in poetry, he considered himself an outsider of the literary world, even the encounters with Robert Frost and Hemingway remained unhappy.

Analyses of and Comments on His Representative Poems

Wallace Stevens' Poems

Stevens' poems are quite often packed with special images, especially musical imagism. Figurative statements are brought into play to convey subtle ideas. What's more, his poems also emphasize meaning and emotion supported by variations in rhythm and sound. Thus, his poems are considered as willfully difficult and are not easy to comprehend or paraphrase. But he was also regarded as an eminent abstractionist and a provocative thinker. In his ideas, reality was the product of the imagination as it shapes the world. Stevens considered the world and our perception of the world to be separate. To make sense of the world is to construct a worldview through an active exercise of the imagination.

Among his poems, "Anecdote of the Jar" published in his collection of poems *Harmonium* was considered as his masterpiece, in which he talked about human arts or creation's superiority over wilderness in nature. He perceived in a different way when most of his peers thought ill of the modern technology and creation, which broke the harmony of nature. The same thing happened when people regarded physical beauty was inferior to spiritual beauty, and he wrote the poems "Peter Quince at the Clavier" in 1915 about the sensual beauty and desire. Physical beauty triggered art and it was the permanent. Stevens' idea about beauty was different from Plato's who emphasized the spiritual love rather than the physical love. He highlighted the significance on the enjoyment of sensual emotions, delighting in depicting the world as revealed to the senses. In Stevens' poems, he talked of hedonism. In the "The Emperor of Ice-Cream" written in 1922, it tells a story about people thought of sensuality when a woman is going to be buried. In this way he wanted to tell us life and appetite went on when death occurred.

Wallace Stevens' Modernist Poetry

Most of Wallace Stevens' topics were concerning the relationship between reality, poetry, and imagination. Stevens considered there were two kinds of realities. One was the objective reality: the perceptions by the five senses. The other was the subjective reality: mental world dominated by imagination. He explored the notion of poetry as the supreme fusion of the creative imagination and objective reality. His theory of poetry is the theory of life. Stevens considered poetry as a mode of thinking.

What he enjoyed most was the climate, nature, the sky, and the natural aspect. However, he did hold the perspective of a romanist, he viewed it in a different angle. He thought nature was submissive to human's creation. The world was fantastic because of human's interference.

Wallace Steven was opposed to T. S. Eliot's pessimistic attitude. He took the initials of a new poetic lyricism. If T. S. Eliot created waste land to present the modern barren world, then Stevens tried to reconstruct the meaningless world through the use of arts and imagination. In the society, art was a thread that collects everything in the world. Any society without art was unimaginable. Although the faith to God was fading, he held faith in poetry. When people doubted about God, it was necessary to believe in something else, such as poetry, a thing created by imagination. It was the important role of the poets to point out the order and faith through arts and poems.

Stevens was very much an atheist, and his poetry has a strong atheistic undercurrent, as in "The Man with the Blue Guitar": "Poetry // Exceeding music must take the place / Of empty heaven and its hymns."

Anecdote of the Jar (1919)

Contents Summary

The following is the paraphrase of the original:

I placed a jar on the hill of Tennessee,
It was round.
It made the untidy wilderness orderly.
The hill became the center.

The wilderness was submissive to the jar;
The jar tamed the wilderness.
The round jar was put on the ground.
It was tall and like a harbor in the air.

It was in charge of everywhere
Although it was gray without decoration.
It did not give life like a bird or bush
But it was unique in Tennessee.

"Anecdote of the Jar" is a poem from Wallace Stevens' first book of poetry, *Harmonium*. It was first published in 1919. The poem is mainly about the relationship between nature, art, and human beings. A plain and round jar is put on the top of a hill in a wild environment. According to Stevens, the basis of art comes from creative consciousness of human beings, thus the jar may serve as a controller of the slovenly wilderness. In this poem, Stevens forced the readers to feel the confusion and chaos presented between the jar and its surroundings, two of which form an analogy with a sculpture at that moment. It invites different interpretations from different perspectives ever since, ranging from a new critical angle to a poststructuralist perspective concerning with linguistic disjunction. A feminist perspective reveals a poem concerned with male dominance over a traditionally feminized landscape. A cultural critic might find a sense of industrial imperialism.

Themes

The poet thinks that nature is a disordered world and only ideas can make it united as a whole. In fact, "the slovenly wilderness" is the symbol of crudity and ignorance, which indicates that the world is in a state of chaos. "Wilderness in Tennessee" is the symbol of nature. The jar is the design of a created object embodying a human, cultural purpose. Being put on the top of a hill, it gives a sense of human purpose through nature. "The wilderness rose up to it, / And sprawled around." The jar is controlling the outside, the wilderness, and compels a "surrounding."

The jar does not have life as animals, or have the power as a king, but it has its unique specialty, which overshadows other ordinary creatures in nature; it tames the wilderness. "It took dominion everywhere." While as a piece of beautiful and irreplaceable art work, it also represents imaginative creativity and makes the slovenly wilderness orderly. Here, Stevens is less interested in describing the objects presented than the imaginative ideas played out between them. What's more, a poet should find beauty pleasure and meaning in the chaotic world and sordidness of reality.

Some scholars notice something peculiar in this poem. Generally speaking, a jar contains what is inside it. However, the jar "contains" what is outside of it, because civilization or art created by man, is composed within the jar. In the opening stanza, Stevens mentions that the jar was round, and then he repeats that in the second stanza: it was "round upon the ground." The jar's roundness exerts a centripetal force on the "slovenly wilderness." The shape is a symbolic artifact that expresses its desire to dominate all that is senseless or shapeless or wild. The geometric feature of the jar does "contain" what is outside of it. But ironically, at the end of the poem, the jar "was gray and bare." It implies that art without the support of reality is not with life. "It did not give of bird or bush." It will not be of use to a bird or bush and it does not have real life as plants and birds. Emptily, it "contains" the wilderness. It becomes part of what surrounds it. The poet may suggest art also depends on reality, the physical world. We need to accept the real world as it is. The last two lines enforce this statement with two negatives. This sudden shift proves more thinking about the relationship between art and nature. It, in some sense, expresses man's manipulation over the natural elements.

Some compare the poem with its famous romantic precursor—Keats, who wrote "Ode to a Grecian Urn." Keats viewed the Grecian urn as "a friend to man" in the final stanza of the poem. He reinforced his belief that classical Greek art was idealistic and captured Greek virtues, which forms the basis of the poem. There is paradoxical relationship between the poem's world and reality. While this poem of Wallace Stevens concerns the relationship with man's creation and nature. The jar becomes the object of imaginative creation of man which surpasses nature. More is emphasized on the object itself. The jar is placed in a strange environment and divorced from its practical function. And equal emphasis is placed upon the gifted perceiver rather than the craftsman who made the jar. The sense of an object as an event rather than a thing of sense characterizes as a modern poem.

The "I" of the poem places a tall, round jar on the top of a hill. In this sense, it may suggest the poet should shoulder the responsibility to recreate an aesthetic order in the disordered world. Poems are the instruments to make people see the scattered life whole again. In T. S. Eliot's eyes, modernization and creations of human beings, altogether with the desire of man destroy the harmony of the world. The two world wars greatly damaged the world as well as the spiritual world of man. However, Wallace Stevens placed the jar higher than other things in nature, which suggests that he holds a positive attitude upon human's creation and imagination. Civilization is originated from wildness, but it is superior to the original wildness. Although it is higher than others, it does not mean that the jar can replace the position of the wilderness. The jar and the wilderness together knit the whole picture, and they are closely related to each other. Nature and human beings are depending on each other. Human beings as well as nature are indispensable.

Stevens' poems are obviously marked with imagism because the imagists hold that the most effective means is through the use of one dominant image. In this poem, Stevens made use of one dominant image—the jar, but compared with the imagists who often catch the momentary expression of the real world, Stevens' poem is pure imagination rather than the impression of momentary feeling from the real world. As the leader of imagist movement, Pound's image was often concerned with history, mythology, and cultural traditions. While according to Stevens, imagism was split into two, the world of the reality and the world of imagination. What's more, Stevens' imagism is movable and dynamic.

Literary Techniques

The poem makes use of metaphor. The poem "Anecdote of the Jar" is a metaphor for humans' existence in nature. Industry and the urbanization of the early twentieth century largely changed the landscape of nature. By the 1950s and 1960s, technology formed the American way of life, because human beings stamp their sign everywhere in the world. The poem contains a modern pastoral theme to create an existence of "harmony" surrounding where man attempts to order wilderness against nature's inert state. The jar made the wilderness "no longer wild" and therefore inhabitable for humankind's pastoral vision.

The poem also is tinged with surrealism. Surrealism is best known for its visual artworks and writings. It has the element of surprise, unexpected juxtapositions. The poet purposely puts the relatively discordant verbal images and physical objects together so as to create a feeling of surreal. It is strange, not like reality, like a dream. In this poem, the jar and the slovenly wilderness are placed together to produce the effect of being surreal.

The Emperor of Ice-Cream (1922)

Contents Summary

This poem was published in 1922 alluring pleasures of the senses. The story in the poem can be divided into two equal stanzas: one for the kitchen where the ice cream is being made; one for the bedroom where the corpse waits for decent covering. Faced with slovenly and sensual life in the kitchen and cold death on the bed, one must recognize the true face of life. The poem goes like this: it happened in a poor residential place in the United States. People of Latin-American ancestry live in the neighborhood and roll cigars to earn money. A muscular cigar maker was asked to make ice cream to serve the visitors who help "lay out" (arrange for decent viewing) the corpse in the bedroom. Both the symbolic kitchen stanza and the symbolic bedroom stanza end with the same line echoed by the title: "The only emperor is the emperor of ice-cream." In earlier times, the wake took place in the home of the deceased. Besides paying their last respects to the dead person, visitors often ate, drank, and told stories. In "The Emperor of Ice-Cream," the narrator tells what will happen before and during the wake. There will be the ice-cream, and men from the neighborhood will bring flowers. The dresser for the dead woman lacks three glass knobs that is a symbol of luxury. The dead woman will lie in her bedroom under a bedsheet. Her bedding may be too short to cover both head and feet. Feet are the earthen root, but the sheet cannot mask them, which may suggest poverty in lifetime and finally in death. Her prone body, mocking how the wench lived, lies flat in the indignity of death. "If her horny feet protrude," those limbs protruding tell us "how cold she is, and dumb." She made beautiful embroidery the day she was alive. But now the embroidery covers her face and body but exposes her callused feet. Art is exposed as too inert in its powers to cover up death.

So a wench is dead, stretched out cold at the ice-cream party. The visitors will socialize and have fun, not with mourning for the loss of a neighbor. The woman's death presents an opportunity for her acquaintances to hold a party. The pleasure they will derive from the occasion apparently matters more than the memory of the deceased woman they are supposed to be mourning. The "muscular" one is called for before "dawdling wenches." The cigar has phallic connotations and "concupiscent curds" evoke gender issues. No doubt, the women will pay more attention to the muscular man who makes the "concupiscent curds." The flowers are juxtaposed with last month's newspapers—something fresh is contrasted with something stale. Appetizer is symbolized as sensuality in the ice-cream. The muscular man and the ice- cream represent sensual or physical pleasure. In turn, the "boys" will no doubt want to live it up with the "wenches," even if they are attending a funeral. Everyone wants to seize the day, the temporary pleasure.

 **Themes**

The poet appears to speak from a godlike, distant perspective even though he uses imperative mood and second-person point of view in almost all the sentences. He is the person to help "lay out" (arrange for decent viewing) the corpse in the bedroom. Stevens seems to suggest in this poem what people perceive are the concupiscent pleasures and what people should embrace is reality, namely, death. But the verses "Let the lamp affix its beam" implies to say that let light show itself. As a seeing eye celebrates an inner light in mortal darkness, a comeback optics of imagining sunrise is reborn at sunset. Whether the narrator approves of the partying about to take place is unknown. He (or she) leaves it up to the reader to pass judgment on its propriety. It may also signify that life will continue to attach importance to the festive moods despite gruesome realities like poverty and death.

There is a peculiar phenomenon presenting in this poem. A series of commands from an unknown master of ceremonies, directing the neighbors in their funeral duties: "Call the roller of big cigars, / The muscular one, and bid him whip / In kitchen cups concupiscent curds. /... // Take from the dresser ... / ... that sheet /... / And spread it so as to cover her face." The orders have echoed by the title as well as the last sentence: "The only emperor is the emperor of ice-cream." The coldness of the ice-cream may refer to the fact that life goes on although the reality is harsh.

The only god of this world is the cold god of persistent life and appetite.

Literary Techniques

The poem is full of metaphysics or exoticism in this piece. It resisted explication for some decades, perhaps because no one took the trouble to deduce its implicit meaning. Some suggest it derives from Stevens' mother's death ten years earlier. Symbolically, it represents the bitter moment of choosing life over death, at a time when life seems particularly lonely, lustful, and sordid. It is an indictment on the superficiality and absolute materialism of Americans.

Peter Quince at the Clavier (1915)

Contents Summary

"Peter Quince at the Clavier" is a poem from Wallace Stevens' first book of poetry, *Harmonium*. The poem was first published in 1915 in the "little magazine," *Others: A Magazine of the New Verse*.

Peter Quince in the title is the director of the naive troupe of tradesmen-players in Shakespeare's *Midsummer Night's Dream* (1595). He is a comic figure. The title gives us the ironic image of Peter Quince at the delicate instrument, his rough hands attempting to play. The somewhat awkward man at his instrument wishes to find some adequate chords to communicate his desire, which later he compares to the lust of the elders in the story of Susanna, which is told in the book of Daniel of the biblical apocrypha. Peter Quince suggests that desire is the origin of art; beauty plays on the spirit of the perceiver just as the perceiver plays on the keys of his instrument. There is a correspondence between the dynamic of arousal and that of artistry.

The two events of the poem—Quince at the clavier and Susanna and the elders in the garden—seem to occur simultaneously. A fair Hebrew wife named Susanna was falsely accused by lecherous voyeurs. As she bathes in her garden, having sent her attendants away, the red-eyed elders are bewitched into yearning for the sight of Susanna bathing. When she makes her way back to her house, they accost her, threatening to claim that she was meeting a young man in the garden unless she agrees to have sex with them. She refuses to be blackmailed and is arrested and about to be put to death for promiscuity when a young man named Daniel interrupts the proceedings, shouting that the elders should be questioned to prevent the death of an innocent. After being separated, the two men are questioned about details (cross-examination) of what they saw but disagree about the tree under which Susanna supposedly met her lover. The first says they were under a mastic. The second says they were under an evergreen oak tree. The great difference in size between mastic and an oak makes the elders' lie plain to all the observers. The false accusers are put to death and virtue triumphs.

Themes

The poem gives direct expression of sexual desire. But Peter Quince has dimensions beyond Susanna's ablutions and the elders' desire.

In this poem, a beautiful woman's humiliating encounter with lustful elders gives further meditation on the nature of beauty. And it suggests the woman's physical beauty exist forever in memory and through death in the union of body and nature: "The body dies; the body's beauty lives. / So evenings die, in their green going, / A wave, interminably flowing." The poem's Part IV contains a stunning inversion of Platonism beauty. Instead of saying that beauty is an abstract unchanging Platonic form existing perfectly in a world separate from the five senses, or an abstract unchanging concept in the mind, the poem says that, paradoxically, "Beauty is momentary in the mind": only transient beauty in the flesh is immortal. The poem may suggest that desire is the origin of art.

Literary Techniques

Musical elements are prominent in this poem. According to Stevens, poetry is music into words, and words into music. The poem develops the theme that "music is feeling" by combining the poetic devices of alliteration, assonance, and consonance with puns on musical terms to suggest the sounds of the musical instruments mentioned, as in this passage describing the feelings of the lascivious elders:

> The basses of their beings throb
> In witching chords, and their thin blood
> Pulse pizzicati of Hosanna.

Stevens created an excellent example of his musical imagism. There are three imagist poetic principles: 1, Direct treatment of poetic subjects. 2, Elimination of ornamental words. 3, Rhythmical composition in the sequence of the musical phrase rather than in the sequence of a "metronome." Stevens' "Peter Quince at the Clavier" is a case in point to bring music and poetry closer together. At the beginning of the first section there is tenderly reflective music. In contrast to this, there is the sudden intrusion of the bass music at the end. The throbbing and pulsing are made acute through the repetition of the b and p sounds. "Pulse pizzicati of Hosanna" is mimicking the plucking of strings to suggest sexual itch. The woman's situation is emphasized by descriptions of sounds from nature and musical instruments. In Section II of the poem, Susanna's thinking is subtly expressed through a few rhymes, but it is interrupted by the crash of the cymbal and the roaring horns. In Section III, the nervous rhythms and the couplets create a mincing, simpering music. "And as they whispered, the refrain / Was like a willow swept by rain." The music of Section Ⅳ is stately and sweeping. This section also evokes a sense of the continuity underlying change, partially by the use of the series of four rhymes ending in "-ing," which creates a long delaying effect.

In the poem, colors are also used to present the feelings. Stevens made use of color images, such as "blue-shadowed silk," "green evening," "in the green water," and even the "red-eyed elders." This is a reminder that he insisted also on the analogy between poetry and painting.

In sum, certain literary techniques are used in the poem: 1) allusions of the Bible and Shakespeare's work present; 2) musical and color elements naturally interwoven within the poem; 3) tensions formed in its plot and its rhetoric.

Bibliography

Doggett, Frank A. *Wallace Stevens: A Celebration.* Princeton: Princeton University Press, 1980.

Rehder, Robert. *The Poetry of Wallace Stevens.* London: Macmillan Press, 1988.

http://en.wikipedia.org/wiki/Wallace_Stevens 2012-05-03

http://wenku.baidu.com/view/8cb7d56db84ae45c3b358ca7.html 2013-03-09

http://wenku.baidu.com/view/d560b565783e0912a2162a4f.html 2012-05-04

http://www.english.illinois.edu/maps/poets/s_z/stevens/stevens.htm 2012-04-30

T. S. Eliot

His Life and Writing Career

His Life

T. S. Eliot is a shortened name for Thomas Stearns Eliot (1888—1965). Eliot was born into a middle-class family from New England on September 26, 1888. His father was a successful businessman and his mother wrote poetry. His four sisters were between eleven and nineteen years older; his brother was eight years older. He was the youngest of seven children and his parents were both 44 years old when he was born. Known to family and friends as Tom, he was named after his grandfather on his mother's side Thomas Stearns. Several elements contribute to his way on literature. Firstly, when he was a child Eliot had to overcome physical limitations and thus he had little interaction with other children; hence, he was a little bit timid and deep in thinking. Secondly, his mother Charlotte Champe Stearns, a former teacher, was an amateur poet with a taste for Emerson. Thirdly, Eliot's talent also was credited to his hometown which filled his imagination with literary vision. From 1898 to 1905, Eliot attended Smith Academy, where he studied languages included Latin, Ancient Greek, French, and German. He began to write poetry when he was 14. His first published poem "A Fable for Feasters" was written as a school exercise and was published in the *Smith Academy Record* in February 1905 and later in *The Harvard Advocate*, Harvard University's student magazine. After graduation, Eliot attended Milton Academy in Massachusetts for a preparatory year and he studied philosophy at Harvard from 1906 to 1909. He earned his bachelor's degree within three years instead of four. Eliot moved to Paris one year later and studied philosophy there. He was back at Harvard studying Indian philosophy in 1911—1914, and was awarded a scholarship to Merton College, Oxford in 1914.

In London he met his wife Vivienne Haigh-Wood, a Cambridge governess, who married him in 1915, but the marriage was not supposed to be a happy one. For her, it was to save the poet by keeping him in England, and to him, it brought the state of mind out of which came "The Waste Land." By 1916, he had completed a PhD dissertation for Harvard on knowledge and experience. On June 29, 1927 Eliot converted to Anglicanism and in November he took British citizenship. He specifically identified himself as classicist in literature, royalist in politics, and Anglo-catholic in religion. By 1932 Harvard offered him a professorship, Eliot left Vivienne in England and thought about the separation. His work *Four Quartets* led to his being awarded the Nobel Prize in literature in 1948. On January 10, 1957, Eliot at the age of 68 married Esmé Valerie Fletcher, who was 32. Eliot died of emphysema in London on January 4, 1965 due to his heavy smoking. In accordance with Eliot's wishes, his ashes were taken to St. Michael's Church in East Coker, the village from which his ancestors had immigrated to America. Eliot has been one of the most daring innovators of the twentieth century. He never compromised either with the public or indeed with language itself. In his idea, poetry should aim at a representation of the complexities of modern civilization.

 His Writing Career

T. S. Eliot settled in England for many years. There he became a schoolmaster and a bank clerk, but eventually he became the literary editor for the publishing house Faber & Faber. It paved the way later for him to become a director. He founded and edited the influential literary journal *The Criterion*, which published from October 1922 to January 1939. Eliot's goal was to make it a literary review. The first issue of the magazine included Eliot's "The Waste Land." It received contributions from Virginia Woolf, Ezra Pound, E. M. Forster, and W. B. Yeats.

T. S. Eliot was a playwright, literary critic, and one of the most important English-language poets of the 20th century. He had been one of the most daring innovators of twentieth-century poetry. Following his belief that poetry should aim at a representation of the complexities of modern civilization in language, he was famous for his description and concern for the spiritual barrenness of the modern people in his masterpieces. "The Love Song of J. Alfred Prufrock" (1915) was followed by some of the best-known poems in the English language, including "Gerontion" (1920), "The Waste Land" (1922), "The Hollow Men" (1925), "Ash Wednesday" (1930), and "Four Quartets" (1945). Those poems were notoriously obscure in understanding for their various languages and allusions from afar. His works as well as his nationality invited a lot of arguments. He was born an American, but on June 29, 1927 Eliot converted to Anglicanism from Unitarianism, and in November that year he took British citizenship. This is the reason why both American literature and British literature claim T. S. Eliot as their writer.

T. S. Eliot was a spokesman of modernity. He portrayed the modern world as the waste land and the modern people as hollow men. In addition to his poetry he also wrote dramas such as *Murder in the Cathedral* (1935), *The Family Reunion* (1939), *The Cocktail Party* (1949), *The Confidential Clerk* (1954), and *The Elder Statesman* (1959). Eliot also made significant contributions to literary criticism. He wrote such critic books as *The Sacred Wood* (1920), *Essays on Style and Order* (1929), *Elizabethan Essays* (1934), *and After Strange Gods* (1934). He dominated criticism in the period between two world wars and shaped the tastes and the critical vocabulary of a generation. He insisted that poetry should be impersonal and the poet's private life and the world he lived in have nothing to do with a true understanding of his works, which strongly influenced the school of new criticism at that time. His perspective of viewing the world and his genius and talents in conveying his idea exerted a great influence on modern literature and poets to come.

Analyses of and Comments on His Representative Poems

T. S. Eliot's Poems

"The Love Song of J. Alfred Prufrock," begun in February 1910 and published in Chicago in June 1915, is the poem that made his name and also is seen as a masterpiece of the modernist movement. He successfully portrayed a modern everyman with the method of using dramatic interior monologue. It somewhat established his fame in the literature world. "The Waste Land," a 434-line poem published in 1922 was regarded as the representative of the modernist movement and the disillusionment of the post-war generation. It is of obscure nature with satire, prophecy, and changes of speaker, location, and time. "The Waste Land" is another name for the modern world at that time. "The Hollow Men" appeared in 1925 and altogether with "The Waste Land" constructed his main work in the 1920s. It is concerned most with post-World War I Europe, in which the poet expressed the difficulty of hope and religious conversion. Eliot wrote that he produced the title "The Hollow Men" by combining the titles of the romance "The Hollow Land" with the poem "The Broken Men," but the title derives more from the character Kurtz in Joseph Conrad's *Heart of Darkness* who is referred to as "hollow at the core." "The Hollow Men" contains some of Eliot's most famous lines, notably its conclusion: "This is the way the world ends/ Not with a bang but a whimper."

"Ash Wednesday" (1930) is the first long poem written by Eliot after his 1927 conversion to Anglicanism. The poem itself is a transition in style. It deals with the aspiration to move from spiritual barrenness to hope for human salvation. But personally, Eliot regarded "Four Quartets" as his masterpiece, and it is the work that led to his being awarded the Nobel Prize in literature in 1948 "for his outstanding, pioneer contribution to present-day poetry." "Four Quartets" is a set of four poems that were published individually over a six-year period. It consists of four long poems, each first published separately: "Burnt Norton" (1936), "East Coker" (1940), "The Dry Salvages" (1941), and "Little Gidding" (1942). They represent the meditations on man's relationship with time, the universe, and the divine. Eliot combines his Anglo-Catholicism with eastern and western religious and cultural traditions. Both "Ash Wednesday" and "Four Quartets" are regarded as confessional poetry.

T. S. Eliot's Modernist Poetry

There is no exaggeration to say that T. S. Eliot shaped the taste and the form of the modern poems. As a talent in language, he mastered a variety of languages and knew many myths, fables, and stories. Allusions are seen everywhere, which prevent people from understanding. That may partly explains the reason why his poems are notoriously difficult to comprehend. His poems are for the elites rather than the common people. In addition to the allusions, the scenes in his poems shift quickly from one to another: past to present, home to abroad. They juxtapose together to make the poem appear in the reader's mind like montage the film technique. In his poems even the dead people or the people from myth are to tell their stories and talk to the living people. It seems the poems are not organized by logic but with random thoughts. And at the same time, by using the fragmentary pieces in the poems, T. S. Eliot intended to present the mental state of modern people. In the wake of WWI, buildings as well as civilization were broken into pieces. The waste land appeared in physical world as well as in mental world. People witnessed the tragedy of wars and they never knew whether they would be still living tomorrow, thus they refused to think of tomorrow and lingered in the street thinking of the past. T. S. Eliot's poetry presented the spiritual state at that time: the people as hollow men and the world as waste land. His disillusioned view largely influenced the poets to come. They saw the world with their sorrowful eyes, thought with an empty mind, and felt with sentimental heart.

The Love Song of J. Alfred Prufrock (1915)

 ## Contents Summary

The poem is commonly known as "Prufrock." It started in 1910 and published in Chicago in 1915, describing a middle-aged man Prufrock's journey one evening in an attempt to seek women. Prufrock, a modern everyman, is a kind of tragic figure caught in a sense of defeated idealism and tortured by unsatisfied desires. The poem represents his inability to live a meaningful existence in the modern world.

The pronouns "I," "us," and "you" produce a sense of uncertainty. "I" should be the speaker, of course, but "J. Alfred Prufrock" suggests no certain identity. Compared with Robert Browning's dramatic monologue, which is to explore the inner feeling of the historical characters, J. Alfred Prufrock is nobody but an invented person. To think who is "you" in the poem and what is the relationship between "you" and "I" eventually forms "us." Some critics suggest that "you" is the implied reader whoever reads this poem, and some suggest that "you" is the imagined person that Prufrock keeps in mind in order to accompany him to overcome his timidity, but others with Freudian ideas in mind argue that "you" is another aspect of the same person: their relationship is the ego and superego.

Through the random thoughts going through a person's head, the poem is psychological rather than logical. Similarly, critics dispute whether Prufrock is going somewhere during the course of the poem. Prufrock uses various outdoor images: the sky, streets, cheap restaurants and hotels, fog, which enable people to think that Prufrock is on his way to an afternoon tea. Others, however, believe that Prufrock is not physically going anywhere, but rather, is playing through it in his mind.

The title "the love song" usually reminds us of the romantic language the man uses in the courtship for a woman and more often the boy will think highly of the beauty of the girl and simultaneously boast of his strength and power. But Profrock presents his negative sides. He is neither a prophet (Lazarus) nor a tragic hero (Hamlet). He is eager for women while his cowardness and timidity prevent him from moving forward. He is somewhat an anti-hero of modern time who is lacking the heroic qualities of a traditional hero such as courage, honesty, heroism, and idealism.

They will say: "How his hair is growing thin!" "But how his arms and legs are thin!" Prufrock is concerned about his hair and teeth. Collar mounting firmly to the thin and the simple pin show his concern over aging. Prufrock thinks that he has passed his prime of life and he is no more attractive and handsome, which causes his indecisiveness, but "Do I dare / Disturb the universe?" enormously exaggerates the crippling fear. How can an ordinary court generate such a huge power to disturb the universe It is a typical modern cultured man who is good at empty thinking while lacking in a step forward. And "there will be time, there will be time," the repetitions endlessly delay his action.

The women are no better portrayed. Women in sawdust restaurants with oyster-shells are no upper class ladies, but they are "talking of Michelangelo," an Italian renaissance painter, sculptor, architect, poet, and engineer who exerted an unparalleled influence on the development of western art. Michelangelo was considered the greatest living artist in his lifetime, and ever since then he has been held to be one of the greatest artists of all time. How can the women come and go in a cheap restaurant talk of Michelangelo? It is just a way to show a pretentious artistic style or a false or exaggerated interest in art.

Themes

Significance of the poem: the story of J. Alfred Prufrock is the one that many people can relate to their own personal feelings and desires. He is the image of an ineffectual sorrowful, tragic 20th century western man, possibly the modern intellectual who is divided between passion and timidity, between desire and impotence. This is the first poem of importance by Eliot, one of the most memorable pieces because of its unflinching undisguised satire on the genteel society, showing the emptiness, the listlessness, and the boredom of these men and women in superb, effectively ironic style.

Literary Techniques

Simile The evening is compared to a patient who is etherized. Modern people are so inert that they are paralyzed bodily as well as mentally. The image of the evening is in fact the projection of Prufrock's mind.

Different Languages It may suggest the poet's ability in mastering different languages and simultaneously expressing his ideas more thoroughly. Or it is conveying the idea that the phenomenon is a universal one at that time.

Allusions "I know the voices dying with a dying fall" echoes Orsino's first lines in Shakespeare's *Twelfth Night*. Phrases such as, "there will be time" and "there is time" are also reminiscent of the opening line of English metaphysical poet Andrew Marvell (1621—1678) 's poem. In the final section of the poem, Prufrock rejects the idea that he is Prince Hamlet.

Color "The yellow fog" and "yellow smoke" appear in the poem. The color of yellow represents weakness and morbidity. The images of "fog" and "smoke" are characterized by passiveness and listlessness which are typical of Prufrock's existence.

Irony The very title of the poem can serve as a good example. It is not a love song but a story of a love failure. The name is a combination of two contradictory words "prude and frock." In fact, Alfred was a great emperor in the British history, but the character here is a nobody, which adds more to the ironic effect. The images of sawdust restaurants with oyster-shells make readers feel languor and decay rather than the warmth of love.

The Waste Land (1922)

Contents Summary

T. S. Eliot composed "The Waste Land" in the autumn of 1921, while taking a vacation in Switzerland. Before returning to London, he visited Ezra Pound at Paris and left the draft with him. Pound blue-penciled it and reduced its length which was nearly twice as long as its present form. So T. S. Eliot dedicated the poem to him. In October 1922, Eliot published the poem in *The Criterion*. The first appearance of the poem in the US was in the November 1922 issue of *The Dial* magazine.

The title may refer to the desert, a symbolic situation after WW I. In fact, the title of the poem draws its significance from the Fisher King story, which is a part of the Grail legend. As the story goes, the Fisher King sins against God, who then punishes him by making him sexually impotent. The disability of the King is reflected on his land, so that his kingdom becomes a waste land. Hence is the title. To restore the King and his land to fertility, a quest (search) is undertaken to search for the Holy Grail, the cup which is said to have been used by Jesus Christ at the Last Supper. Thus the story of the Fisher King and the quest of the Holy Grail serve as the governing myth of "The Waste Land". The poem established his position as the leader of a whole generation of writers who were called as "Waste Land Painters" like Hemingway and Faulkner.

Themes

It concerns the spiritual crisis of postwar Europe of the 1920s. "The Waste Land" is a 434-line modernist poem, consisting of 5 parts: 1) The Burial of the Dead; 2) A Game of Chess; 3) The Fire Sermon; 4) Death by Water; 5) What the Thunder Said.

The epigraph in the beginning of the poem talks about the Sibyl from the Greek mythology. Sibyl was a famous prophetess. She was given the power of prophesy and a-thousand-year life by Apollo. She forgot to ask for eternal youth and she shrank into withered old age. At last, she preserved herself within a jar. When the boys asked her, "Sibyl, what do you want?" She answered, "I want to die." Death alone offers escape; death alone promises the end, and therefore a new beginning. Here, death and life are easily blurred. Death can spring life, and life in turn necessitates death. The quotation is followed by a dedication to Ezra Pound, who blue-penciled this poem.

In the first section, the poem begins with a description of the seasons. The paradox is there at the very beginning of the poem: April is the cruelest month. Shouldn't it be the kindest? The lovely image of lilacs in the spring is here associated with "the dead land." In spring, "memory and desire" mix. The poet becomes acutely aware of what he is missing, of what he has lost, and of what has passed him by. The narrator clings to memories that would seem to suggest life in all its vibrancy and wonder: summer rain in Munich, coffee in a German park, sledding with a cousin in the days of childhood. The second stanza returns to the tone of the opening lines, describing a land of "stony rubbish"—dead tree, dry stone quite simply the "waste land" of the poem's title. Eliot used biblical language to construct a sort of dialogue between the narrator—the "son of man"—and a higher power. The former is desperately searching for some sign of life, but all he can find are dry stones, dead trees, and "a heap of broken images." There is no relief from the beating sun, and no trace of water. Suddenly Eliot switches to German, quoting directly from German composer Richard Wagner (1813—1883) 's *Tristan and Isolde*. In Wagner's opera, Isolde, on her way to Ireland, overhears a sailor singing this song, which brings with it ruminations of love promised and of a future of possibilities. After this digression, Eliot offers the reader "hyacinth girl." Looking upon the beloved girl, he "knew nothing"; that is to say, faced with love, beauty, and "the heart of light," he saw only "silence." From here Eliot switches abruptly to a more prosaic mode, introducing Madame Sosostris. This fortune-teller is known across Europe for her skills with Tarot cards. The narrator remembers meeting her when she had "a bad cold." Her meeting with the narrator concludes with a hasty bit of business. The final stanza of this first section of "The Waste Land " begins with the image of an "unreal city" echoing Baudelaire's "fourmillante cite," in which a crowd of people flows over London Bridge while a "brown fog" hangs like a wintry cloud over the proceedings. The narrator sees a man he recognizes named Stetson. He cries out to him, and it appears that the two men fought together in a war. He then asks Stetson whether the corpse he planted last year in his garden has begun to sprout.

The next section, "A Game of Chess," shifts the narrator from the streets of London to a gilded drawing room, in which sits a rich lady who complains about her nerves and wonders what to do. The poem drifts again to a pub where two Cockney women gossip. Within a few stanzas, we have moved from the upper class to London's lower class.

The third section, "The Fire Sermon," opens with an image of a river. The narrator sits on the banks where he sees maidens sing a song of lament, one of them crying over her loss of innocence to a similarly lustful man.

"Death by Water," the fourth section of the poem, describes a dead Phoenician lying in the water, perhaps the same drowned sailor of whom Madame Sosostris spoke.

The fifth section, "What the Thunder Said," is the ending, which shifts from the sea to rocks and mountains. The narrator cries for rain, and it finally comes. The thunder generates three-pronged dictum sprung from the Brihadaranyaka Upanishad: "Datta, dayadhvam, damyata": to give, to sympathize, and to control. It seems to suggest the collapse of civilization, corresponding with the scene that "London bridge is falling down falling down falling down."

 ## Literary Techniques

The poem has been called "one of the most important poems of the 20th century." In spite of the fact that the poem is full of satires, allusions, and prophecies, the poem has become a familiar touchstone of modern literature. The past and present are perfectly interwoven together to give a sense of historic and mythic meaning. The modern emptiness and sterility are vividly presented. The hero is the common and unknown people, thus the poem largely reveals the mental state of modern man. Eliot's poems are often quoted, among which famous phrases, such as "April is the cruelest month" and "I will show you fear in a handful of dust" are frequently used. The poem is known for its obscure nature with satire and prophecy. Despite this, it has become a touchstone of modern literature, a poetic counterpart to James Joyce's *Ulysses*.

Some literary techniques are used in the poem:

Various Places and Languages They represent modernity and internationality.

Allusions The Fisher King's sin and quest for Holy Grail are presented to make the poem a whole one in form and in meaning.

Stream of Consciousness Because of the use of stream of consciousness, it is often difficult to determine what is meant to be interpreted literally or symbolically.

Bibliography

Chinitz, David. *A Companion to T. S. Eliot*. New Jersey: Wiley-Blackwell, 2009.

Moody, Anthony David. *The Cambridge Companion to T. S. Eliot*. Shanghai: Shanghai Foreign Language Education Press, 2000.

Tamplin, Ronald. *A Preface to T. S. Eliot*. Beijing: Peking University Press, 2005.

http://en.wikipedia.org/wiki/T._S._Eliot 2012–01–10

http://en.wikipedia.org/wiki/The_Hollow_Men 2013-03-17

http://www.english.illinois.edu/maps/poets/a_f/eliot/eliot.htm 2011-12-10

http://www.gradesaver.com/the-waste-land/study-guide/short-summary/ 2013-02-19

http://www.nobelprize.org/nobel_prizes/literature/laureates/1948/eliot-bio.html 2013-03-17

F. Scott Fitzgerald

His Life and Writing Career

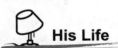

His Life

Francis Scott Key Fitzgerald (1896—1940) is usually viewed as the spokesman of the Jazz Age and the Roaring Twenties in the American history, an epoch characterized by booming wealth, exuberance, excessive consumption as well as decadence and carelessness. Of all American writers concerned with the inventions of modernism, F. Scott Fitzgerald was the most autobiographical. "Sometimes," Fitzgerald once said, "I don't know whether I'm real or whether I'm a character in one of my own novels." It is, in a sense, true in that many of Fitzgerald's works are vivid portraits of his and his wife's lavish lifestyle and eventual downfall as Fitzgerald descended into alcoholism and his wife, Zelda, into madness.

Fitzgerald was born in Saint Paul, Minnesota—the Mid-West, "the provinces" of America. He was the namesake and second cousin three times removed of Francis Scott Key, the author of the US. national anthem. His father Edward Fitzgerald (1853—1931) was an unsuccessful manufacturer of wicker furniture in Saint Paul and later dismissed from his job as a salesman in upstate New York. After that, the family went back to Saint Paul and lived a comfortable and respectable life on his mother Mary ("Mollie") McQuillan (1860—1936) 's inheritance. Fitzgerald attended the St. Paul Academy and at the age of 13, got his first piece of writing—a detective story published in the school newspaper. At the age of 15, he was sent to the Newman School, a prestigious Catholic preparatory school in New Jersey, where he met Father Sigourney Fay, who noticed his incipient talent with written word and encouraged him to pursue his literary ambitions. After graduating from the Newman School in 1913, Fitzgerald decided to stay in New Jersey to continue his artistic development at Princeton University. Although talented in writing, he was a failure in terms of academic performances and finally dropped out of school in 1917 to join the army. The war ended just before Fitzgerald saw combat—he actually never left the country. While stationed in Alabama, he met the most important woman in his life, Zelda Sayre, an outshining eighteen-year-old southern belle, and fell in love with her immediately. The two were engaged, but Zelda was not willing to marry him until the publication of his first novel *This Side of Paradise* (1920) was a spectacular success. The two got married eventually and a year later, their daughter (only child) Frances Scott ("Scottie") Fitzgerald was born.

Young, seemingly wealthy and beautiful, the Fitzgeralds soon became literary celebrities in New York and embarked on an extravagant and reckless lifestyle that earned him a reputation as a playboy. Throughout the rest of his career, Fitzgerald supported his family financially by writing great numbers of short stories for popular publications such as *The Saturday Evening Post* and *Esquire*. In 1922, Fitzgerald published his second novel, *The Beautiful and the Damned*, which helped to cement his status as one of the great chroniclers and satirists of the culture of wealth, extravagance and ambition that emerged during the affluent 1920s—which Fitzgerald christened "the Jazz Age." "It was an age of miracles," Fitzgerald wrote, "it was an age of art, it was an age of excess, and it was an age of satire." The public attention helped to sell Fitzgerald's stories and to make him the most highly paid magazine fiction writer of the twenties, but gradually he could hardly make ends meet because of the couple's opulent lifestyle.

In 1924, the Fitzgeralds moved to France and remained there until the end of 1926, alternating between Paris and the Riviera. In France, Fitzgerald befriended Gertrude Stein and Ernest Hemingway, whom he admired greatly. And he wrote, revised, and published his masterpiece *The Great Gatsby* (1925). However, contrary to Fitzgerald's expectations, *the Great Gatsby* was not as financially successful as his previous novels, although critics thought highly of it. From the late 1920s until his death, Fitzgerald suffered one misfortune after another—Zelda's affair with a French aviator and her mental illness, his own unsuccessful stint of screenwriting in Hollywood back in the United States and his drinking and financial problems. The Fitzgeralds returned to France in 1929, where Zelda suffered her first breakdown and Fitzgerald had to work on short stories to pay for his wife's psychiatric treatment. They returned to America and rented a house in Montgomery, Alabama. Zelda remained in and out of mental hospitals, but while she was hospitalized, she wrote *Save Me the Waltz*, an autobiographical novel, which Fitzgerald regarded as pre-empting the material that he was using in his novel-in-progress, *Tender Is the Night* (1934). Although it was his most ambitious novel, it was a commercial failure and its merits were matters of critical dispute. For several years Fitzgerald lived near Baltimore and made several failed efforts to write.

Drunk, ill, in debt, and unable to write commercial stories, Fitzgerald went to Hollywood alone in the summer of 1937 to write screen scripts. Although he managed to earn a considerable amount of money to pay off most of his debts, he was unable to save. His trips east to visit Zelda were disastrous. In California, Fitzgerald fell in love with a movie columnist, Sheilah Graham. In 1939, he began his Hollywood novel, *The Love of the Last Tycoon* (which was published posthumously and incomplete as *The Last Tycoon* in 1941) and had written more than half of a working draft when he died of a heart attack in Graham's apartment on December 21, 1940 at the age of 44. Zelda Fitzgerald perished in a fire at Highland Hospital in 1948.

F. Scott Fitzgerald died believing himself a failure. None of his works received anything more than modest commercial or critical success during his lifetime. However, since his death Fitzgerald has gained a reputation as one of the preeminent authors in the history of American literature due almost entirely to the enormous posthumous success of *The Great Gatsby*. As perhaps the quintessential American novel, as well as a definitive social history of the Jazz Age, *The Great Gatsby* has become required reading for virtually every American high school student for the past half century, and had a transportive effect on generation after generation of readers.

His Writing Career

Literary opinion makers used to be reluctant to accord Fitzgerald full marks as a serious craftsman. His reputation as a drinker inspired the myth that he was an irresponsible writer; yet he was a painstaking reviser whose fiction went through layers of drafts. Fitzgerald's clear, lyrical, colorful, and witty style evoked the emotions associated with time and place. When critics objected to Fitzgerald's concern with love and success, his response was: "But, my God! It was my material, and it was all I had to deal with." His manuscripts corroborate his conscientious craftsmanship. Even in his commercial stories, "there was one little drop of something not blood, not a tear, not my seed, but me more intimately than these, in every story, it was the extra I had."

Like most writers, Fitzgerald's thematic interests ran deeper than wider. Whether exploring the inevitability of loss and the thin line that separates failure from success, the quest for self-determination, the effects of class and money on morality, the attenuating values of the 1920s, or the dangers of dissolution and the struggle to maintain self-discipline, he rarely sought to reinvent himself to patent his imprimatur. As he insists in "One Hundred False Starts," a good writer must repeat himself: "Otherwise, one would have to confess to having no individuality at all." The chief theme of Fitzgerald's work was aspiration—the idealism he regarded as defining American character. Another major theme was mutability or loss.

Fitzgerald wrote altogether five novels in his life, including an unfinished one. As one of the earliest examples of a novel about college life, his first novel *This Side of Paradise* (1920) was accepted as the voice of the younger generation in a society increasingly oriented toward youth. He combined the traditional narrative and rhetorical gifts of a good fiction writer, it appeared, with a thoroughly modern sensibility. Perhaps the definitive novel of the *Lost Generation*, it tells the story of Amory Blaine, a handsome, wealthy Princeton student who halfhearted involves himself in literary cults, "liberal" student activities and a series of empty flirtations with young women. When he finally does fall truly in love, however, the young woman rejects him for another. After serving in France during the war, Blaine returns to embark on a career in advertising. Still young, but already cynical and world-weary, he exemplifies the young men and women of the 1920s, described by Fitzgerald as "a new generation grown up to find all Gods dead, all wars fought, all faiths in man shaken."

His second novel *The Beautiful and Damned* (1922) provides a portrait of the eastern elite during the Jazz Age, exploring New York café society. It tells the story of Anthony Patch (a 1920s socialite and presumptive heir to a tycoon's fortune), his relationship with his wife Gloria, his service in the army, and alcoholism. As with his other novels, Fitzgerald's characters are complex, especially in their marriage and intimacy, much like how he treats intimacy in *Tender Is the Night*. The book is believed to be largely based on Fitzgerald's relationship and marriage with Zelda Fitzgerald.

With his third novel *The Great Gatsby*, Fitzgerald made a conscious departure from the writing process of his previous novels. Fitzgerald set out, as he put it, to "make something new— something extraordinary and beautiful and simple and intricately patterned." And, to achieve this, the first and most important choice he made was to drop the third-person narrator of his two previous novels. Instead of an omniscient viewpoint, there is a fictional narrator, Nick Carraway, a man who is only slightly involved in the action but who is profoundly affected by it. The structure of *The Great Gatsby* is compact; the style is dazzling; and its images of automobiles, parties, and garbage heaps seem to capture the contradictions of a consumer society. It is *The Great Gatsby* that establishes Fitzgerald's status as one of the most important American writers.

His fourth novel *Tender Is the Night* (1934) follows the decline of a young American psychiatrist whose personal energies are sapped, and his career corroded equally by his marriage to a beautiful and wealthy patient and his own weakness of character ("character" was one of Fitzgerald's favorite concepts). As in *The Great Gatsby*, the character begins as a disciple of the work ethic and turns into a pursuer of wealth, and the American dream accordingly turns into a nightmare. Although the novel was not sold well when it was published, it is considered now as another Fitzgerald's masterpiece, aside from *The Great Gatsby*.

According to *Publishers Weekly*'s 1993 review of the edition reconstructed by Fitzgerald scholar Matthew J. Bruccoli, Fitzgerald's last and unfinished novel *The Love of the Last Tycoon* is "generally considered a roman a clef," inspired by the life of film producer Irving Thalberg, on whom protagonist Monroe Stahr is based. The story follows Stahr's rise to power in Hollywood, and his conflicts with rival Pat Brady, a character based on studio head Louis B. Mayer. Fitzgerald wrote the novel in a blend of first person and third person omniscient narrative. While the story is ostensibly told by Cecelia, many scenes are narrated in which she is not present. Occasionally a scene will be presented twice, once through Cecelia and once through a third party. The revised edition of *The Love of the Last Tycoon* won the Choice Outstanding Academic Books award of 1995.

At the peak of his fame, Fitzgerald so flaunted the connection between his life and his writing that the resulting facade of self-absorption became a defining facet of his literary persona. Yet interpreting Fitzgerald's protagonists as versions of himself underestimates the amount of imaginative transformation that went into his fiction. While the autobiographical impetus behind a certain plot or motif is often easily identified, his works usually deviate from authorial actualities to serve a literary purpose. Fitzgerald was certainly the poet laureate of the Jazz Age and his way of writing about that age, and its aftermath, laid bare fundamental issues—about American and modern society and how "we" define ourselves as human beings. He was no doubt a romantic, but a romantic with a firm grip on reality, a cold, knowing eye. For Fitzgerald, the personal was the political; he saw the quality of private experience as gauge of society, a way of understanding history. That is why his fiction is an intimate disclosure of its author and his times and of ourselves, the "we" of his audience, as well.

In addition to his novels, Fitzgerald wrote many short stories that treat themes of youth and promise along with despair and age. Four collections were published in his lifetime—*Flappers and Philosophers* (1921), *Tales of the Jazz Age* (1922), *All the Sad Young Men* (1926), and *Taps at Reveille* (1935), and six after his death—*Afternoon of an Author* (1957), *Babylon Revisited and Other Stories* (1960), *The Pat Hobby Stories* (1962), *The Basil and Josephine Stories* (1973), *The Price Was High: Fifty Uncollected Stories* (1979), and *The Short Stories of F. Scott Fitzgerald* (1989). Some of his most notable stories include "The Diamond as Big as the Ritz," "The Curious Case of Benjamin Button," "The Camel's Back," and "The Last of the Belles."

Analysis of and Comment on His Representative Novel

The Great Gatsby (1925)

Plot Summary

The Great Gatsby is a story told by Nick Carraway, a young man who has moved from the Midwest to West Egg, Long Island, seeking his fortune as a bond salesman in the summer of 1922. He rents a house in the West Egg district of Long Island, a wealthy but unfashionable area populated by the new rich, a group who have made their fortunes too recently to have established social connections and who are prone to garish displays of wealth. Nick's next-door neighbor in West Egg is a mysterious man named Jay Gatsby, who lives in a gigantic Gothic mansion and throws extravagant parties every Saturday night.

Nick is unlike the other inhabitants of West Egg—he was educated at Yale and has social connections in East Egg, a fashionable area of Long Island home to the established upper class. Nick drives out to East Egg one evening for dinner with his cousin, Daisy Buchanan, and her husband, Tom, an erstwhile classmate of Nick's at Yale. Daisy and Tom introduce Nick to Jordan Baker, a beautiful, cynical young woman with whom Nick begins a romantic relationship. Nick also learns a bit about Daisy and Tom's marriage: Jordan tells him that Tom has a lover, Myrtle Wilson, who lives in the Valley of Ashes, a gray industrial dumping ground between West Egg and New York City. Not long after this revelation, Nick travels to New York City with Tom and Myrtle. At a vulgar, gaudy party in the apartment that Tom keeps for the affair, Myrtle begins to taunt Tom about Daisy, and Tom responds by breaking her nose.

As the summer progresses, Nick eventually garners an invitation to one of Gatsby's legendary parties. He encounters Jordan Baker at the party, and they meet Gatsby himself, a surprisingly young man who affects an English accent, has a remarkable smile, and calls everyone "old sport." Gatsby asks to speak to Jordan alone, and, through Jordan, Nick later learns more about his mysterious neighbor. Gatsby tells Jordan that he knew Daisy in Louisville in 1917 and is deeply in love with her. He spends many nights staring at the green light at the end of her dock, across the bay from his mansion. Gatsby's extravagant lifestyle and wild parties are simply an attempt to impress Daisy. Gatsby now wants Nick to arrange a reunion between himself and Daisy, but he is afraid that Daisy will refuse to see him if she knows that he still loves her. Nick invites Daisy to have tea at his house, without telling her that Gatsby will also be there. After an initially awkward reunion, Gatsby and Daisy reestablish their connection. Their love rekindled, and they begin an affair.

After a short time, Tom grows increasingly suspicious of his wife's relationship with Gatsby. At a luncheon at the Buchanans' house, Gatsby stares at Daisy with such undisguised passion that Tom realizes Gatsby is in love with her. Though Tom is himself involved in an extramarital affair, he is deeply outraged by the thought that his wife could be unfaithful to him. He forces the group to drive into New York City, where he confronts Gatsby in a suite at the Plaza Hotel. Tom asserts that he and Daisy have a history that Gatsby could never understand, and he announces to his wife that Gatsby is a criminal—his fortune comes from bootlegging alcohol and other illegal activities. Daisy realizes that her allegiance is to Tom, and Tom contemptuously sends her back to East Egg with Gatsby, attempting to prove that Gatsby cannot hurt him.

When Nick, Jordan, and Tom drive through the Valley of Ashes, however, they discover that Gatsby's car has struck and killed Myrtle, Tom's lover. They rush back to Long Island, where Nick learns from Gatsby that Daisy was driving the car when it struck Myrtle, but that Gatsby intends to take the blame. The action then switches back to Wilson who, distraught over his wife's death, sneaks out and goes looking for the driver who killed Myrtle. Nick retraces Wilson's journey, which placed him, by early afternoon, at Gatsby's house. Wilson murders Gatsby and then turns the gun on himself.

After Gatsby's death, Nick is left to help make arrangements for his burial. What is most perplexing, though, is that no one seems overly concerned with Gatsby's death. Daisy and Tom mysteriously leave on a trip and all the people who so eagerly attended his parties, drinking his liquor and eating his food, refuse to become involved. Even Meyer Wolfshiem, Gatsby's business partner, refuses to publicly mourn his friend's death. Only a few people attend Gatsby's funeral— Gatsby's father Henry Gatz, a few servants, the postman, and the minister at the graveside. Despite all his popularity during his lifetime, in his death, Gatsby is completely forgotten.

Nick, completely disillusioned with what he has experienced in the East, prepares to head back to the Midwest. Before leaving, he sees Tom Buchannan one last time. Their discussion reveals that Tom was the impetus behind Gatsby's death. When Wilson came to his house, he told Wilson that Gatsby owned the car that killed Myrtle. In Tom's mind, he had helped justice along. Nick, disgusted by the carelessness and cruel nature of Tom, Daisy, and those like them, leaves Tom, proud of his own integrity.

On the last night before leaving, Nick goes to Gatsby's mansion, then to the shore where Gatsby once stood, arms outstretched toward the green light. The novel ends prophetically, with Nick noting how we are all a little like Gatsby, boats moving up a river, going forward but continually feeling the pull of the past.

Themes

The Decline of the American Dream in the 1920s On the surface, *The Great Gatsby* is a story of the thwarted love between a man and a woman. The main theme of the novel, however, encompasses a much larger, less romantic scope. Though all of its action takes place over a mere few months during the summer of 1922 and is set in a circumscribed geographical area in the vicinity of Long Island, New York, *The Great Gatsby* is a highly symbolic meditation on 1920s America as a whole, in particular the disintegration of the American dream in an era of unprecedented prosperity and material excess.

Fitzgerald portrays the 1920s as an era of decayed social and moral values, evidenced in its overarching cynicism, greed, and empty pursuit of pleasure. The reckless jubilance that led to decadent parties and wild jazz music—epitomized in *The Great Gatsby* by the opulent parties that Gatsby throws every Saturday night—resulted ultimately in the corruption of the American dream, as the unrestrained desire for money and pleasure surpassed more noble goals. When

World War I ended in 1918, the generation of young Americans who had fought the war became intensely disillusioned, as the brutal carnage that they had just faced made the Victorian social morality of early-twentieth-century America seem like stuffy, empty hypocrisy. The dizzying rise of the stock market in the aftermath of the war led to a sudden, sustained increase in the national wealth and a newfound materialism, as people began to spend and consume at unprecedented levels. A person from any social background could, potentially, make a fortune, but the American aristocracy—families with old wealth—scorned the newly rich industrialists and speculators. Additionally, the passage of the *Eighteenth Amendment* in 1919, which banned the sale of alcohol, created a thriving underworld designed to satisfy the massive demand for bootleg liquor among rich and poor alike.

Fitzgerald positions the characters of *The Great Gatsby* as emblems of these social trends. Nick and Gatsby, both of whom fought in World War I, exhibit the newfound cosmopolitanism and cynicism that resulted from the war. The various social climbers and ambitious speculators who attend Gatsby's parties evidence the greedy scramble for wealth. The clash between "old money" and "new money" manifests itself in the novel's symbolic geography: East Egg represents the established aristocracy, West Egg the self-made rich. Meyer Wolfshiem and Gatsby's fortune symbolize the rise of organized crime and bootlegging.

As Fitzgerald saw it (and as Nick explains in Chapter 9), the American dream was originally about discovery, individualism, and the pursuit of happiness. In the 1920s depicted in the novel, however, easy money and relaxed social values have corrupted this dream, especially on the East Coast. The main plotline of the novel reflects this assessment, as Gatsby's dream of loving Daisy is ruined by the difference in their respective social statuses, his resorting to crime to make enough money to impress her, and the rampant materialism that characterizes her lifestyle. Additionally, places and objects in *The Great Gatsby* have meaning only because characters instill them with meaning: the eyes of Doctor T. J. Eckleburg best exemplify this idea. In Nick's mind, the ability to create meaningful symbols constitutes a central component of the American dream, as early Americans invested their new nation with their own ideals and values.

Nick compares the green bulk of America rising from the ocean to the green light at the end of Daisy's dock. Just as Americans have given America meaning through their dreams for their own lives, Gatsby instills Daisy with a kind of idealized perfection that she neither deserves nor possesses. Gatsby's dream is ruined by the unworthiness of its object, just as the American dream in the 1920s is ruined by the unworthiness of its object—money and pleasure. Like 1920s Americans in general, fruitlessly seeking a bygone era in which their dreams had value, Gatsby longs to re-create a vanished past—his time in Louisville with Daisy—but is incapable of doing so. When his dream crumbles, all that is left for Gatsby to do is die; all Nick can do is move back to Minnesota, where American values have not decayed.

The Hollowness of the Upper Class   One of the major topics explored in *The Great Gatsby* is the sociology of wealth, specifically, how the newly minted millionaires of the 1920s differ from and relate to the old aristocracy of the country's richest families. In the novel, West Egg and its denizens represent the newly rich, while East Egg and its denizens, especially Daisy and Tom, represent the old aristocracy. Fitzgerald portrays the newly rich as being vulgar, gaudy, ostentatious, and lacking in social graces and taste. Gatsby, for example, lives in a monstrously ornate mansion, wears a pink suit, drives a Rolls-Royce, and does not pick up on subtle social signals, such as the insincerity of the Sloanes' invitation to lunch. In contrast, the old aristocracy possesses grace, taste, subtlety, and elegance, epitomized by the Buchanans' tasteful home and the flowing white dresses of Daisy and Jordan Baker.

What the old aristocracy possesses is in taste, however, it seems to lack in heart, as the East Eggers prove themselves careless, inconsiderate bullies who are so used to money's ability to ease their minds that they never worry about hurting others. The Buchanans exemplify this stereotype when, at the end of the novel, they simply move to a new house far away rather than condescend to attend Gatsby's funeral. Gatsby, on the other hand, whose recent wealth derives from criminal activity, has a sincere and loyal heart, remaining outside Daisy's window until four in the morning in Chapter 7 simply to make sure that Tom does not hurt her. Ironically, Gatsby's good qualities (loyalty and love) lead to his death, as he takes the blame for killing Myrtle rather than letting Daisy be punished, and the Buchanans' bad qualities (fickleness and selfishness) allow them to remove themselves from the tragedy not only physically but psychologically.

Literary Techniques

Fitzgerald relies heavily on images to function as symbols to serve a thematic purpose. For example, the green light, which is situated at the end of Daisy's East Egg dock and barely visible from Gatsby's West Egg lawn, represents Gatsby's hopes and dreams for the future. Gatsby associates it with Daisy, and in Chapter 1 he reaches toward it in the darkness as a guiding light to lead him to his goal. Because Gatsby's quest for Daisy is broadly associated with the American dream, the green light also symbolizes that more generalized ideal. In Chapter 9, Nick compares the green light to how America, rising out of the ocean, must have looked to early settlers of the new nation.

Another symbol is the Valley of Ashes between West Egg and New York City consisting of a long stretch of desolate land created by the dumping of industrial ashes. It represents the moral and social decay that results from the uninhibited pursuit of wealth, as the rich indulge themselves with regard for nothing but their own pleasure. The Valley of Ashes also symbolizes the plight of the poor, like George Wilson, who live among the dirty ashes and lose their vitality as a result.

Instead of an omniscient viewpoint, Fitzgerald adopted a dual narrative system with a first-person narrator—Nick. Partly influenced by Joseph Conrad, this technique is able to filter action and meaning through Nick, who is at once involved with the action and profoundly affected by it. To some extent, Nick is quite like the protagonist Jay Gatsby. Both are young people from the Midwest trying to prove themselves in the East. The East, and in particular its cities, have become for them a new frontier, a neutral space in which their dreams of wealth, measureless power, and mobility may perhaps be realized. And both of them have a love affair with charismatic woman that ends in disillusion: Gatsby with Daisy and Nick with Jordan. This creates a bond of sympathy between the two men. Nick is looking back on an action already completed that, as we know from the beginning, ended in disaster, some "foul dust" that "floated in the wake" of Gatsby's dreams; he is also recording how he grew to sympathize with, like, and admire Gatsby. Like, however, does not mean approval, and it does not inhibit criticism. Nick has had "advantages" that Gatsby, born to poverty as James Gatz, has not had. He has a reserve, a common sense and even an incurable honesty that make him quite different from the subject of his meditations. That helps to create distance, enables him to criticize Gatsby and the high romanticism he embodies, and it makes his commentary vividly plural; Nick is, as he himself puts it, "within and without, simultaneously enchanted and repelled" by the hero he describes. The use of Nick as a narrator, in effect, enables Fitzgerald to maintain a balance for the first time in his career between the two sides of his character. The idealist, the romantic who believed in possibility and perfectibility, and the pragmatist, the realist, convinced that life is circumscribed, nasty, brutish, and short: these opposing tendencies are both allowed their full play, the drama of the narration is the tension between them. "The test of a first-rate intelligence," Fitzgerald was later to say in his autobiographical essay "The Crack-Up" "is the ability to hold two opposed ideas in the mind at the same time, and still retain the ability to function." That is precisely what he does in *The Great Gatsby*, thanks to the use of Nick Carraway as a narrator: by his own stringent standards, the book is the product not only of refined sensibility and a strenuous act of imaginative sympathy but also of "a first-rate intelligence."

As many critics have pointed out, the method Fitzgerald adopts in *The Great Gatsby* is a brilliant one. He starts the novel in the present, giving us, in the first three chapters, a glimpse of the four main locales of the novel: Daisy's house in East Egg (Chapter 1); the Valley of Ashes and New York (Chapter 2); and Gatsby's house in West Egg (Chapter 3). Having established the characters and setting in the first three chapters, he then narrates the main events of the story in Chapters 4 to 9, using Chapters 4, 6, and 7 to gradually reveal the story of Gatsby's past. The past and present come together at the end of the novel in Chapter 9.

Fitzgerald gives us the information as Nick gets it, just as we might find out information about a friend or acquaintance in real life, in bits and pieces over a period of time. Since we don't want or cannot absorb much information about a character until we truly become interested in him, Fitzgerald waits to take us into the past until close to the middle of the novel. As the story moves toward its climax, we find out more and more about the central figure from Nick until we, too, are in a privileged position and can understand why Gatsby behaves as he does.

Thus the key to the structure of the novel is the combination of the first person narrative and the gradual revelation of the past as the narrator finds out more and more. The two devices work extremely effectively together, but neither would work very well alone.

Bibliography

Baym, Nina. *The Norton Anthology of American Literature, Shorter Fifth Edition*. New York & London: W. W. Norton & Company, 1999. 2124–2125.

Curnutt, Kirk. *The Cambridge Introduction to F. Scott Fitzgerald*. Shanghai: Shanghai Foreign Language Education Press, 2008. 13–27, 41, 44, 53.

Fitzgerald, F. S. *This Side of Paradise*. New York: Dover Publications, Inc., 1996.

Gray, Richard. *A History of American Literature*. Cornwall: Blackwell Publishing Ltd., 2004. 435–440.

Gross, Dalton & Mary Jean Gross. *Understanding the Great Gatsby*. Beijing: China Renmin University Press, 2008. 2–5, 17–25.

Oakes, E. H. *American Writers*. New York: Facts on File, Inc., 2004. 126–128.

Prigozy, Ruth. *F. Scott Fitzgerald*. Cambridge: Cambridge University Press, 2002. 1–27.

http://en.wikipedia.org/wiki/F._Scott_Fitzgerald 2013-02-05

http://en.wikipedia.org/wiki/The_Beautiful_and_Damned 2013-02-06

http://en.wikipedia.org/wiki/The_Great_Gatsby 2013-02-06

http://en.wikipedia.org/wiki/The_Love_of_the_Last_Tycoon 2013-02-06

http://www.biography.com/people/f-scott-fitzgerald-9296261?page=1 2013-02-05

http://www.cliffsnotes.com/study_guide/literature/great-gatsby/book-summary.html 2013-02-07

http://www.studyworld.com/studyworld_studynotes/great_gatsby/themes.htm 2013-02-07

Ernest Hemingway

His Life and Writing Career

His Life

Ernest Miller Hemingway (1899—1961) was an American author and journalist. The prime of his artistic creation was between the mid-1920s and the mid-1950s, during which he produced most of his works. As a prolific writer, he published seven novels, six short story collections, and two nonfiction works in his life time, while three novels, four collections of short stories, and three nonfiction works were published posthumously, many of which are ranked among the classics of American literature. Being the spokesman for the Lost Generation, Hemingway, in his books, well captured and reflected the mood of his generation and his time. His philosophy and beliefs were embodied in the characters he portrayed known as the "Hemingway hero." He experimented with new and effective techniques and developed his unique style, influential in the 20th century and beyond. His ideas about literary creation were well summarized in his "iceberg theory." Hemingway was awarded the Pulitzer Prize for fiction in 1953 and the Nobel Prize in literature in 1954.

Hemingway was born on July 21, 1899, in Oak Park, Illinois. His father was a physician and his mother was a musician. His father loved outdoor sports like hunting and fishing. When he was a child, his father taught him to hunt, fish, and camp in the woods and lakes, which cultivated his love for outdoor adventure. He took part in a number of sports, such as boxing, track and field, water polo, and football when he was at high school. Throughout his life, he remained a sports lover, fascinated by bullfighting, deep-sea fishing, and big game hunting. This fondness had a great influence on his writing. His writing practice began as early as when he was a teenager. When he was a school boy, he took a journalism class and contributed to the school newspaper. This laid the foundation for his writing. Hemingway worked as a journalist before becoming a novelist.

After graduating from high school, he went to work for *The Kansas City Star* as a reporter. The six-month working experience as a reporter laid the foundation for his later writing style. In 1918, Hemingway was recruited as a voluntary ambulance driver working with the Red Cross. While serving in the Italian front, he was seriously wounded. This war experience was to be the basis for his novel *A Farewell to Arms* (1928) and it had a lasting effect on his life and writing as well.

Back to the United States, he worked with a commercial journal for some time and then on Sherwood Anderson's advice, he went to Paris, where he worked as a foreign correspondent for the Canadian *Toronto Star*. Paris was then the centre where many modernist writers and artists lived. In Paris, Hemingway got acquainted with such modernist writers as Gertrude Stein, James Joyce, and Ezra Pound, who, among other modernist writers and artists of the 1920s, exerted an immense influence on him. Stein, the leading figure of modernism in Paris, became Hemingway's mentor. The term "Lost Generation" she used to refer to the expatriate artists and writers became popular with the publication of his first novel *The Sun Also Rises* (1926). The novel portrays the post-war expatriate generation, the so called Lost Generation. It was well received and established his reputation as an important writer and the spokesman for the post-World War I generation. Hemingway visited Spain in 1923, where for the first time, he watched/participated the fiesta and became fascinated by bullfighting. It was shortly after the fiesta when he began to write the draft of what would become *The Sun Also Rises*, which involved the fiesta as its background. Also in Spain, during the summer of 1929, Hemingway worked on his next work, *Death in the Afternoon* (1932), a non fiction book about the ceremony and traditions of Spanish bullfighting, covering the theme of fear, death, and courage. In 1933 Hemingway embarked on a 10-week journey to East Africa. This experience provided material for Hemingway's second work of nonfiction *Green Hills of Africa* (1935) as well as for the short stories "The Snows of Kilimanjaro" and "The Short Happy Life of Francis Macomber." On his return from abroad, in early 1934, he began to work on *Green Hills of Africa*, which was published in 1935.

In 1936, the Spanish Civil War broke out. It was fought from 1936 to 1939 between the Republicans and the Nationalists. In 1937 Hemingway went to Spain to work as a correspondent for the North American Newspaper Alliance (NANA). What he observed while reporting on the war provided material for his novel *For Whom the Bell Tolls* (1940). The novel tells a story about a young American, Robert Jordan, in the International Brigades attached to a republican guerrilla unit, fighting heroically for the Republicans in the Spanish Civil War. It was an immediate success. It was sold half a million copies within months and was nominated for a Pulitzer Prize. As an important novel in ten years, it successfully re-established Hemingway's literary reputation. It is regarded as one of Hemingway's best works. Also in 1937 while he was in Spain, his novel *To Have and Have Not* was published. Like *The Torrents of Spring* (1926), it is also set in the United States. It is a social commentary on 1930s.

In 1946, Hemingway began working on *The Garden of Eden* (1986), his second posthumously published novel. He worked on it for 15 years. In this novel, Hemingway explores the male-female relationships and the reversal of gender roles. In 1950, *Across the River and into the Trees* came out. It was inspired by his platonic love affair with the then 19-year-old girl he fell in love with while traveling in Europe in 1948. The book met with negative reviews. Critics began to doubt his literary talent. To answer their doubt, the following year, Hemingway wrote the draft of *The Old Man and the Sea* (1952) in eight weeks. Published in 1952, it turned out to be his last major novel. It was well received both by the reading public and the critics. It reached five and a half million people when published in *Life* magazine, which sold 5,318,650 copies within 48 hours. The novel not only restored his reputation but also made him internationally famous. It was awarded the Pulitzer Prize for Fiction in 1953 and contributed to the awarding of the Nobel Prize in Literature to Hemingway in 1954. In 1957, Hemingway began to work on *A Moveable Feast* and finished it in 1959. It is a set of memoirs about his years in Europe, especially in Paris, when he was a young writer in the American expatriate circle of writers in 1920s. The book was published posthumously in 1964. On July 2, 1961, Hemingway committed suicide.

 ## His Writing Career

Hemingway was a very productive writer with distinguishing mastery of modern art. His major works include *The Sun Also Rises* (1926), *A Farewell to Arms* (1929), *For Whom the Bell Tolls* (1940) and *The Old Man and the Sea* (1951). When he was an apprentice in literature, he took such established writers as Anderson as his mentors. *Three Stories and Ten Poems* (1923), his first published work and also his first short story collection, is a good example of Anderson's influence both in theme and style. His first novel, *The Torrents of Spring* (1926) is a parody of Anderson's style.

In Our Time (1925), Hemingway's first collection of short stories, is of great importance in his writing career. Its publication earned him a place among the most promising American writers of the period. And it is in this book that Hemingway invented a recurrent semi-autobiographical character Nick Adams, established the primary themes resonant in his later stories and novels and almost formed a distinctive style of his own. The book was first published in Paris in 1924 with the title *In Our Time*. The 1925 volume contains several well-known stories, including the Nick Adams stories, stories with Nick Adams as the protagonist mainly about his initiation and adolescence. They are "Indian Camp," "The Doctor and the Doctor's Wife," "The End of Something," "The Three-Day Blow," "The Battler," "Big Two-Hearted River," and so on. Nick Adams was Hemingway's semi-autobiographical character who appeared repeatedly in his later stories and novels. The first story with Nick Adams as the protagonist was "Indian Camp", one of Hemingway's greatest short stories, first published in 1924 in a literary magazine in Paris and republished in *In Our Time*. Nick Adams was the initial prototype/a character type of Hemingway hero. In "Indian Camp," an initiation story, Nick Adams is exposed to childbirth and to violent death—an experience that causes young Nick to face the grisly reality and learn to live in grace under pressure. In the last story of the collection, "The Big-Two Hearted River," Nick Adams is once more confronted with the issues of life and death and endeavors to cope with them.

The world in which Nick Adams grows up is one of violence, disorder, and death. His physical wound in the war results in his psychological and emotional wound, he turns to nature for solace and learns to cope with them with grace and dignity. Starting with Nick Adams, this type of Hemingway hero dominates almost all of Hemingway's later stories and novels. It appears not only in such collections as *Men Without Women* (1927) and *Winner Takes Nothing* (1933) but also in such novels as *The Sun Also Rises* (1926), *A Farewell to Arms* (1928), *For Whom the Bell Tolls* (1940), and *The Old Man and the Sea* (1952). Jake Barnes, the protagonist of *The Sun Also Rises* suffers from the physical impotence caused by the war. Caught in a world of violence, disorder, and meaninglessness, he can do nothing but rely on himself and combat against fate with heroism. Likewise, the protagonist of *A Farewell to Arms,* Frederic Henry, thrusts into a world of killing, death, and chaos, fights on his own against odds with grace under pressure. Both Jake Barnes and Frederic Henry have war experiences and both are disillusioned at the war and the world. The horrible reality alienates them from the society and makes them turn inwardly for strength and fight a solitary fight against a hostile force. Robert Jordan in *For Whom the Bell Tolls* (1940), too, fights fiercely a battle with the slim chance of winning it. Unlike Jake Barnes and Frederic Henry, he is not fighting single-handedly but he is fighting for a cause—democracy. Hemingway hero is presented at its fullest in *The Old Man and the Sea*. Santiago, an old Cuban fisherman, fights a battle with a great marlin. Though he is fully aware of the futility of his effort, yet he keeps on fighting because this is the way to display his unbeatable spirit. Santiago is the epitomized of Hemingway hero. Nick Adams, Jake Barnes, Frederic Henry, and Santiago all adhere to the same principle or the code of honor.

In *The Old Man and the Sea* the Hemingway hero, or the "code hero," is shown to be one who complies with the "code of honor" that "…a man is not made for defeat…A man can be destroyed but not defeated." This "code of honor" is summed up as "grace under pressure." The Hemingway hero lives out this code while confronting adversity and death. Hemingway holds a very negative and pessimistic world view. The world to him is one that is "all a nothing" and "all nada" ("A Clean Well-Lighted Place"). This nihilistic world view is well illustrated by the fictional world he creates. His world is one full of chaos, killing, violence, and death, without meaning and hope. The true Hemingway code hero is fully aware that the universe without God is indifferent, horrific, chaotic, and meaningless. He learns that he is the one to create meaning and order through his personal values, such as integrity, dignity, courage, and so on. He knows that life is full of tension and pain and that there is no possibility of winning the struggle with it. A true Hemingway hero endures the pains of life without complaint and keeps on fighting with "despairing courage" because what matters is his heroism exercised during his fighting and by so doing he succeeds in living out his "code of honor" that is "grace under pressure."

Besides "grace under pressure," death is another common theme of Hemingway's work, which is established in stories as early as "Indian Camp." In this story, Nick Adams is made to witness the death of the father who commits suicide, an event that shapes his personality. The theme of death is central in Hemingway's writings.

Another primary theme permeating much of Hemingway's subsequent work is war, the destructive quality of war. This is evident in *The Sun Also Rises*. Jake Barnes gets wounded in the war, leaving him physically impotent. The destructive effect of war is even more notably exemplified in *A Farewell to Arms*, where war and death go hand in hand. Death is the most horrific reality. It is a mysterious power, unpredictable and inescapable. The war, a futile struggle of man against man, is an example of the indifference of the universe, the death it causes being an extending consequence of the cruel world. Death is prevailing. Catherine's death is such an example. The theme of war and death is also uttered through Henry: "But they killed you in the end. You could count on that. Stay around and they would kill you" (the final chapter).

Obviously Hemingway's world view is the result of the influence of nihilism and existentialism. As his books demonstrate, life is suffering, resulting from purposeless, meaningless, and valueless of living, and from the loneliness and uselessness of man's effort, as well as from the indifference of the universe and the society. This suffering is intensified by the sense of emptiness and meaningless it generates. Another distinctive characteristic of modern life is absurdity, a product of the so-called development of civilization, modernization, and material-orientedness of the modern society, in which man gets lost, alienated as order-taking machines and killing machines as in purposeless wars. Hemingway hero is meant to seek and create meaning out of the meaningless world. This is where the meaning of his books lies and where the power of his books comes from. And this is one reason why his books endure.

Hemingway is indebted to his literary precursors such as Sherwood Anderson, Gertrude Stein and others, when it comes to writing style. In his literary apprenticeship, Hemingway learned from them, but over the years he had developed a unique style. Hemingway called his style the iceberg theory, which he explained in *Death in the Afternoon* (1932), "The dignity of movement of an iceberg is due to only one-eighth of it being above water." This style is also referred to as the "theory of omission," that is to "get the most from the least." Below the seemingly simple surface of factual description or narration lies the real meaning of the work.

Right from his first volume of short stories *In Our Time* (1925), Hemingway began to employ his iceberg theory of writing. A good example is "Big Two-Hearted River," the last story of the collection. In this story, the author describes in great detail the activities carried out by Nick, underneath these activities is hidden the emotional turmoil. Nick's physical wound and internal war are hinted at instead of being made explicit. Meaning is established through his action.

Hemingway is well-known for his simple style of writing or the economical style of writing, characterized by a spare, reportorial prose based on simple sentence structure and use of simple diction. This is in part due to the fact that Hemingway was a journalist before becoming a novelist. He learned the economical writing techniques from writing for newspapers. Hence, the journalistic style of omission. His distinctive style gained the recognition even with the publication of *In Our Time* (1925). Its author was praised for his use of spare language about 70 percent of the sentences are simple sentences. Linguistically, Hemingway's prose style is simple, clear, direct, and precise. His diction is simple, concrete, and fundamental. His sentences are short, simple, declarative, and sometimes ungrammatical. He favored the repetition of words, phrases, and sentence structures and habitually used the word "and" to replace commas. Sometimes this simplicity is even to the point of monotony. Yet, much is conveyed through this simplicity. In fact, the minimum use of words can achieve the strongest effect. The short simple sentences are laden with implications as well as strong emotions. This is the way Hemingway applied his principle to "get the most from the least."

Hemingway's style can also be seen as an achievement of the revolution he accomplished along with Ezra Pound, T. S. Eliot, and James Joyce in literary style and language, a reaction against the elaborate style of 19th century writers. His influence in style as a modern writer is so immense that it is beyond time and space. In 1954, when Hemingway was awarded the Nobel Prize for literature, his citation by the Nobel Prize Committee spoke highly of "his powerful style-forming mastery of the art" of creating modern fiction.

His major published books are: *In Our Time* (1925), *The Sun Also Rises* (1926), *Death in the Afternoon* (1929), *A Farewell to Arms* (1929), *To Have and Have Not* (1937), *For Whom the Bell Tolls* (1940), *Across the River and into the Trees* (1950), *The Old Man and the Sea* (1951), *A Moveable Feast* (1964, posthumous).

Analyses of and Comments on His Representative Novels

The Sun Also Rises (1926)

Plot Summary

Jake Barnes is the protagonist. He is an expatriate American journalist living in Paris. He gets wounded in a war, leaving him physically impotent. Brett Ashley, an Englishwoman, is his lover. She is a new woman, twice-divorced, with numerous love affairs.

The story opens with Jake playing tennis with his college friend Robert Cohn. He picks up a prostitute (Georgette), and accidentally meets Brett and Count Mippipopolous in a nightclub.

Brett and Jake leave together by taxi. On the way, she tells him that she loves him, but they know their love cannot last long.

Bill Gorton from New York and Brett's fiancé Mike Campbell from Scotland have just arrived and join Jake. Jake and Bill travel to Spain with the intention to meet Robert Cohn north of Pamplona for a fishing trip. Cohn, however, leaves for Pamplona to wait for Brett and Mike. Cohn used to be Brett's lover. Although she is engaged to Mike, he still wants to keep the relationship with her. With their absence, Jake and Bill spend five days peacefully, fishing the streams near Burguete. After that they rejoin Cohn and Brett in Pamplona, where they indulge in drinking.

Cohn is becoming less and less welcome in the group who insult him with anti-semitic remarks. Now comes the fiesta, during which the group enjoy themselves by drinking, eating, watching the running of the bulls, attending bullfights, and they quarrel with each other, too. At Montoya's hotel, Jake introduces Brett to Romero, a 19-year-old matador. Brett is so attracted by him that she seduces him, resulting in jealousy as well as fistfights among the men. Jake, Campbell, Cohn, and Romero each love Brett. After the fiesta, sober again, they leave Pamplona for different places. Brett had left with Romero, but later she decided to go back to Mike. In a cheap hotel, without money, she sends Jake a telegram for help when he is about to return to Paris. The novel ends with Jake and Brett in a taxi.

Themes

The themes of *The Sun Also Rises* are implied in its two epigraphs. The first refers to the post-war generation, the Lost Generation, including the young English and American expatriates and those involved in the war. They were disillusioned with the old ideals and values as well as western civilization in general and at the same time they could find no trustworthy spiritual guides. The war left them with a psychic trauma, frustrations, and a sense of emptiness, to which they reacted with cynical hedonism. Jake's wound is a metaphor for the disability of the entire generation. The other epigraph is a long quotation from Ecclesiastes. Hemingway used it to convey his world view, that is, the universe is indifferent to human sufferings. It has its own law, its own purpose and value. It is immortal. What one can do in the face of adversity is to face up to it, accept the grim reality, and bear with it with grace and courage.

Jake Barnes is the representative of the Lost Generation and an example of Hemingway hero. The novel vividly presents his spiritual growth, from one indulging in seeking sensory pleasure to escape the painful reality to one learning to confront it with courage and live with dignity. Three places and events are vital to his spiritual journey. They are Paris—the symbol of the waste land, the trout streams of the Irati River symbolizing the restorative power of nature, and the bullfight—metaphor for courage and the power of dominance.

Jake is the representative of those "battered" by the war both physically and mentally or either physically or mentally. His wound is the symbol of the devastation done by the war on the whole post-war generation physically, mentally, and morally. His sexual impotence implies the spiritual inadequacy and decadence of the entire generation, the signal of the decline in morality and the values of the period. Jake and his company, Brett, Cohn, Mike, and Bill are shown wandering in Paris seeking momentary solace by drinking, eating, and playing. By so doing, they try to forget pain and escape from reality. Paris is like the waste land devoid of vitality, and above all, morality, with its dwellers living pointlessly without thought and feeling. Different from others, Jake struggles to learn how to live with purpose and dignity in the world of emptiness and meaninglessness, despite all the odds.

Jake's fishing with Bill Gorton on their way from Paris to Pamplona prepares him for his spiritual enhancement in Spain. The tranquility of nature makes him settle down and feel life with a fresh feeling. Fishing is obviously a symbolic activity separating him from his old dispirited life in Paris. The trout streams of the Irati River at Burguete signals a sort of spiritual rebirth, a recovery of health after the emotional crisis.

Jake's return to health is achieved through his watching the bullfight in Spain. Bullfight is a central metaphor in the novel. It serves as a paradigm for the game of life and death. Jake discovers in the primitive game of Spain about the Spaniard's tragic sense of life and death. He comes to accept suffering and death as they are because they are inescapable realities. This realization helps to heal his psychological wounds in a way. Another lesson Jake draws from bullfight is given by Romero. Romero is a code hero. As a torero, he must learn to live with fear and death. In the bullring, he confronts violence and death with skill and courage so that he attains honor and dignity. The ultimate act of domination over the death of the bull is demonstrated in the last moments of the bullfight, in the act of the final sword thrust. The way Romero conducts bullfighting exemplifies a kind of disciplined and courageous life. His ability to dominate the bull symbolizes his ability to control and dominate his fate. Jake sees the similarity between the torero and himself. From the bullfight, he acquires a model of masculine conduct displayed by Romero when he performs bullfight with courage and grace. He becomes mature, his psychological wounds healed, his confidence restored. Now he is a man with integrity, discipline, and control.

Other themes including love, death, and the nature of masculinity are also explored.

Literary Techniques

The Iceberg Theory Hemingway's writing style is characterized by his application of his iceberg theory, also known as the "theory of omission." This is a sort of minimalistic style with a focus on the surface descriptions of the landscapes or activities of the characters while the themes lurking underneath. Hemingway believes the true meaning of a piece of writing lies below the surface just like the movement of an iceberg with only one-eighth of it being above water. Hemingway applied his iceberg theory excellently in *The Sun Also Rises*. Much of the book is devoted to the description of the activities of the characters, their excessive drinking, partying, and seeking sensory pleasure. Underneath this frenzy and absurd behavior are the disillusion, the frustrations, and helplessness. The spiritual crisis the post-war generation suffers from is not presented but implied. The description of the bullfighting scene is another good example illustrating Hemingway's use of his iceberg theory. Hemingway's description focuses on the bullfighter. It is detached, reportive, with short and simple sentences typical of his writing style. What's happening in the bullring is the one-eighth above water while the implications it carries is the seven-eighths under the water. Obviously the bullfighting scene is essential in conveying the meaning or the theme of the novel. However, it is concealed under the surface story. It invites the reader to detect and savor.

Symbolism   A concrete application of his iceberg theory is the use of symbolism. Jake Barnes' wound is an important symbol symbolizing the physical and spiritual sufferings the First World War imposed on the Lost Generation as well as those involved in the war. And Jake Barnes' sexual impotence caused by the "wound" stands for the spiritual impotence, that is, the spiritual decay, the disillusion, and the frustrations of the Lost Generation in particular and that of the post-war westerners in general. In the novel, Jake Barnes' sexual impotence is only hinted at by means of understatement, and its symbolic meaning is implied. In the middle section of the novel, the author elaborates the fishing trip Jake Barnes takes with his friends. Obviously the hard facts convey something else, a different message about the action. Here the trip stands for self-examination, self-rediscovery and above all, rebirth. Likewise, the underlying truth the scene of bullfighting bears is also presented via symbolism. Bullfighting functions as a symbol for the real world, a world of life and death. The matadors dancing in the bullring are heroes who are confident and courageous enough to face up to death and skillfully triumph over death and end up as the one to dominate rather than being dominated. The bullring epitomizes the real world. Another dominant symbol in the novel is the symbol of taxi. The story begins with Jake Barnes taking taxi and ends with Jake Barnes meeting Brett in a taxi, and throughout the story, now and then, Jake Barnes and his friends are shown wandering around aimlessly by taxi. Their physical action is used to provide an interpretation of the nature of man's existence. Here, taxi symbolizes the taxi takers' aimless, purposeless, and meaningless state of existence and their endless quest for meaning as well. But this symbolic meaning is what under the water. What is above the water is the author's factual representation of the characters' actions.

Hemingway's concrete application of his iceberg theory is also exemplified by his use of understatement, presenting images and scenes without explanations to convey meanings and themes, and his restrained use of description to depict characters and actions.

The Sun Also Rises was regarded as one of the first American modernist novels, which marked the real rise of American modern novels. It emerged with brand-new themes, characters, and features both in form and style. After World War I, Hemingway and other modernists "lost faith in the central institutions of western civilization." As a revolt against the elaborate style of 19th century writers, they created a style in which meaning is established through dialogue, through action, and so on, and in which little is stated explicitly. Hemingway's novel, *The Sun Also Rises*, written on the iceberg theory is a good case in point.

The Old Man and the Sea (1952)

 ### Plot Summary

The Old Man and the Sea is Hemingway's final work published during his lifetime. It was awarded the Pulitzer Prize for Fiction in 1953 and was specifically cited by the Nobel Prize Committee as contributing to the awarding of the Nobel Prize in literature to Hemingway in 1954. The success of the book won Hemingway an international recognition.

The novella's overall structure can be divided into three parts based on the three phases of Santiago's journey, a cycle from the land to the sea and then back to the land again.

Eighty-four days have passed and Santiago, an old, experienced Cuban fisherman, has not caught a fish in the familiar waters of the Gulf of Mexico north of his seacoast village in Cuba. He is considered to be the most unlucky person. It is for that reason that Manolin, his young apprentice, was forced to leave him by his parents. Santiago began to teach him to fish when he was just five. Manolin still visits him each night when he comes back from fishing. He offers to help him and gets him food. The two usually talk about American baseball, especially the player Joe DiMaggio.

On the eighty-fifth day, Santiago sets out alone in his skiff. He sails far out onto the Gulf. By noon of the first day, a big fish takes his bait. It must be a marlin. It is so big that Santiago is unable to pull it in but instead it is pulling his skiff. Two days and two nights pass in this manner, though wounded by the struggle with it, Santiago refers to him as a brother out of compassion and appreciation for him.

On the third day of the ordeal, both the old man and the fish are worn out. The old man puts an end to the long battle between them by stabbing the marlin with a harpoon with all the strength left in him. Santiago straps the marlin to the side of his skiff and heads home.

The trail of blood left by the marlin in the water attracts sharks. Santiago fights a heroic battle with them, killing five of them and driving the others away, but they keep coming. By nightfall the sharks have almost devoured the entire marlin, leaving only a skeleton with its backbone, its tail, and its head. Finally reaching the shore before dawn on the next day, Santiago struggles on his way home. Reaching home, he throws himself onto his bed and falls into a deep sleep.

Santiago is still asleep the next morning when Manolin comes to check on him. Manolin cries at the sight of the old man's injured hands and quietly goes out to get him some coffee. A group of fishermen gather around the boat where the fish's skeleton is still attached. One of them measures it to be 18 feet (5.5 m) from nose to tail. Manolin brings the old man newspapers and coffee. When the old man wakes, Manolin tells the old man that he wants to come back to fish with him for he still has much to learn from him. Santiago asks what his family will say, the young man replies that he doesn't care and so they promise to fish together once again. Manolin tells the old man to get well, for there is much he can teach him, and then asks how much the old man suffered. Santiago replies that he suffered a lot. Manolin says he'll get him some medicine for his hands.

That afternoon, some tourists at the terrace see the remains of the marlin. They mistaken it for a shark and remark to one another that they didn't know sharks had such beautiful tails. Back in his shack, with the boy beside him, Santiago sleeps again and dreams of his youth—of lions on an African beach.

Themes

Grace under Pressure   One central theme of the novella is the recurrent theme in Hemingway's novels, that is, living with "grace under pressure," which is demonstrated by his "code hero" Santiago, an old fishing man. Santiago possesses many of Hemingway code heroes' characteristics, a man of action, who never shies away from adversity and lives by his own beliefs or codes. Santiago describes himself as "a strange old man." He is strange in the sense that he is unconventional in his community. And what makes him unconventional is his philosophy and internal code of behavior. He remains dedicated to them and to his passion for his profession above concerns for material gain or survival. He sees his profession as a more spiritual way of life and a part of nature's order in the eternal cycle in which all creatures are brothers sharing the common condition of being both predator and prey. It is his dedication to his craft that separates him from the pragmatic fishermen motivated by money. Santiago is a man of action, who faces up to his odds, 84 days without catching a fish and begins his solitary quest for the big fish. Far out at the sea, he fights single-handed a gallant battle against the repeated attacks of the vicious sharks. Exhausted and helpless as he is, he never gives up. Now and then he draws his inspiration and confidence from religion, baseball, memories of his own youth, his love for Manolin, and so on. He is a man who is able to keep alive in himself the hope and dreams to withstand suffering. He lives up to his conviction that "A man can be destroyed but not defeated." For Santiago, what matters most in life is to live with great fervor and nobility following his beliefs, to do his best to use his skills and nature's gifts, and to accept inevitable destruction with dignity. What ennobles and makes him a success is his perseverance against overwhelming odds. He accepts the formidable challenge and sees it through to the end. Whether he wins or loses his battle with the great fish is less important than fighting a good and honorable fight in which he exercises his heroism. Despite a lifetime of hardships he suffers from, he is still a man in charge. His eyes remain young, cheerful, and undefeated. He has successfully reasserted his identity as a great fisherman, proving once again his dedication to his craft and the value of his philosophy, the basis of that dedication. The skeleton of the marlin stands as the testimony of the old man's failure and the symbol of his spiritual triumph, too.

Suffering and Redemption   An underlying theme of the novella is religious, the theme of suffering and redemption. The novel is rich in its religious images and allusions, esp. the allusions to the crucifixion. Santiago, the old fisherman, can be interpreted as the incarnation of Jesus Christ. He is compared with Christ in His struggle to redeem fallen man. The early descriptions of him suggest that he has endured many ordeals. He is old, thin and gaunt, with deep wrinkles on the back of his neck and blotches of skin cancer on his face and hands and with scars on his hands from handling heavy fish on cords, all of which is the consequence of a long life of hard work and meager existence. Besides, he never had children and his wife has died. Indeed, he is a poor man whose best days are behind him. Worse still, as a fisherman, he has gone 84 day without catching a fish. Amid the sneer and despise of his fellow fishermen, he embarks on a solitary fishing trip. Far out at sea, he undergoes a three-day ordeal, the worst ordeal of all, suffering piercing injury to the palms of his hands and back, experiencing extreme thirst, struggling with the marlin and the attacking sharks, through which he demonstrates "what a man can do and what a man endures" and proves that he is indeed "a strange old man," who can be "destroyed but not defeated." Returning from the trip, exhausted, staggering and falling, he carries the mast up the hill toward home while keeps looking back at the marlin's skeleton. It is an allusion to Christ carrying the cross to Golgotha. When he reaches home and finally lies down in bed, he sleeps with his arms straight out. Again, it alludes to Christ, the crucified Christ. Christ submits to the crucifixion for the redemption of mankind. Likewise, Santiago must accept his suffering and defeat so as to redeem his individual life. His trip to the sea is a trip of self-redemption and self-reassertion. Its meaning is affirmed by the skeleton of the marlin and Manolin the boy. The skeleton, the evidence of Santiago's epic catch, is already becoming the stuff of legend, which turns out to be a vehicle for the intrinsic values of his existence. Manolin helps Santiago recognize that he has succeeded in reasserting his identity as an incomparable fisherman dedicated to his craft and the value of his belief. As the story goes, the next morning, when Santiago finally awakens and tells Manolin, "They beat me," Manolin replies, "He didn't beat you. Not the fish." His redemption is achieved through his suffering and endurance. Here, the Hemingway code hero and the God-like figure merge into one whose greatness lies in their firmness in holding on to their beliefs, their courage to endure ordeals and their unbeatable spirit of never giving up as well as accepting destruction with dignity.

Santiago arises high above those caught between the two world wars, who were disillusioned with traditional values and ideals, even disenchanted with life, indulging in hedonism, leading an aimless and meaningless life. Santiago's experience of self-redemption and self-reassertion might offer inspiration, courage, and hope to them. In this sense, his trip at the sea is beyond its own significance. Just like Christ who sacrifices his life for the redemption of mankind and whose resurrection also gives hope and the promise of eternal life, Santiago endures all the hardships and sufferings so as to save all the men. In this way, the image of the old man and the image of God merge into one. They both have the sense of responsibility, the spirit of self-sacrifice and fraternity, and above all, personal strength which comes within. This might explain Hemingway's intention in identifying the ordinary old man in real life with the biblical figure, the God. Through this image, Hemingway affirms the values and meanings of life.

The Natural Order and Man's Role in It   The novella also explores the theme of the natural order and man's role in it. The story revolves around Santiago's journey from the land to the sea and then back to the land again. This cyclical journey forms the basic structure of the novel and more importantly it suggests the condition of human life and the nature of the natural world.

All living creatures are interdependent in the universe. The natural order binds together all creatures in mutual dependency and a common fate. Recognizing his connection to nature, Santiago affectionately refers to the sea as *la mar* (the Spanish feminine), beautiful, temperamenta, and emotional. He loves her and knows quite well that as part of nature, it can be very cruel occasionally. Rowing alone, he feels he is at one with nature. He hears the flying fish and regards them as friends. He feels sympathy for the delicate sea birds that must cope with an ocean at times beautiful and cruel for survival. Santiago affirms his place in the natural order and his kinship with all other living creatures. This kind of relationship is more intensely dramatized through his interaction with the marlin. From the moment Santiago feels the marlin's first tug at the other end of the line, he feels connected to it. This connection becomes more intimate as they remain locked in the life-and-death battle for three days. He first sympathizes with and admires the fish and then empathizes and identifies with it. Out in the middle of the sea, they are both alone without help. Santiago finds in it the same qualities he possesses and admires: nobility of spirit, endurance, beauty, and dignity. He even wonders if it is sinful to kill it for whatever purposes. He eventually decides that he kills it because he is a fisherman. He is born to be a fisherman just as the fish is born to be a fish. They coexist in a world where "everything kills everything else" and where they are locked in the natural cycle of predator and prey. He has to do what he is destined to do and what his role in the eternal nature demands. Just as he says, "I love you and respect you very much. But I will kill you dead before this day ends." The marlin's death represents his victory. Yet shortly after his victory, he is attacked by the first shark. Victor as he is, he inevitably must fall subject to nature's endless cycle of predator and prey. Like the marlin, he must lose and become victim. The shark, as the predator, only assumes its rightful place in the natural order and does what it is born to do, just as what Santiago does. All creatures are predator and prey, but they also nourish one another, which is symbolized by Santiago's eating the marlin's flesh to sustain himself. By taking part of it, he becomes one with it. The two of them reach a kind of communion. And the marlin's death is not meaningless.

Here the fundamental message is that in the natural world where "everything kills everything else" and also nourishes everything else, all creatures are interdependent, and they all remain subject to nature and the eventual destruction in the natural order. The meaning of individual life in nature's endless cycle is to live with great enthusiasm, making good use of one's skills, and whatever offered by nature, and then accepting the eventual destruction with dignity. Similarly, life is an endless cycle. This natural cycle of life consists of a passage from youth to old age and a passing on of whatever one generation possesses and values to the next generation, just as Santiago's relationship with Manolin suggests. Santiago is mentor, spiritual father, old man, or old age while Manolin is pupil, son, boy, or youth. Santiago is the great fisherman and Manolin his apprentice faithful to him and what he represents. In giving the marlin's spear to the boy, the old man is passing on whatever he possesses and values to him, his successor. In accepting the marlin's spear from the old man, Manolin accepts for all time Santiago's legacy. By dramatizing Santiago's connection with nature and the other creatures and his relationship with the boy, Hemingway affirms on a deeper level of the values and meanings of individual life.

 ## Literary Techniques

The Iceberg Theory Hemingway's application of his iceberg theory in this novella is to the utmost. One primary way to apply his iceberg principle is the use of religious allusions. From its first paragraphs, the novella is laden with religious images and allusions which are what under the water, expanding and deepening its spectrum in meaning. The central allusion is that to the crucified Christ. On the surface, Santiago is an ordinary old fisherman, yet various inexplicit evidences suggest his association with Jesus Christ in a variety of ways. In fact, he can be interpreted as the incarnation of Jesus Christ. The details concerning Santiago's plight, his fishing trip out at sea and his returning are surface stories, what underlies is the message about man's suffering and redemption. Like Christ who submits to the crucifixion for the redemption of mankind, Santiago must accept his suffering and defeat so as to redeem his individual life. His trip to the sea is suggestive of a trip of self-redemption and self-reassertion. Just like Christ who sacrifices his life for the redemption of mankind, Santiago endures all the hardships and sufferings so as to save himself and all the men.

Hemingway's application of his iceberg theory also lies in the allegorical quality of the old man's story. On the surface, it is a realistic story about an old fisherman and a young man who loves him, and the old man's battle with a giant fish. Yet it is a story with under-the-surface meanings. It is similar to an allegory. Likewise, the characters become more than themselves— they become archetypes. Santiago becomes an archetype representing the human condition. And his story becomes everyone's story. It is truly universal and genuinely uplifting, too. Ultimately, his heroic struggle not only redeems himself but inspires and saves those around him.

Resorting to resonances from historical and factual references is again an effective method Hemingway used to apply his iceberg theory. These references provide background information, establish the story's cultural context, and advance the plot. On top of that, they indirectly reveal the characters, and contribute to the story's integral thematic dimensions. For example, having read yesterday's newspaper, Santiago tells the boy about "the baseball" by referring to Joe DiMaggio. His reference to DiMaggio predicts his upcoming battle at sea and reflects his deep faith in the indomitability of the human spirit Joe DiMaggio stands for. By associating the old fisherman with the great baseball player, Hemingway reveals his endurance and indomitable spirit and strengthens one central theme of the story, as well.

Hemingway prefers to use the detailed description of activities to reveal characters and convey themes. On the surface, these descriptions are realistic, yet they touch on the story's multiple themes and reveal layers of meaning and larger significances embraced in the story. Take the section at the sea for example. In this section, the old man's fishing process is described in great detail. This elaboration demonstrates Santiago's considerable skill as a fisherman, his commitment and devotion to his profession, and his capacity to cultivate and draw upon the inspiration to sustain himself in the face of hardship. Here we see that Santiago, though stuck in plight, is still a man in charge, confronting all the new challenges with calm and ease. The descriptive details resonate with the ever-expanding meanings of the story.

The materialization of Hemingway's iceberg theory is also achieved by the use of symbolism. Among the various symbols scattering in the novella, the sea, baseball and the baseball player Joe DiMaggio, and the lions are the dominant symbols. The sea not only serves as the setting of the story, but also symbolizes the universe. The old man affectionately refers to it as *la mar*, the feminine. Alone at sea, he is at one with it. Yet, as part of the universe, it is also cruel, full of danger and challenges. It stands for the battle field where the old man's battle against nature is unfolded. The more vicious and fierce the sea is, the more heroic, and tragic the old man's combat against it is. The sea is undefeatable. Similarly, the old man is unbeatable in spirit. Against the background of the sea, the old man's courage and strength is highly intensified. Baseball and the great baseball player Joe DiMaggio play an important role as symbols. Again and again, they are mentioned or appear in the old man's talk with the boy or in his memories. Baseball is a very competitive and demanding game, challenging one's courage and endurance. DiMaggio stands for the indomitability of the human spirit. Hemingway again and again connects Santiago to the great DiMaggio to show that like DiMaggio the old man also possesses such noble spirit. When

Santiago is alone far out at the sea, he dreams of young lions on the beach in Africa, where he sailed as a young man. On the one hand, the lions are a source of inspiration for him, and on the other hand, he identifies himself with them. The lions are symbolic of qualities such as courage, strength, grace, and dignity—all the qualities of a fighter that Santiago appreciates, admires, and cherishes. Back home after accomplishing his heroic feat at the sea, the old man dreams of the lions again when he falls asleep. It seems to suggest that he feels relieved that, though no longer a young man, he still maintains the spirit represented by the lions and that he has exercised and exhibited that spirit to the fullest. That's what matters. The sea, baseball and the baseball player, and the lions are actually interrelated symbols which coordinately and indirectly reveal the protagonist and the central theme of the novella, the theme that is articulated by the old man himself, "…a man is not made for defeat… A man can be destroyed but not defeated."

Stream of Consciousness This technique is employed in the story's middle part when Santiago is alone at sea, with no one to talk to. The narrative increasingly shifts from the omniscient narrator to Santiago's perspective by entering his mind. Sometimes, Santiago is made to talk aloud to himself, sometimes a third-person narration of his thoughts is presented, at other times, the narrative drifts subtly from either of these into a kind of interior monologue. To present this limited stream of consciousness, Hemingway lets the seemingly disorganized thoughts leap into the old man's fatigued mind. In fact, they are loosely connected through recurring images, allusions, actions, and themes.

Shift in the Point of View The story begins and ends with a third-person, omniscient narration, which is limited to and concentrates on Santiago and his actions without dipping into his thoughts, while the part at sea, when Santiago is alone, with no one to talk to, is narrated from Santiago's perspective by entering into his mind. The shift in the point of view is conducive to establishing a certain psychic distance. The two parts of the story that take place on land benefit from this psychic distance in that the emotional impact aroused by Santiago's plight at the story's beginning and the tragedy of his defeat at the story's end make itself acutely felt. This detached reporting is typical of Hemingway's writing style.

Bibliography

常耀信 . 美国文学简史 . 天津：南开大学出版社，1995.

胡荫桐 . 美国文学教程 . 天津：南开大学出版社，1995.

李维屏 . 英美现代主义文学概观 . 上海外语教育出版社，1998.

吴伟仁 . 美国文学史及选读 . 北京：外语教学与研究出版社，1993.

杨金才主撰．新编美国文学史（第三卷）．上海外语教育出版社，2002．

Berman, Ronald. *Translating Modernism: Fitzgerald and Hemingway*. Tuscaloosa: The University of Alabama Press, 2009.

Donaldson, Scott. *The Cambridge Companion to Ernest Hemingway*. Shanghai: Shanghai Foreign Language Educarton Press，2000．

Hays, P. L. *Teaching Hemingway's The Sun Also Rises*. Moscow: University of Idaho Press, 2003.

Wikipedia, the free encyclopedia. http://en.wikipedia.org/wiki/Slaughterhouse-Five 2012-08-14

William Faulkner

His Life and Writing Career

His Life

William Cuthbert Faulkner (1897—1962) was an American writer primarily known and acclaimed for his novels and short stories though he also wrote poetry, essays, and screenplays during his career. He was one of the greatest modern writers of the 20th century and the outstanding representative of the southern renaissance and the southern literature of the United States. He was awarded Nobel Prize in literature in 1949. He received the Pulitzer Prize for fiction respectively in 1955 and 1963.

William Cuthbert Faulkner was born in New Albany, Mississippi. On September 21, 1902, only a few days prior to his fifth birthday, his family moved to Oxford, Mississippi and settled there, where he lived for the rest of his life. Faulkner was the first of four sons in the Faulkner family with a long history tracing back to the time of the Civil War. His great-grandfather, after whom he was named, William Clark Faulkner, was the pride of the family. He was a successful businessman who built a railroad, a writer with two novels and a play, and a Civil War hero. The Faulkner family called him "Old Colonel," and enjoyed telling his stories, which exerted a great influence on Faulkner and which were to be one important source of his later literary creation. His father Murry Cuthbert Faulkner (1870—1932) worked on the family railroad, then he ran his own business and ended up as a business manager of the University of Mississippi. Murry enjoyed the outdoors sports and taught his sons such sports as hunting, tracking, and fishing. His mother Maud Butler (1871—1960) and his maternal grandmother Lelia Butler who liked reading, painting, and photographing played a crucial role in cultivating Faulkner's artistic imagination. Maud put emphasis on her children's education and taught them to read before sending them to public school and exposed them to the classical works of especially English writers. Another important person who had a great influence on Faulkner in the Faulkner family was Caroline Barr, the black woman who raised him from infancy. Her lifelong education Faulkner received was essential to his preoccupation with the politics of sexuality and race as a writer.

Faulkner didn't have much formal schooling. He only attended two years of high school in Oxford. Yet he had his self-education beyond classroom by reading widely in his grandfather's library and listening to stories told to him by his elders, including war stories, stories of the Civil War, slavery, the Ku Klux Klan, and the Faulkner family. He was greatly influenced by the history of his family, his home state of Mississippi where he was born and raised and the history and culture of the American South altogether. His sense of humor, his sense of the tragic position of black and white Americans, his characterization of southern characters, and his timeless themes all bear the mark of his home state.

Faulkner began writing poetry in adolescence. Among the first to discover his talent and artistic potential was Philip Stone whom he met at the age of seventeen. A literary mentor to him, Stone made it possible for him to read extensively, discussed literature with him, and introduced him to the rising writers such as James Joyce, Frost, Pound, and Sherwood Anderson. His literary horizons were greatly expanded. His literary influences are deep and wide.

In 1918, Faulkner enlisted in the Royal Air Force in Canada, there he was trained as a pilot. When he was still in training, the First World War came to a close. He returned to Oxford and then spent a year or so studying languages and English literature at the University of Mississippi. In 1925, he moved to New Orleans, Louisiana, then a literary center, where the little magazine, *Double Dealer*, published avant-garde poetry. It was there he came to learn about James Joyce, Joseph Conrad, and Sigmund Freud. And it was there he got acquainted with Sherwood Anderson. Under his influence and help, Faulkner began to attempt fiction writing, the result of which was his first novel, *Soldiers' Pay* (1926). Anderson offered help in the publication of this novel and Faulkner's second novel, *Mosquitoes* (1927). In 1925, Faulkner spent six months traveling in Europe and met his idol James Joyce. Instead of settling in Paris like most intellectuals of his generation did, he decided to return to his hometown to be a "provincial" writer. During the summer of 1927, Faulkner wrote his first novel with his fictional Yoknapatawpha County as its setting. It was *Flags in the Dust*, which was based on the traditions and history of the South, in which Faulkner was brought up. It was first rejected by the publisher. When it finally came out in 1928, it was entitled *Sartoris*. Its publication marked the establishment of his fictional world, the fictional county of Yoknapatawpha County, and the end of his literary apprenticeship. In the fall of 1928, at the age of thirty, Faulkner began working on *The Sound and the Fury* (1929) in a much more experimental style. The novel turned out to be a masterpiece of American modern literature.

In 1929 Faulkner married Estelle Oldham, who brought with her two children from her previous marriage. To support his new family as a writer, Faulkner had to work as a screenwriter in Hollywood. Throughout the 1930s and 1940s, Faulkner continued to find work as a screenwriter. Meanwhile he continued to work on his fictional county, the Yoknapatawpha County. During this period, his major works came out one after another, including *As I Lay Dying* (1930), *Light in August* (1932), *Absalom, Absalom!* (1936), and *Go Down, Moses* (1942).

In both 1957 and 1958, Faulkner served as writer-in-residence at the University of Virginia at Charlottesville. He was seriously injured in a horse-riding accident in 1959, and died from a myocardial infarction at the age of 64, on July 6, 1962.

His Writing Career

Faulkner began his writing career by writing poetry. As a matter of fact, he wrote two volumes of poetry, published in small printings, *The Marble Faun* (1924) and *A Green Bough* (1933). He did not write his first novel until 1925. With the encouragement and help of Sherwood Anderson, he wrote and published his first novel, *Soldiers' Pay* (1926). It is about a wounded soldier returning home, a "waste land." It presented the disillusionment prevailing after the First World War and fell into the category of the works of the "Lost Generation." In 1927, again with the help of Sherwood Anderson, he published his second novel *Mosquitoes* (1927). Like his first novel, it was not well received either. The publication of his third novel *Sartoris* (1929) revealed that Faulkner had began to develop his own style. As the first of his Yoknapatawpha series, this novel signaled the beginning of his constructing his famous Yoknapatawpha Saga, which is composed of 14 novels and many short stories. Set in his fictional county, Yoknapatawpha County, these novels and stories give a vivid presentation of the rise and fall of the big old southern families and the destiny of several generations, a panorama of the southern society after the Civil War. His Yoknapatawpha County became the most well-known "miniature world" in the 20th century literature. Faulkner's maturity as a writer was marked by his next novel *The Sound and the Fury* (1929). The novel tells the story of the inevitable deterioration of the Compson family, an old aristocratic family in the South. As it is revealed its tragedy is rooted in its lack of love and humanity. In technique it is experimental and innovative. It uses the stream of consciousness technique to present the inner realities of the characters so successfully that it is acclaimed as the first American stream of consciousness novel in the real sense, representing the highest achievement of American novels in this genre. With the publication of this novel, the first period of Faulkner's literary career drew to a close and the second period of his literary creation began.

His second period, the main creative period extended from 1930 to 1942. During this period, Faulkner successively published two collections of short stories and nine novels. Most of them are components of the Yoknapatawpha Saga and are ranked among the modern classics. *As I Lay Dying* (1930), another stream of consciousness novel by Faulkner, further established his leading position in American stream of consciousness fiction writing. Composed of 59 monologues, the novel narrates in great detail the unusual journey a poor white family takes to bury their mother, reveals the thoughts and feelings of the family members on the journey, and conveys the meanings of life through them. *These 13* (1931), his first short story collection, includes many of his most acclaimed and most frequently anthologized stories, including "A Rose for Emily," "Red Leaves," "That Evening Sun," and "Dry September." *Light in August* (1932), a realistic novel, revolves around racial problems. It exposes the evils of racial discrimination and appeals compassion and understanding. *Absalom, Absalom!* (1936), a fable about the South, focuses on the theme of doom brought about by the denial of humanity. *The Hamlet* (1940), the first volume of a trilogy, tells stories about the Snopes. *Go Down, Moses* (1942), a collection of short stories, is again about moral injustice responsible for the decline of southern civilization.

In the third period of his literary career, Faulkner spent some years writing screenplays in Hollywood. It was between 1942 and 1945. In his later years, he produced five novels, including *Intruder in the Dust* (1948), *A Fable* (1954), the other two volumes of the trilogy concerning the Snopes stories: *The Town* (1957) and *The Mansion* (1959), which wind up his Yoknapatawpha Saga, and *The Reivers* (1962).

Although his work was published as early as 1919, and most of his works were published during the 1920s and 1930s, Faulkner remained relatively unknown until he was awarded Nobel Prize in literature in 1949. Worse still, in the 1940s, his works were treated with indifference and even hostility. They were thought to be pessimistic and full of violence. The experimental technique employed in them was considered as bewildering. The 13 novels including his most celebrated novels such as *The Sound and the Fury* (1929), *As I Lay Dying* (1930), *Light in August* (1932), and *Absalom, Absalom!* (1936) as well as numerous short stories he published from the early 1920s to the outbreak of World War Ⅱ constituted the basis of his reputation and accounted for his being awarded the Nobel Prize in 1949. What is sad about it is that they were written by an obscure writer out of the need for money.

In spite of that, Faulkner was a serious writer with a strong sense of the South. He was, first of all, a southern writer, deeply rooted in the history, tradition, and culture of his hometown, Mississippi, devoting all his life working on this "postage stamp of native soil." He not only modeled his fictional Yoknapatawpha County on it but also made people there and even the members of his family the prototypes for his fictional characters. He drew heavily on what his hometown could provide for his literary creation, its tormented history, the civil war tales, local legends and his own family history he was raised on, and painted an extraordinary portrait of a community united by a common heritage with his Yoknapatawpha stories. With the South as the basis for his literature, he reflected the changes the old society went through and the impact of the changes upon its people, the conflicts between the old and new, the past and present. He probed into the root of the decline of a number of southern aristocratic families, presented their inevitable doom brought about by their own evil deeds—driving the native Indians out of their land, establishing the institution of slavery and so on, and further demonstrated the disintegration of the southern society, the decline of southern tradition and the southern civilization as a result of that. He mercilessly exposed the evils of slavery, racism, the lack of love and humanity of the aristocrats. He is the champion of the illiterate poor white, working-class southerners, the Negro, the Indians who were the original owners of the land. Their kindness is expressed in their relation to nature and their ability to love. It is the proud who are doomed and the humble who endure. Faulkner's vision of the South is complex and even contradictory. He elegizes the agrarian virtues of the Old South, but at the same time he sees clearly the guilt conducted by the institution of slavery. His stories convey a kind of nostalgia for a past golden age. This southern complex makes itself intensely felt and adds a touch of sadness and complexity to his works.

Faulkner was more than a southern writer. His books explore a wide range of human experience both regional and universal, transcending time and space. He was a modern writer concerned with modern man's plight and dilemma in general. With the cosmos of his own, he portrayed characters and explored the themes to reflect the life of the southerners in particular and the situation of the post-war modern man in general. Both were caught between the old and the new, the past and the present, confronted with a world of swift changes, a world falling apart. Both were disenchanted with life, finding themselves living in an absurd, sterile, and meaningless world. Spiritual deterioration and nihilism were shared characteristics of modern life. The post-war world was a spiritual waste land. The root of the spiritual decadence, as his stories reveal, is the loss of love and the denial of humanity.

Faulkner was more than a writer. He was a humanist preoccupied with the general human situation. His works explore the basic human nature and the basic patterns of human behavior, expose the lack of love and humanity of the aristocrats, and celebrate the humanistic brilliance of the unprivileged—the poor whites, the blacks, and the primitives. He values such virtues as honor, pride, pity, justice, courage, love, and compassion which are rare to modern life. In his Nobel Prize acceptance speech, he said "…I decline to accept the end of man… I believe that man will not merely endure, he will prevail. He is immortal, not because he alone among creatures has an inexhaustible voice, but because he has a soul, a spirit capable of compassion, and sacrifice, and endurance…" He once said to the effect that if he belonged to any school then he belonged to the school of humanitarianism.

Faulkner was a modernist ceaselessly experimenting with modern techniques in order to represent precisely the reality as he saw it. His experiments in the dislocation of narrative time and his use of stream-of-consciousness technique categorized him as among the avant-garde. He believed that it is the writer's responsibility to truthfully represent the reality and the most important and the most significant reality is the inner reality of man. In his works, he used interior monologue, free association, montage, and the dislocation of time to represent the spiritual world and spiritual chaos of his characters. For example, in *The Sound and the Fury*, a masterpiece of modernism, he used such new techniques as stream-of-consciousness, juxtaposition, counterpoint, flashback, montage, symbolism, and so on. His achievement in the use of stream-of-consciousness technique is parallel to that of James Joys and Virginia Woolf. His verbal innovations and labyrinthine organization of his novels, his sense of time: time as a completed whole, seamless are all evidence of his being a modern writer. Faulkner developed his unique style—an integration of modernistic techniques and the southern literary tradition. He was awarded Nobel Prize in literature in 1949 for "his powerful and artistically unique contribution to the modern American novel."

His major published books are: *Sartoris* (1929), *The Sound and the Fury* (1929), *As I Lay Dying* (1930), *These 13* (1931), *Light in August* (1932), *Absalom, Absalom!* (1936), and *Go Down, Moses* (1942).

Analysis of and Comment on His Representative Novel

The Sound and the Fury (1929)

Plot Summary

The Sound and the Fury was Faulkner's first critically-acclaimed novel published in 1929. It is one of the greatest modern novels of the world and may be the greatest southern novel ever written. Set in the fictional Yoknapatawpha County, the novel revolves around the Compson family, former southern aristocrats who are struggling to deal with the decline of their family and its reputation. It is composed of four distinct sections. The first section, April 7, 1928, is written from the perspective of Benjamin "Benjy" Compson, a 33-year-old man with severe mental handicaps. The second section, June 2, 1910, centers in Benjy's older brother, Quentin Compson, and the events leading up to his suicide. The third section, April 6, 1928, is narrated from the perspective of Jason, Quentin's cynical younger brother. The fourth section, the final one, set a day after the first, on April 8, 1928, is related from a third person omniscient point of view, which primarily focuses on Dilsey, one of the Compsons' black servants.

Part 1: April 7, 1928

This section of the novel is narrated by Benjamin "Benjy" Compson, covering the period 1898—1928. Benjy's narrative develops in a nonlinear manner. It is a series of non-chronological events presented in stream of consciousness. The opening scene presents Benjy accompanied by Luster, a servant boy, watching golfers on the nearby golf course while waiting to hear them call "caddie"—the name of his favorite sibling. Upon hearing one of them calling for his golf caddie, Benjy's mind recalls the memories of his sister Caddy. His mind focuses on one critical scene in 1898 when their grandmother died. During the funeral, the four Compson children were forbidden to stay inside. Caddy climbed a tree in the yard to see what was going on there, and while looking inside, her brothers—Quentin, Jason, and Benjy—looked up and noticed that her underwear was muddy. Other crucial memories presented through Benjy's mind are his change of name (from Maury, after his uncle) in 1900 when he was discovered to be handicapped; the marriage and divorce of Caddy (1910), and his castration, a result of his attack on a girl when he is not under supervision.

Part 2: June 2, 1910

This section focuses on Quentin, a freshman at Harvard. He is presented wandering the streets of Cambridge, thinking about death and his sister Caddy. He is concerned very much about Caddy's virginity and purity. Preoccupied with southern ideals of chivalry, he is ready to protect women, especially his sister. Quentin is horrified to find that Caddy has lost her virginity and purity. He turns to his father for advice but is only told that virginity is an invention of men and should not be serious about it. Quentin fails to prove his father wrong though he has tried to. Shortly before Quentin leaves for Harvard in the fall of 1909, Caddy becomes pregnant. To protect her, Quentin tells his father that they have committed incest. He feels he should be responsible for her sin. Caddy then marries another man Herbert Head whom Quentin dislikes but Caddy is determined to do so because she must marry before the child is born. But Herbert finds out that he is not the father of the child and the marriage ends up in Caddy's being sent away. Quentin is wandering through Harvard, heartbroken over losing Caddy, thinking sadly of the decline of the South after the American Civil War. Unable to come to terms with the amorality of the world around him, he commits suicide.

Part 3: April 6, 1928

The third section is narrated by Jason, the third child of the Compson family. The narrative takes place the day before Benjy's section, on Good Friday. Jason's narration is straightforward, a reflection of his single-minded pursuit for material wealth. After his father's death, he becomes the financial supporter of the family. Due to the burden of the family, he becomes bitter and cynical. When this section begins, Jason decides to leave work to search for Caddy's daughter Miss Quentin of whom he is the guardian. Miss Quentin has run away again. In both of them there exist two conflicting predominant traits of the Compson family: Miss Quentin's recklessness and passion which is inherited from her grandfather and, ultimately, from the Compson side and Jason's ruthless cynicism which passes down from his mother's side.

Part 4: April 8, 1928

This section focuses on Dilsey, a black servant. April 8, 1928, is Easter Sunday, on which Dilsey takes her family and Benjy to church. Though mistreated and abused by the Compsons, she nevertheless remains loyal. With the help of her grandson Luster, She cares for Benjy. Her strength comes from her faith.

Meanwhile, the family discovers that Miss Quentin has run away with a carnival worker, taking with her the money which her mother Caddy sends to support her but was embezzled by Jason and her uncle Jason's life savings. Therefore, he sets off once again to find her on his own, but ends up in failure.

After church, Dilsey's grandson Luster drives Benjy to the graveyard, but he drives the wrong way around a monument. Benjy begins to cry. His hysterical sobbing and violent outburst can only be stopped by Jason.

Themes

Love *The Sound and the Fury* explores the root of the deterioration of an old aristocratic family in the Old South. A variety of reasons attributes to the downfall of the family, but one main reason appears to be the family's inability to express and share normal love. Disillusioned with life and the society in which he lives, Mr. Compson indulges in alcoholism and nihilism with little attention or love to spare for others, and Mrs. Compson is obsessed with self-pity and excessive concern for the family's "good name" so much so that she is unable to carry out her duty as a loving mother. Of the four children, Caddy takes care of Benjy with love, yet, in her own search for love, she loses her virginity. Quentin puts an end to his own life in disappointment with his dreams of love and old ideals. What Jason loves is nothing but himself and money. Caddy's daughter, Miss Quentin, reenacts her mother's false pursuit of love.

In contrast to the members of the Compson's family, Dilsey Gibson, the Compsons' black cook, possesses just what they don't have: love and compassion though she is at the bottom of the segregated Old South society. She takes care of the Compson's family and children instead of Mrs. Compson. She never treats Benjy as an idiot, instead, she loves him just as she loves other children. With her story, the author celebrates such values as love and compassion.

Death The central theme of the novel is death, which is symbolized by the decline of a once noble southern family whose ancestry traces back to the US Civil War hero General Compson. The Compson family is doomed due to such vices as racism, greed, selfishness, and the psychological inadequacy of individuals to cope with changes which were responsible for the problems in the

South. It is deteriorating with its money dwindling, its ancestral home decaying, its land holdings shrinking and, most importantly, its loss of religious faith and Caddy's loss of virginity. There is no promising future for the young generation of the aristocratic Compsons. Benjy is insane and cannot marry, Quentin commits suicide, and Jason refuses to marry. Caddy marries, but gets divorced. Caddy's daughter, Miss Quentin rejects the family and runs off with a man. The world these people live in is one of decadence and sterility, a waste land devoid of vitality and humanity. Gone with the decline of the Compson family are the traditional ideals, values, and the traditional morality as well as the old system.

Time Each of the four sections of the novel is entitled with a precise time, which is a marker of a particular occurrence and suggestive of the theme of the novel, that is time. Faulkner's idea of time is based on the theory of time of French philosopher, Henri-Louis Bergson (1859—1941). Faulkner agrees with him on his concept of psychological time, a continuous, successive, and seamless time, which cannot be measured by second, minute, or hour, but it is related to one's stream of consciousness flowing from the present to the past in reflection or to the future in imagination. Faulkner probes the characters' interior reality by presenting their psychological time or sense of time with stream of consciousness so as to reveal their relationship to the future, to the world around them, to their concepts of freedom, and to the way they view themselves.

With little or no sense of the passage of time Benjy lives outside of time. For him, time exists not as past, present, and future, but rather as a chaotic mix of them. Life to him is a cyclical progress rather than a linear one. He cannot progress in any way. Neither can his family. It can never progress to arrive at an ending, a resolution of past problems. In a way, Benjy is the symbol of his family's doom. In contrast to Benjy who has no knowledge of time, Quentin is obsessed with it so much so that he watches shadows, breaks watches, and divides his day into clear sections. In addition, Quentin is obsessed with what time brings. To him, time is both obsessive and futile. An anachronism, he transcends time by putting an end to his own life. Quentin perceives humanity as one of continual loss with slim hope of recovery. His suicide is one more sign of the growing regression of the family. Mr. Compson holds that "clocks slay time" and that "time is dead as long as it is being clicked off by little wheels; only when the clock stops does time come to life." Jason, the final Compson brother, longs to possess time and makes use of it for his financial gain. Money provides the only value he can place on life and the only means by which he can prove his humanity. In Benjy's world, there are more past remembrances than present-day occurrences. Quentin's world is full of constant recalling of his past, and he longs in vain to change the past in order to embrace the future. Jason does not waste his time longing to change the past, but he is unable to come to terms with the past. Different to them all, Dilsey is capable of living in the present because her sense of time is much larger than that of the Compsons. Her vision of time, family, and humanity is larger and more positive than the others.

Literary Techniques

Stream of Consciousness *The Sound and the Fury* is a psychological novel. Faulkner uses the stream-of-consciousness technique in the first three sections of it. These sections are narrated by the three brothers of the Compsons in first-person point of view. Their thought patterns and modes of expression are presented while they try with desperation and hopelessness in their own way to mourn the loss of their sister, Caddy. By tracking their mental movement, the novel traces the decline of the traditional values of the southern society. Benjy's section is narrated in a nonlinear manner, covering the period 1898—1928. Benjy's narrative consists of a series of non-chronological events presented in a seamless stream of consciousness. It is full of highly disjointed narration, free association, frequent chronological leaps, interior monologues, presenting a picture of the chaotic flow of consciousness, the mental state of an idiot. Faulkner uses italics to indicate significant shifts in the narrative. In the opening scene, Benjy is seen watching golfers on the nearby golf course waiting to hear them call caddie. The sound of the word "caddie" triggers the flow of his memories of his sister, Caddy, his change of name, the marriage and divorce of Caddy, and his castration. As an idiot, he lives permanently in the present. For him, there is no past or future. The scenes or what is happening before his eyes can immediately take him back to the past or disturb his reflections and cause his thinking to leap into another past event. Therefore, in his narrative, the present and the past, and various kinds of past events at all levels are smashed into fragments and pieced together. Though chronologically incoherent, Benjy's narrative gives objectively a glimpse into the true motivations of many characters. Like Benjy's section, Quentin's narrative is not strictly linear. Quentin is shown wandering the streets of Cambridge, contemplating death, and remembering his sister Caddy. To demonstrate the confusion and chaos generated by Quentin's severe depression and deteriorating state of mind, the chronological events are entangled together. What's more, this section, especially the end of it, is written in a rambling series of words, phrases, and sentences with no separation indicating where one thought ends and another begins, completely disregarding grammar, spelling, or punctuation. This section gives the novel's best example of Faulkner's employment of the stream-of-consciousness technique. The third section is narrated by Jason. The stream-of-consciousness technique is once more used. But here, Jason's narrative is more straightforward.

Multiple Point of View Multiple point of view is another important technique adopted in the novel. Faulkner breaks the limit of the first person point of view by effectively using the multiple first person point of view. The first three sections are related respectively by the three brothers of the Compsons in the first person narrative. The three characters, Benjy, Quentin, and Jason, living separately in their own world, observe the world in his own way. Through them, Faulkner presents glimpses of the thoughts and deeds of everyone in the family. Many of the same events are related in the three sections, each from a different point of view. They are overlapping and interwoven. They provide insights into them from different perspectives and put emphasis on different themes. For example, the three brothers tell the story of the central character Caddy, her sexuality, her early pregnancy, and her quick and unhappy marriage, from their own perspectives through interior monologues. Their accounts reveal their different impressions of, views on, attitudes toward, and passions for her. The information from any one point of view is subjective, rambling, fragmented, and one-sided, but the information from the three narrators when assembled will produce an overall impression of her on the reader, and in return this impression will reflect the narrators' personalities and biases. In the novel, besides the main lines of the story, significant details are embedded in a mass of information, allusion, and conjecture. Put together, all of them come to present a comprehensive and authentic and chronological picture of the Compson family, its history, its problems and their causes, the desires, concerns and worries of the family members, and above all, its inevitable decay.

Other prominent techniques used in the novel are: flashback, juxtaposition, the use of time, and so on. Flashback is used to represent what happened in the past, linking the past and the present. For example, Chapter 1 takes place on Saturday, April 7, 1928, the day before Easter, but flashes back frequently to previous years. Chapter 2 takes place on June 2, 1910. It also flashes back to previous years. Juxtaposition is employed to highlight the presentation of a state of mind or attitude of a character through interior monologues. Time used as negotiation between the past and the present makes Faulkner's novel a brilliant example of modern technique. The playing with time as a technique that Faulkner employs in the novel becomes a hallmark of a new literary form and a fine example of modernist aesthetics.

Bibliography

常耀信. 美国文学简史. 天津：南开大学出版社，1995.

胡荫桐. 美国文学教程. 天津：南开大学出版社，1995.

李维屏. 英美现代主义文学概观. 上海：上海外语教育出版社，1998.

吴伟仁. 美国文学史及选读. 北京：外语教学与研究出版社，1993.

肖明翰. 威廉·福克纳研究. 北京：外语教学与研究出版社，1997.

杨金才. 新编美国文学史（第三卷）. 上海：上海外语教育出版社，2002.

Weinstein, P. M. *The Cambridge Companion to William Faulkner*. Shanghai: Shanghai Foreign Language Education Press, 2000.

Wikipedia, the free encyclopedia. http://en.wikipedia.org/wiki/Slaughterhouse-Five 2012-08-14

Eugene O'Neill

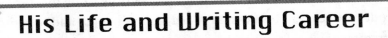

His Life and Writing Career

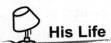

His Life

Eugene Gladstone O'Neill (1888—1953) is generally acclaimed as one of the greatest American playwrights, who influence American drama extensively and profoundly. He is the first to fully explore serious themes as subject matter for the theater. Some critics hold that O'Neill has been ranked, along with William Shakespeare and George Bernard Shaw, as one of the three greatest playwrights in English language theater. O'Neill has won four Pulitzer Prizes for his plays: *Beyond the Horizon* (1918); *Anna Christie* (1920); *Strange Interlude* (1928); and *Long Day's Journey into Night* (1941). Moreover, he is so far the only American playwright who has won the Nobel Prize in literature to award "for the power, honesty, and deep-felt emotions of his dramatic works, which embody an original concept of tragedy"(1936). The power of his drama lies not only in its external action, but also in the depth of his characterization and the deep concerns for human fate. O'Neill is credited with raising American dramatic theater from its narrow origins to an art form respected around the world. He is regarded as America's premier playwright.

The son of a professional actor, O'Neill was brought up on the road and acquired a precocious knowledge of the theater. His mother, Ella Quinlan O'Neill, was the emotionally fragile daughter of a wealthy father who died when she was seventeen. O'Neill's mother never recovered from the death of her second son, Edmund, who had died of measles at the age of two, and she became addicted to morphine as a result of Eugene's difficult birth.

His early years were profoundly affected by the pressures of his mother's recurring mental illness and his father's coldness, which he later vividly portrayed in *Long Day's Journey into Night* (1941). Although he was a voracious reader, O'Neill was a poor student; he preferred to spend his adolescence in barrooms with his profligate brother James. After expulsion from Princeton University for his frequent drinking, and a brief, unsuccessful marriage, O'Neill attempted suicide, and then left his family for a life at sea. O'Neill spent several years as a sailor, during which time he suffered from depression and severe alcoholism. O'Neill lived for six years as a wanderer, working occasionally as a sailor and spending a great deal of time as an unemployed drifter in Buenos Aires, Liverpool, and New York City. O'Neill would later jokingly refer to this time of his life as his "real education."

O'Neill's parents and elder brother Jamie (who drank himself to death at the age of 45) died within three years of one another, not long after he had begun to make his mark in the theater. Despite his depression he had a deep love for the sea, and it became a prominent theme in many of his plays, several of which are set onboard ships like the ones that he worked on. The turning point in his life came in 1912, when he suffered a mild attack of tuberculosis. While convalescing in a dramatist he spent the next several years assiduously studying his craft.

O'Neill briefly found employment during this period as a writer for the New London Telegraph, dabbling in playwriting from time to time. It wasn't, however, until his experience at Gaylord Farms Sanatorium (where he was recovering from tuberculosis) that he experienced an epiphany and devoted his life to writing plays. O'Neill enrolled in the famous playwriting course taught by George Pierce Baker at Harvard University, spending 1914—1915 writing prolifically, though he would later disown all his writings from this period. In 1916, O'Neill had his first big break, when he joined the Provincetown Players, a raggedy band of young writers, artists, and actors who had assembled in the tiny coastal village of Provincetown. Although many other writers wrote plays for the company to perform, O'Neill soon became their biggest attraction. During this period, O'Neill concentrated primarily on writing small, one-act plays that drew heavily from his experiences at sea. *Bound East for Cardiff* (1914) would become the most famous of these, and it would ultimately be O'Neill's first work to be performed in New York City, to rave reviews.

Following the success of *Bound East for Cardiff*, O'Neill moved back to New York and became a regular on the Greenwich Village literary scene, where he also befriended many radicals, most notably US Communist Party founder John Reed. In 1920, O'Neill's first full-length play, *Beyond the Horizon*, was produced on Broadway. O'Neill would win a Pulitzer Prize for the play, and soon after he became a major literary celebrity. His productivity during this period was legendary; he wrote several plays a year, obsessively revising earlier drafts of plays for reproduction. In 1929, O'Neill moved to the Loire Valley of northwest France. Later, he moved to Danville, California, in 1937, living there until 1944.

After suffering from multiple health problems over many years, O'Neill ultimately began to suffer from a severe tremor in his hands which made it impossible for him to write. He attempted to write via dictation, but found it impossible to compose by that method; O'Neill never wrote another play for the remaining ten years of his life.

O'Neill died from the advanced stages of Parkinson's disease in room 401 of the Shelton Hotel in Boston, on November 27, 1953, at the age of 65. He was interred in the Forest Hills Cemetery in Jamaica Plain, Massachusetts.

His Writing Career

O'Neill's writing career can be divided into five somewhat distinct periods. The first, the period of his dramatic apprenticeship, lea ds nothing of consequence to his reputation. Included in the period is his first collection, *Thirst, and Other One Act Plays*, and the so-called *Lost Plays*, works so poor that O'Neill made no attempt to publish them. O'Neill first gained recognition during his second period which was devoted primarily to one act plays about the sea. According to some critics O'Neill's initial production, *Bound East for Cardiff* (1914), marks the first departure from nineteenth-century melodrama and the beginning of serious American theater. All of these plays are slice-of-life dramas dealing with the delusions and obsessions of common people. He is particularly representative of this period with its naturalistic style, its tragic irony and its use of the sea as symbol of malignant fate.

During his third period, 1920—1924, O'Neill turned to no longer plays. Foremost among these is *Desire Under the Elms* (1925), one of O'Neill's few conventional tragedies, which examines the power of repressed sexuality in a staid New England town. Throughout this period O'Neill exploited many experimental dramatic techniques. His most successful experiments were with symbolism in *The Emperor Jones* (1920) and expressionism in *The Hairy Ape* (1922), a grim play in which a brutish laborer is destroyed by industrial civilization.

O'Neill's fourth, sometimes called his "cosmic" period extends to 1935. Throughout this era he was preoccupied with the problems of identity and the nature of fate, and these vast, sprawling plays are often much longer than traditional productions. O'Neill was still experimenting heavily with theatrical techniques and he successfully utilized such effects as masks, split personalities and stream of consciousness monologues. The most important play of this era, *Mourning Becomes Electra* (1931), is a powerful examination of the ways that guilt, jealousy, and sexual passion lead to the downfall of an old New England family. Uncharacteristic of this period, and of O'Neill's career as a whole, is *Ah, Wilderness!* (1933), a nostalgic and idealistic comedy about adolescence that critics find one of his most unpretentious and thus most successful works.

Despite his award of the Nobel Prize in literature in 1936, O'Neill's reputation declined steadily after 1935. It was not until after his death that the plays of his last period gained recognition. Of these, *The Iceman Cometh* (1939), a realistic study of the fragility of illusions, is generally considered his masterpiece, while *Long Day's Journey into Night* (1941), a portrait of a tormented, destructive family, is called one of the most powerful dramas in American theater.

O'Neill's third wife and literary executor, Carlotta Monterey, to whom *Long Day's Journey into Night* is dedicated, recounted that O'Neill's oldest son asked his father that the play should not be published or performed because of the negative light cast on his father's family. O'Neill acquiesced, depositing the play with his publishers with the injunction that it not appear until twenty-five years after his own death. However, according to Monterey, O'Neill believed his son's suicide removed this constraint. After O'Neill's death, she authorized the play's production in 1956 in Sweden—a country O'Neill had always felt was particularly receptive to his drama and it debuted in the United States later that year.

It is generally agreed that O'Neill wrote some of the most important and some of the most lackluster of modern dramas. In his plays he experimented with almost every dramatic innovation of the early twentieth century. Unfortunately, experimentation with theatrical effects sometimes became an end in itself, and techniques could not enhance such puerile, poorly conceived works as *Lazarus Laughed* (1925—26) and *The Great God Brown* (1926). For this reason O'Neill's most realistic plays are considered his best. Similarly, while O'Neill was a master at sketching character, he also wrote melodramatic, needlessly verbose dialogue. It is such seeming contradictions that make O'Neill's work fascinating to contemporary critics; they often attack several elements of his plays while applauding the ultimate effects. O'Neill is universally acknowledged as an important tragedian who is credited with creating the traditions of twentieth-century American drama and is as integral to modern world literature as Bertolt Brecht and August Strindberg.

Some clear and indisputable summaries on O'Neill's accomplishments and status are justifiable. Firstly, almost all the critics share a conviction that O'Neill has made American theater a serious endeavor. Before O'Neill, American theater is usually an escapist' entertainment. It is from O'Neill on that the American drama starts to highlight its political, moral and social significance. His greatest contribution to American drama also lies in his tremendous impact on many dramatists of later generations who are able to aim high and handle serious subjects in a serious manner. O'Neill takes his art seriously and is totally committed to his work. The playwright has made American drama significant and serious, and thus renders it powerfully enough to compete with its European counterparts. In some sense without O'Neill the American drama will have been nothing.

Secondly, O'Neill is acclaimed as the boldest American literary experimenter for his technical inventiveness. During his early writing the application of realism has brought a new slight in sharp contrast with the former entertainment plays. The playwright has applied various techniques during his creation career. Later, O'Neill returns to realism with his serious contemplation on human fate and human history. O'Neill's application of sound, light, gesture, movement, and setting is highly emotive and impressing, for he expresses an instinctive understanding of the theater and what the audience wants. He "was able to make demands on that audience in the face of opposition from producers and directors. He took risks, and usually his audience went along with him, responding to his sincerity of purpose."

Beyond the Horizon (1918) is written by Eugene O'Neill in1920. It was O'Neill's first full-length work, and he became the winner of the 1920 Pulitzer Prize in drama. The play focuses on the portrait of a family, and particularly two brothers Andrew and Robert. In the first act of the play, Robert is about to go off to sea with their uncle Dick, a sea captain while Andrew looks forward to marrying his sweetheart Ruth and working on the family farm as he starts a family.

The Emperor Jones (1920) is Eugene O'Neill's most important play written in the technique of expressionism, which tells the tale of Brutus Jones, an African-American man who kills a man, goes to prison, escapes to a Caribbean island, and sets himself up as emperor. The play recounts his story in flashbacks as Brutus makes his way through the forest in an attempt to escape former subjects who have rebelled against him. The play displays an uneasy mix of expressionism and realism, which is also characteristic of several other O'Neill's plays, including *The Hairy Ape* (1922). It was O'Neill's first play to receive great critical acclaim and box-office success, and the one that launched his career.

Strange Interlude in 1928 is an expressionist play about a woman who tries to control her father, her husband and, her lover by various means to compensate for the dead aviator that she once loved. Her attempts to indulge her mothering instinct are repeatedly frustrated, first when she attempts to take care of her father and then later when she can not have a child by her husband because his family's history in insanity. Finally, she had a child by her lover. The play is widely known for its 5-hour length and its use of expressionist techniques such as masks, asides, and an onstage chorus that delivers the internal thoughts of each character.

The Iceman Cometh in 1939 is perhaps the finest of O'Neill's tragedies. The story is set in a dockside bar of the lower west side of New York City. It concerns a group of drunken derelicts who spend their time in the back room of Henry Hope's saloon where they discuss their hopeless lives. One man wants to get back into the police force, another to be re-placed as a politician. Their daily routines are shattered when Hickey, a salesman and the sin of a preacher, appears as a messiah, and encourages them to start rehabilitation. They find out that their new hero is himself a madman and murderer, who has killed his wife, and lapse once more into their comfortable world of whiskey.

Long Day's Journey into Night in 1941 is an autobiographical play in four acts. The action takes place during a single day in August in 1912 at the summer home of the Tyrone family. The members of the family are the father, James Tyrone, and actor; the drug-addicted mother, Mary; the elder brother, Jamie; and Edmund, based on O'Neill himself, who is stricken with tuberculosis. The play explores the tragic nature of family relations, and questions the possibility of forgiveness and redemption.

Eugene O'Neill's outstanding plays include: *Beyond the Horizon* (1918), *Anna Christie* (1920), *The Emperor Jones* (1920), *The Hairy Ape* (1922), *All God's Chillun Got Wings* (1924), *Desire Under the Elms* (1925), *Lazarus Laughed* (1925—1926), *The Great God Brown* (1926), *Strange Interlude* (1928), *Mourning Becomes Electra* (1931), *Ah, Wilderness!* (1933), *The Iceman Cometh* (1939), *Long Day's Journey into Night* (1941), *A Moon for the Misbegotten* (1943), *A Touch of the Poet* (1942), and *More Stately Mansions* (1967).

Analysis of and Comment on His Representative Play

The Hairy Ape (1922)

Plot Summary

The Hairy Ape is an expressionistic play. In the play man's miserable position in a mechanical world is symbolically presented. Yank, the "hairy" protagonist, is a strong and sordid stoker on modern ocean liner. He feels that he belongs to the powerful world of steam, steel, and iron until he encounters Mildred Douglas, the daughter of the owner of the steamship line. Seeing Yank, the delicate, supercilious, neurotic, and rich woman becomes horrified. She says, "Oh, the filthy beast" and faints.

The struggle of Yank, a fireman who works aboard a transatlantic liner, is the subject of *The Hairy Ape*. Yank, his real name is Bob Smith, was born in New York City. Yank does not reveal many details of his family history, but, from what he does say, it is clear that it was painful. His mother died of the "tremens" and his father, a shore-worker, was abusive. Yank tells Long that on Saturday nights his parents' fighting was so intense that his parents would break the furniture. Ironically, his parents made him attend church every Sunday morning. After his mother died, Yank ran away from home, tired of lickings and punishment.

Yank, perplexed, goes ashore to find out if he belongs to the modern world. On Fifth Avenue, he finds that the wealthy people are walking idly without seeming to have seen the sailors. Yank, infuriated, insults some of the wealthy people and is arrested and put into prison. In jail, he hears about an organization which would overthrow the capitalist society. But when he wants to work for the organization after his release, he is rejected and tossed out. He stays outside at night, dislocated and lost.

Yank, in the final scene, attempts to find his identity in the zoo. He talks with a gorilla and sets the animal free, hoping to join them and find his sense of belonging, but the animal kills him and throws his body into the cage. Yank belongs nowhere.

This is a symbolic tragedy of modern man who can neither be accepted by his society nor return to his primitive state. The tragedy is a cosmic presentation of modern man's dislocation in an alien world.

The play is divided into 8 scenes. Scene 1 takes place in the firemen's forecastle of a cruise ship, where they sleep. Their racks resemble the bars of a cage. They are sailing from New York, where Yank and the other firemen are talking and singing drunkenly. Yank is shown to be a leader among them. Other featured characters are Long, a socialist, and Paddy, a particularly drunken Irishman.

Scene 2 takes place on the deck, where Mildred Douglas (the rich girl) and her aunt are talking. They are almost constantly arguing.

Scene 3 takes place in the stokehold. Yank and the other firemen take pride in their work. When Mildred comes to visit the stokehold, Mildred hears Yank cursing. When he turns around and she sees him, she is so shocked by him she calls Yank a filthy beast and faints.

Scene 4 also takes place on the ship. Yank is very depressed and the other men try to understand why.

In Scene 5, Yank and Long go to Fifth Avenue in New York. Yank argues with Long about how best to attack the upper class. Long leaves, fearing arrest, and Yank is arrested after attacking a gentleman.

Scene 6 takes place at the prison at Blackwell's Island. Yank tells the prisoners his story and one of the prisoners gives him an article about the Industrial Workers of the World(IWW). Yank tries to escape.

Scene 7 takes place at the IWW office that Yank goes to after his month in jail. They are happy to have him at first because there are not many ship firemen in the union—but he is thrown out after he says that he wants to blow up things, and they think he is a spy.

Scene 8 takes place at the zoo, when Yank is crushed after trying to talk to an ape and releasing it from its cage.

Themes

In the beginning of *The Hairy Ape*, Yank seems fairly content as, if not proud to be a fireman. He defends the ship as his home and insists that the work he does is vital—it is the force that makes the ship go twenty-five knots an hour. Yank's continual references to Paddy (an old Irishman on the same ship) as "dead" and "old" and not "belonging" with the other men aboard the ocean liner reveals Yank's own rejection of freedom. The acceptance and attachment to the modern-ship machine enslaves men like Yank. The need for belonging, without the knowledge of what else to belong to, is dangerous as exemplified by Yank's encounter with Mildred.

Mildred Douglas's reaction to Yank is the catalyst which makes Yank come to class awareness. His attempt to get revenge on Mildred Douglas widens to revenge on the steel industry and finally the entire bourgeois. Throughout this struggle Yank defines "belonging" as power. When he thinks he "belongs" to something he gains strength. When Yank is rejected by a group, he is terribly weak. However, Yank is rejected by all facets of society: his fellow firemen, Mildred, the street goers of Fifth Avenue, the IWW, and finally the ape in the zoo. Yank symbolizes the struggle of modern man within industrial society—he cannot break class or ideological barriers, nor create new ones. Yank is the outsider and eventually just the freak at the zoo for people to cage and point at.

Although Mildred should be considered the antagonist of *The Hairy Ape*, she is equally victimized by class as Yank. Though Mildred has more education and cultural experience than Yank, she still cannot escape her cultural identity. Mildred describes herself as the waste of her father's steel company, as she has felt the benefits, but not the hard work that brought them. She shares with Yank the need to find a sense of usefulness or belonging—the fate of both characters was decided before they were born. Thus, Yank and Mildred desperately search to find an identity that is their own.

The failure of both characters lies in their conscious and unconscious refusal to shed their values and knowledge while searching for a new identity. For example, Mildred will not change out of her white dress and Yank's coal dust is saturated into his skin.

The industrial environment is presented as toxic and dehumanizing; the world of the rich, superficial and dehumanized. Yank has also been interpreted as representative of the human condition, alienated from nature by his isolated consciousness, unable to find belonging in any social group or environment.

The Hairy Ape displays O'Neill's social concern for the oppressed industrial working class. Despite demonstrating in *The Hairy Ape* his clear belief that the capitalist system persecuted the working man, O'Neill is critical of a socialist movement that can not fulfill individual needs or solve unique problems.

O'Neill is a typical representative of American writers though the European tradition can be identified in his plays. O'Neill represents the influence of New England Puritanism in his vivid portrayals of different spectrums in society, but the most striking feature of his creation is the sense of fatality in human lives. The portrayal of the dark side of human existence manifests his inheritances as an American writer. Growing up in a theater but feeling disgusted with the melodrama of his father's day, the playwright wants to reform this situation with his serious thinking and his emotive creations. O'Neill has exerted himself to pave a serious way of dramatization in reflecting life and expressing human life and social problems. Almost all of his plays concern the problems in human life and human history from the physical, psychological, and spiritual dimensions.

Literary Techniques

O'Neill was still experimenting heavily with theatrical techniques and he successfully utilized such effects as masks, split personalities, and stream of consciousness monologues. O'Neill uses the device of symbolic expressionism. The ship symbolizes modern society and Yank the man who struggles to make improvement but is defeated. O'Neill presents his own reaction to the modern state through his central character Yank, for Yank is, according to O'Neill, "every human being." In the drama, when Yank realizes that he is viewed as an object, he starts to muse over his existence. Freedom is badly desired. However, does that mean he is growing? No. People are all in want of freedom, but do we really get it? Contrarily, they are chosen by freedom instead of their choosing. The ship is an epitome of capitalist society. Workers like Yank have to endure cruel treatment. If they want to change, they will definitely meet more miserable situation. Actually, a numerous obstacles and frustrations occur in the way of Yank's seeking for his position, which reflects survival crisis of most modern people. The more people think about, the clearer people realize about freedom. His vengeance only wants to prove the sense of his existence, so he gets to know freedom is the root of bitterness. Faced with this kind of freedom, Yank is sad, isolated and unhopeful. Moreover, all the attempts are in vain. Yank has nothing to do but degenerate—death that is inevitable.

Yank, symbolizing human, hasn't been afoot for the tough task of searching for freedom, therefore the tragedy of Yank becomes a fight between human and self produced with existence of human. In addition, the costume of upper class and the bars that are around the stokehole are also related to expressionism. The former tells that that group of people stick to convention and are nonchalant. The latter shows people are in a cage. *The Hairy Ape* is well worth studying, for it can be considered the first important play that attacks the materialism of American society. It has a strong and political dimension.

One of the most famous naturalistic playwrights, O'Neill was essentially concerned with the miserable position of modern man. For the sense of the tragic, his plays are unsurpassed and unequaled by other American playwrights. But he was against the old naturalism of surface-reality, for he was interested in the inscrutable forces behind life. He liked to create extremes of unhappiness. He treated man as an animal at the mercy of basic urges either in the form of passion or violence and caught or trapped in a meaningless universe. His creative capacity renders his characters as living realities. O'Neill was more interested in the inner conflicts of his characters rather than in social problems. In the study of his characters, he frequently uses his knowledge of Freudian and Jungian psychology.

Bibliography

常耀信. 美国文学简史（第二版修订本）. 天津：南开大学出版社，2006. 290–295.

王卓，李权文主编. 美国文学史. 武汉：华中师范大学出版社，2010. 335–341.

吴瑾瑾主编. 美国文学史. 北京：经济科学出版社，2008. 403–412.

Hall, S. K., ed. *Twentieth-Century Literary Criticism*, *Vol. 6*. Detroit, Michigan: Gale Research Company, 1982. 323–327.

Poupard, Dennis, ed. *Twentieth-Century Literary Criticism*, *Vol. 27*. Detroit, London: Gale Research Inc., 1988. 156–157.

http://en.wikipedia.org/wiki/Eugene_O'Neill 2013-02-15

http://www.newworldencyclopedia.org/entry/Eugene_O'Neill 2013-02-15

Arthur Miller

His Life and Writing Career

His Life

Arthur Asher Miller (1915—2005) was an American playwright and essayist. He was a prominent figure in American theater, writing dramas which are still widely studied and performed worldwide.

Arthur Miller, the son of moderately affluent Jewish-American parents, Isdore and Augusta Miller, was born in Harlem, New York City in 1915. His father owned a coat-manufacturing business, which failed in the Wall Street Crash of 1929, after which, his family moved to humbler quarters in Brooklyn.

Because of the effects of the Great Depression on his family, Miller had no money to attend university in 1932 after he had graduated from high school. After securing a place at the University of Michigan, Miller worked in a number of menial jobs to pay for his tuition.

At the University of Michigan, Miller first majored in journalism and worked as a reporter and night editor for the student paper, *Michigan Daily*. It was during this time that he wrote his first play, *No Villain* (1936). Miller switched his major to English, and subsequently won the Avery Hopwood Award for *No Villain*. The award brought him his first recognition and led him to begin to consider that he could have a career as a playwright. Miller enrolled in a playwriting seminar taught by the influential Professor Kenneth Rowe, who instructed him in his early forays into playwriting. Rowe emphasized how a play is built in order to achieve its intended effect, or what Miller called "the dynamics of play construction." Rowe provided realistic feedback along with much-needed encouragement, and became a lifelong friend. Miller retained strong ties to his alma mater throughout the rest of his life, establishing the university's Arthur Miller Award in 1985 and Arthur Miller Award for Dramatic Writing in 1999, and lending his name to the Arthur Miller Theater in 2000. In 1937, Miller wrote *Honors at Dawn* (1938), which also received the Avery Hopwood Award.

On August 5, 1940, he married his college sweetheart, Mary Slattery, the Catholic daughter of an insurance salesman. The couple had two children, Jane and Robert (a director, writer, and producer whose body of work includes producer of the 1996 movie version of *The Crucible*).

Arthur Miller's eminence as a dramatist is based primarily on four plays he wrote early in his career: *All My Sons* (1947), *Death of a Salesman* (1949), *The Crucible* (1953), and *A View from the Bridge* (one-act, 1955; revised two-act, 1956). Although his later works are generally considered inferior to his early masterpieces, Miller remains among the most important and influential dramatists to emerge in the United States since World War Ⅱ.

In December 2004, the 89-year-old Miller announced that he had been in love with 34-year-old minimalist painter Agnes Barley and had been living with her at his Connecticut farm since 2002, and that they intended to marry. Miller's final play, *Finishing the Picture* (2004), opened at the Goodman Theater, Chicago, in the fall of 2004. He stated that the work was based on the experience of filming *The Misfits* (1957).

Miller died of heart failure after a battle against cancer, pneumonia, and congestive heart disease at his home on the evening of February 10, 2005 at the age of 89.

His Writing Career

In 1940 Miller wrote *The Man Who Had All the Luck* (1940), which was produced in New Jersey in 1940 and won the Theater Guild's National Award. The play closed after four performances and disastrous reviews. In 1947 Miller's play *All My Sons* (1947), the writing of which had commenced in 1941, was a success on Broadway (earning him his first Tony Award, for best author) and his reputation as a playwright was established. With the success of *All My Sons*, he devoted himself entirely to drama.

Miller always acknowledges the strong influence of Henrik Ibsen on his work. He has lerarned from Ibsen the technique of providing information about the past little by little, and in this way false ideas of reality are gradually replaced by the underlying truth.

In 1948 Miller built a small studio in Roxbury, Connecticut. There, in less than a day, he wrote Act II of *Death of a Salesman* (1949). Within six weeks, he completed the rest of the play, one of the classics of world theater.

Death of a Salesman was hailed as an American myth and a contemporary tragedy. Directed by Elia and Kazan, *Death of a Salesman* was premiered on Broadway on February 10, 1959 by the Morosco Theater, and the play was commercially successful and critically acclaimed, winning a Tony Award for best author, the New York Drama Circle Critics' Award, and the Pulitzer Prize for drama. It was the first play to win all three of these major awards. The play was performed 742 times. This play not only won six famous awards but also won him reputation as one of the best American dramatists after the War.

Arthur Miller was summoned by the House Un-American Activities Committee on his political views, but he refused to cooperate. This bitter experience of the "McCarthy Era" led him to write *The Crucible* (1953), in which Miller likened the situation with the House Un-American Activities Committee to the witch hunt in Salem in 1692, opened at the Beck Theater on Broadway on January 22, 1953. Though widely considered only somewhat successful at the time of its initial release, today *The Crucible* is Miller's most frequently produced work throughout the world and was adapted into an opera by Robert Ward which won the Pulitzer Prize for music in 1962. It was now seen to have a more lasting and universal significance than had earlier been apparent. As Robert Martin later maintained, *The Crucible* "has endured beyond the immediate events of its own time. If it was originally seen as a political allegory, it is presently seen by contemporary audiences almost entirely as a distinguished American play by an equally distinguished American playwright."

After *A View from the Bridge* (1955) and *A Memory of Two Mondays* (1955), he abandoned the stage for about eight years. In June 1956, Miller left his first wife Mary Slattery and on June 25 he married Marilyn Monroe. Though Marilyn Monroe was a famous movie star, she was exploited by the film industry. In 1961, Miller began to work on *The Misfits*, starring his wife. Miller later said that the filming was one of the lowest points in his life; shortly before the film's premiere in 1961, the pair divorced. nineteen months later, Monroe died of a possible drug overdose.

He returned to the theater in 1964 with two works, *After the Fall* (1964), and, near the end of the year, *Incident at Vichy* (1964). *After the Fall* is considered Miller's most experimental and, perhaps, most pessimistic piece. That same year, Miller was elected the first American president of International PEN, a position which he held for four years. During this period Miller wrote the penetrating family drama, *The Price*, produced in 1968. It was Miller's most successful play since *Death of a Salesman*. The three plays deal with failure in human relationships and the question of guilt and responsibility of people to each other. These realistic plays explore his old subjects: individual responsibility, contrasting brothers, and alienated generations.

His next work, *The Creation of the World and Other Business* (1972), as series of comic sketches based on the *Biblical Book of Genesis*, met with severe critical disapproval when it was produced on Broadway in 1972, closing after only 20 performances. All of Miller's subsequent works premiered outside of New York. Miller staged the musical *Up from Paradise* (1974), an adaptation of *The Creation of the World* (1972), at his alma mater, the University of Michigan. *The Archbishop's Ceiling* (1977) was presented in 1977 at the Kennedy Center in Washington, D. C.

In the 1980s, Miller produced a number of short pieces. *The American Clock* (1980) is based on Studs Terkel's oral history of the Great Depression, *Hard Times*, and is structured as a series of vignettes that chronicle the hardship and suffering that occurred during that period. *Elegy for a Lady* (1982) and *Some Kind of Love Story* (1982) are two one-act plays that were staged together in 1982. Reviewers have generally regarded these later plays as minor works, inferior to Miller's early masterpiece.

During the early 1990s Miller wrote three new plays, *The Ride Down Mt. Morgan* (1991), *The Last Yankee* (1991), and *Broken Glass* (1994). In 1996, a film of *The Crucible* starring Daniel Day-Lewis and Winona Ryder opened. Miller spent much of 1996 working on the screenplay to the film. *Mr. Peters' Connections* (1998) was staged off-Broadway in 1998, and *Death of a Salesman* was revived on Broadway in 1999 to celebrate its fiftieth anniversary. The play, once again, was a large critical success, winning a Tony Award for best revival of a play.

In 1993, he was awarded the National Medal of Arts. Miller was honored with the PEN/Laura Pels International Foundation for theater award for a master American dramatist in 1998. In 2001 the National Endowment for the Humanities (NEH) selected Miller for the Jefferson Lecture, the US federal government's highest honor for achievement in the humanities. Miller's lecture was entitled "On Politics and the Art of Acting." Miller's lecture analyzed political events (including the US presidential election of 2000) in terms of the "arts of performance," and it drew attacks from some conservatives such as Jay Nordlinger, who called it "a disgrace," and George Will, who argued that Miller was not legitimately a "scholar."

In 1999 Miller was awarded The Dorothy and Lillian Gish Prize, one of the richest prizes in the arts, given annually to "a man or woman who has made an outstanding contribution to the beauty of the world and to mankind's enjoyment and understanding of life." On May 1st, 2002, Miller was awarded Spain's Principe de Asturias Prize for literature as "the undisputed master of modern drama." The following year Miller won the Jerusalem Prize.

Arthur Miller has published many influential plays such as: *No Villain* (1936), *Honors at Dawn* (1938), *The Man Who Had All the Luck* (1940), *All My Sons* (1947), *Death of a Salesman* (1949), *The Crucible* (1953), *A View from the Bridge* (1955), *A Memory of Two Mondays* (1955), *Incident at Vichy* (1964), *After the Fall* (1964) , *The Price* (1968), *The Creation of the World and Other Business* (1972), *Up from Paradise* (1974), *The Archbishop's Ceiling* (1977), *The American Clock* (1980), *Elegy for a Lady* and *Some Kind of Love Story* (1982), *The Ride Down*

Mt. Morgan (1991), *The Last Yankee* (1991), *Broken Glass* (1994), *Mr. Peter's Connections* (1998), *Resurrection Blues* (2002), and *Finishing the Picture* (2004).

Analysis of and Comment on His Representative Play

Death of a Salesman (1949)

Plot Summary

Death of a Salesman is Miller's masterpiece. The play premiered on Broadway in February 1949, running for 742 performances, and has been revived on Broadway four times winning three Tony Awards for best revival. With the production of *Death of a Salesman*, Miller firmly established his reputation as an outstanding American dramatist. This play represents his most powerful dramatization of the clash between the individual and materialistic American society.

Arthur Miller based Willy Loman, the protagonist, on his own uncle, Manny Newman. Miller started writing the play in 1947 after a chance encounter he had with his uncle outside the Colonial Theater in Boston.

Willy Loman is an aging salesman who returns home one night from a sales trip, unable to concentrate on the road. He needs to keep making sales since there are so many payments to make, and they need the money. His wife, Linda, is worried about him, and is completely devoted to him and encourages him to find a job where he does not have to travel anymore. His two adult sons, Happy and Biff, are back in the house for the first time in years, talking about their future job prospects. Both Biff and Willy are determined to ask for better jobs: Biff from Bill Oliver, a successful man whom he knew long ago, and Willy from Howard Wagner, the son of the man who first hired Willy to the firm. Both are unsuccessful.

As the play unfolds, the observer learns about various incidents in the Loman family in the past which account for their present condition. Biff, having always relied on athletics, fails math and does not graduate high school. Willy, having always encouraged Biff not to concentrate on academics since he had such great athletic potential, does not want to be blamed for Biff's failures. Moreover, one day, Biff catches Willy cheating on Linda with another woman in Boston, and his esteem for Willy completely vanishes. Willy thinks Biff is intentionally spiteful to him and only wants to hurt Willy, but soon Willy realizes that Biff just wants Willy to accept him for who he is. Biff says that he is not the business type and just wants to work on a farm in the open air, and he breaks down crying since Willy keeps forcing him to pursue a job with Bill Oliver. Biff says he does not want to lie anymore.

When Willy sees Biff crying, he finally realizes that Biff loves him and has not been trying to hurt him all these years. He wants to make up for it by giving Biff $20,000 with which to start a new business and Willy will get the money by killing himself and collecting the insurance policy. Willy kills himself by crashing the car before Biff can make amends with him. Biff realizes that they have all been living a false dream, but Happy is determined to carry out Willy's dreams. Linda is distraught, especially since she has just paid the last payment on the mortgage but now there is no one to live in the house.

The play doesn't end with Willy's death. The dilemma is projected forward as Biff rejects the dream that hounded his father to his death and Happy dedicates himself to it. The spiritual and the material remain in tension.

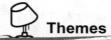

Themes

The Disillusionment of the American Dream　Willy Loman believes wholeheartedly in what he considers the promise of the American Dream—that a "well-liked" and "personally attractive" man in business will indubitably and deservedly acquire the material comforts offered by modern American life. Oddly, his fixation with the superficial qualities of attractiveness and likeability is at odds with a more gritty, more rewarding understanding of the American Dream that identifies hard work without complaint as the key to success. Willy's interpretation of likeability is superficial—he childishly dislikes Bernard because he considers Bernard a nerd. Willy's blind faith in his stunted version of the American Dream leads to his rapid psychological decline when he is unable to accept the disparity between the Dream and his own life.

Willy's life has fallen apart in his hands. Willy seems childlike and relies on others for support. His first name, Willy, reflects this childlike aspect as well as sounding like the question "Will he?" His last name gives the feel of Willy being a "low man," someone low on the social ladder and unlikely to succeed. Derided by the buyers on whom he depends, alienated from his son, Biff, no longer in touch with his life, he plans a suicide that will redeem him. A believer in the dreams paraded as social realities, he finds himself holding nothing that will give meaning to his life, so he revisits his past, searching for the moment when promise had turned to failure, when the myth that had provided his life with structure and purpose had collapsed.

Biff Loman represents Willy's more realistic and depressed side. Biff is Willy's pride and joy. Willy always talks about Biff, and his visits bring great excitement to Willy. However, Biff has been raised with the wrong values, since Willy encourages Biff to ignore his academics, rely on athletics and personality, and to steal. When Biff finally sees that his father is a fake, he becomes lost, since he had relied so heavily on Willy's values in the past to guide him, yet now those values have led him astray. When Biff is pressured into seeing Bill Oliver to ask for a job, he unfortunately steals a fountain pen from Oliver's office. When Biff realizes what he is doing, he sees for the first time that he is not doing what he wants to do but has always been doing what Willy has wanted him to do. He is no one special and if Willy had not puffed him up so much in the past, maybe Biff would have been someone. When Biff tries to confront Willy and get him to see how false his dreams were, Willy refuses to listen, so Biff has to be turned away, which causes him to cry. Willy sees the tears as a symbol of Biff's love for him, which leads him to commit suicide for Biff's sake, but his action was to no avail. At Willy's funeral, Biff accuses Willy of having false dreams, and Biff is glad that he has finally escaped them. Intent on revealing the simple and humble truth behind Willy's fantasy, Biff longs for the territory obscured by his father's blind faith in a skewed, materialist version of the American Dream. Biff's identity crisis is a function of his and his father's disillusionment, which, in order to reclaim his identity, he must expose.

Happy Loman is the neglected son of the family. Throughout his life, he has always been second string to Biff in Willy's eyes. He is moderately successful with a good job and his own apartment, but he still feels lonely, since he knows that he is missing the love and care that his parents pay to Biff. He is always looking for attention from his parents, but rarely gets any, and he even goes as far as to make things up just for attention, such as telling his parents he is going to get married and his determination to carry out the Lomans' dreams of being successful in business. He tries to discourage Biff from telling Willy the truth by keeping up the front that Biff is going into business with Bill Oliver and that Biff and Happy will go into business together as the Loman Brothers, which makes Willy proud. In the end, Happy still tries to live Willy's dream, even though Biff knows they are false. Happy is a doomed, utterly duped figure, destined to be swallowed up by the force of blind ambition that fuels his insatiable sex drive.

Betrayal Willy's primary obsession throughout the play is what he considers to be Biff's betrayal of his ambitions for him. Willy believes that he has every right to expect Biff to fulfill the promise inherent in him. When Biff walks out on Willy's ambitions for him, Willy takes this rejection as a personal affront (he associates it with "insult" and "spite"). Willy, after all, is a salesman, and Biff's ego-crushing rebuff ultimately reflects Willy's inability to sell him on the American Dream—the product in which Willy himself believes most faithfully. Willy assumes that Biff's betrayal stems from Biff's discovery of Willy's affair with the Woman—a betrayal of Linda's love. Whereas Willy feels that Biff has betrayed him, Biff feels that Willy, a "phony little fake," has betrayed him with his unending stream of ego-stroking lies.

Literary Techniques

The play is mostly told from the point of view of the protagonist, Willy, and the previous parts of Willy's life are revealed in the flashback, sometimes during a present day scene. It does this by having a scene begin in the present time, and adding characters onto the stage whom only Willy can see and hear, representing characters and conversations from other times and places.

The play's structure resembles a stream of consciousness account: Willy drifts between his living room downstage to the apron and flashbacks of an idyllic past, and also to fantasized conversations with Ben. When we are in the present the characters abide by the rules of the set, entering only through the stage door to the left; however, when we visit Willy's "past" these rules are removed, with characters openly moving through walls. Whereas the term "flashback" as a form of cinematography for these scenes is often heard, Miller himself rather speaks of "mobile concurrences." In fact, flashbacks would show an objective image of the past. Miller's mobile concurrences, however, rather show highly subjective memories. Furthermore, as Willy's mental state deteriorates, the boundaries between past and present are destroyed, and the two start to exist in parallel.

The real force of the play lay in its method, in a use of time that opened up process and compacted past and present into the same space. How fantastic, Miller said to himself, "a play would be that did not still the mind's simultaneity, did not allow a man to 'forget' and turned him to see present through past and past through present, a form that in itself, quite apart from its content and meaning, would be inescapable as a psychological process and as a collecting point for all that his life in society has poured into him." There were three categories of time in the play: surreal time, psychological time, and the time created by the play as it is perceived by the audience. *Death of a Salesman* was a wholly original creation.

Symbolism   In the play, seeds represent for Willy the opportunity to prove the worth of his labor, both as a salesman and a father. His desperate, nocturnal attempt to grow vegetables signifies his shame about barely being able to put food on the table and having nothing to leave his children when he passes. Willy feels that he has worked hard but fears that he will not be able to help his offspring any more than his own abandoning father helped him. The seeds also symbolize Willy's sense of failure with Biff. Despite the American Dream's formula for success, which Willy considers infallible, Willy's efforts to cultivate and nurture Biff went awry. Realizing that his all-American football star has turned into a lazy bum, Willy takes Biff's failure and lack of ambition as a reflection of his abilities as a father.

Diamonds to Willy represent tangible wealth and, hence, both validation of one's labor (and life) and the ability to pass material goods on to one's offspring, two things that Willy desperately craves. Correlatively, diamonds, the discovery of which made Ben a fortune, symbolize Willy's failure as a salesman. Despite Willy's belief in the American Dream, a belief unwavering to the extent that he passed up the opportunity to go with Ben to Alaska, the Dream's promise of financial security has eluded Willy. At the end of the play, Ben encourages Willy to enter the "jungle" finally and retrieve this elusive diamond—that is, to kill himself for insurance money in order to make his life meaningful.

Willy's strange obsession with the condition of Linda's stockings foreshadows his later flashback to Biff's discovery of him and the Woman in their Boston hotel room. The teenage Biff accuses Willy of giving away Linda's stockings to the woman. Stockings assume a metaphorical weight as the symbol of betrayal and sexual infidelity. New stockings are important for both Willy's pride in being financially successful and thus able to provide for his family and for Willy's ability to ease his guilt about, and suppress the memory of, his betrayal of Linda and Biff.

The rubber hose is a stage prop that reminds the audience of Willy's desperate attempts at suicide. He has apparently attempted to kill himself by inhaling gas, which is, ironically, the very substance essential to one of the most basic elements with which he must equip his home for his family's health and comfort—heat. Literal death by inhaling gas parallels the metaphorical death that Willy feels in his struggle to afford such a basic necessity.

 ## Motifs

Mythic Figures Willy's tendency to mythologize people contributes to his deluded understanding of the world. He speaks of Dave Singleman as a legend and imagines that his death must have been beautifully noble. Willy compares Biff and Happy to the mythic Greek figures Adonis and Hercules because he believes that his sons are pinnacles of "personal attractiveness" and power through "well likedness"; to him, they seem the very incarnation of the American dream.

Willy's mythologizing proves quite nearsighted, however. Willy fails to realize the hopelessness of Singleman's lonely, on-the-job, on-the-road death. Trying to achieve what he considers to be Singleman's heroic status, Willy commits himself to a pathetic death and meaningless legacy (even if Willy's life insurance policy ends up paying off, Biff wants nothing to do with Willy's ambition for him). Similarly, neither Biff nor Happy ends up leading an ideal, godlike life; while Happy does believe in the American dream, it seems likely that he will end up no better off than the decidedly ungodlike Willy.

The American West, Alaska, and the African Jungle These regions represent the potential of instinct to Biff and Willy. Willy's father found success in Alaska and his brother, Ben, became rich in Africa; these exotic locales, especially when compared to Willy's banal Brooklyn neighborhood, crystallize how Willy's obsession with the commercial world of the city has trapped him in an unpleasant reality. Whereas Alaska and the African jungle symbolize Willy's failure, the American West, on the other hand, symbolizes Biff's potential. Biff realizes that he has been content only when working on farms, out in the open. His westward escape from both Willy's delusions and the commercial world of the eastern United States suggests a nineteenth-century pioneer mentality—Biff, unlike Willy, recognizes the importance of the individual.

Bibliography

常耀信. 美国文学简史（第二版修订本）. 天津：南开大学出版社，2006. 305–312.

吴瑾瑾主编. 美国文学史. 北京：经济科学出版社，2008. 424–432.

Bercovitch, Sacvan. *The Cambridge History of American Literature Vol. 7*. Cambridge U.K. and New York: Cambridge University Press, 1999. 20–43.

Draper, J. P. *World Literature Criticism Vol. 4*. Detroit: Gale, 1992. 2359–2365.

http://en.wikipedia.org/wiki/Death_of_a_Salesman 2013-02-15

http://www.newworldencyclopedia.org/entry/Arthur_Miller 2013-02-15

PART VI

AMERICAN LITERATURE IN THE POSTMODERN PERIOD

(1945—   )

Historical Introduction

We are now entering the post-World War II period, the postmodern period. So much has occurred since 1945 that recent American literature, prominently American postmodern literature, dealing with the new experience in the postindustrial society, the postmodern society, the information society, or the society of late capitalism in the context of globalization, has acquired an imposing stature. American ended the decade of the 1930s in an inward-looking mood, concerned with economic issues, unemployment, and the need to heal internal ideological divisions. By the close of World War II, however, that mood had changed. The United States had become a global superpower, committed to the international arena. In the new era of postwar, postcolonial politics, it had come to stand for the "American" way of capitalism, individualism, and the open market, opposed in every respect to the "Russian" or "communist" way of collectivism and the organized economy. A war machine that had managed to treble munitions production in 1941 continued, if in a slightly lower gear. The cessation of conflict did not mean an end to arms production, now that the United States discovered new treats in international socialism, and the next decade or so saw the rapid expansion of what one president was to term the military-industrial complex: a compact between military interests, eager to acquire ever newer and more powerful armaments, and industrial interests, just as eager to produce them, that was to prove satisfactory and profitable to both. The only nation to emerge from World War II with its manufacturing plant intact and its economy strengthened, America presented itself to the rest of the world—and, in particular, to Europe—as an economic miracle.

The business of America was not only to flourish its economic abundance but also, perhaps, to dictate the terms as modern culture, at least to its western allies, and to other parts of the globe where it claimed a right of intervention and control. As the 1940s passed into the 1950s, America seemed to set the style in everything, from high art to advanced technology to popular culture. In Eisenhower, the president from 1952 to 1960, Americans also had someone at the head of state whose main aim seemed to be to preserve this economic abundance and cultural hegemony through a strategy of masterly inactivity. Like Ronald Reagan thirty years later, Eisenhower made a dramatic exhibition of not working too hard; as he apparently saw it, his job as president was to leave Americans alone to go about their business, and to discourage the state from any interference in the day-to-day life of the individual. If self-help was to be encouraged, then citizens had to be left to themselves, to work hard and then to enjoy the material comforts thereby earned. Many intellectuals and artists—although by no means all of them—participated in this era of consensus. This was the so-called value-free sociology; much of the literal intelligentsia acted on the assumption that it was possible to exercise the critical function untouched by social or political problems; and many writers withdrew from active involvement in issues of public concern or ideology into formalism, abstraction, or mythmaking.

No consensus, however, is quite as complete as it seems, just as no society is without its areas of dissent. Abundance breeds its own anxieties, not least the fear of losing the comforts one enjoys; in many ways, the calm society is the one most susceptible to sudden, radical fits of panic. In literature, related insecurities in a preoccupation with evil, the possible eruption of weariness, guilt, and remorse, into the rhythms of routine experience. In the political life of the period perhaps the most significant expression of this fear of invasion, subversion, or even destruction by covert agencies was the phenomenon known as McCarthyism. Joseph McCarthy was a young senator from Wisconsin who had a self-appointed mission to wage war on anything he saw as communist subversion. Exploiting his position on the Un-American Activities Committee, playing on popular anxieties about the growing power of Russia and the possible presence of an "enemy within," he embarked on a modern-day witch-hunt, the result of which was that many people were sacked from their jobs and blacklisted on the mere suspicion of belonging to the Communist Party. Guilt was established by smear; loss of job followed on false witness, and a cast of characters that included Hollywood scriptwriters, intellectuals, and academics suddenly found themselves the subject of vicious public abuse.

One crucial fear that McCarthy exploited was the fear of the betrayal of atomic secrets. America had unleashed strange and terrible forces when it dropped atom bombs on Hiroshima and Nagasaki. The bomb cast its shadow over the immediate postwar decades, just as it has done ever since; and the discovery that certain people in the United States, Canada, and Britain had passed atomic secrets to the Russians, who could now explode nuclear weapons of their own, clearly exacerbated public anxieties about hidden enemies and conspiracies, and made it that much easier for McCarthy and his committee flourish. Fear of the potential nuclear capability of the enemy, allied to this suspicion of a powerful enemy within, also increased the tensions of what Winston Churchill christened the Cold War: that policy of brinkmanship between the United States and Russia, their respective satellite states and allies, that was based on the premise that the two superpowers were engaged in a life-or-death struggle for global supremacy. Eisenhower years was more than just a useful weapon in the hands of certain ambitious politicians, helping to generate policies of confrontation and containment.

By the late 1950s this threat—and, more specifically, the bomb that embodied it—had become a potent symbol for the destructive potential of the new society: the dark side of those forces that had created apparently limitless wealth. Everywhere in the culture there were signs of revolt. There was a renewed spirit of rebelliousness, opposition to a social and economic order that had produced the possibility of global death. In music, the emergence of rock and roll, derived mainly from black musical forms, signaled a reluctance to accept the consensual mores, and the blandness, of white middle-class America: which is why, until they were absorbed into the mainstream, performers were perceived by political and religious leaders as such a potent threat, offering a gesture of defiance to "civilized standards." In the movies, similarly, new heroes appeared dramatizing an oppositional stance to the dominant culture. And in literature, too, there were analogous developments. Two key fictional texts of the period were *The Catcher in the Rye* (1951) by J. D. Salinger and *On the Road* (1957) by Jack Kerouac. Radically dissimilar as these two books were, they had in common heroes at odds with modern urban-technological life: outsiders who moved between fragile mysticism and outright disaffiliation in their search for an alternative to the orthodox culture. They were willing, in effect, to say no, in thunder, just as earlier American heroes had been. This was also true of many writers of the period who bore witness to a gradual slipping away from the formalism and abstraction—and, to some extent, the conformism—of the postwar years and toward renewed feelings of freedom, individualism, and commitment. Recovering the impulse toward the personal, sometimes to the point of the confessional, and the urge toward an individual, perhaps even idiosyncratic beat, they gave voice to a growing sense of resistance to the social norms. Reinventing the old American allegiance to the rebellious self, and weaving together personal and historical traumas, they sought in their line and language for a road to liberation: a way of realizing their fundamental estrangement. No cultural development is seamless, and it would be wrong to suggest that the story of the first two decades after World War II is one, simply, of abundance and anxiety merging into revolt and repudiation of fixed forms.

President John F. Kennedy spoke in terms of a general direction or tendency at his inaugural in January 1961. He brought with him to office the expectation of great change, an optimism and confidence about the character of the United States and its role in the world that many Americans were eager to share. His words were ambitious and struck a responsive chord in the heart of the nation. "We stand today on the edge of a new frontier," Kennedy declared, "a frontier of unknown opportunities and perils... I am asking each of you to be pioneers on that new frontier." The appeal to the apparently timeless myth of the West, pioneering and conquest captures the confidence, the ambition, the sense of potential, and the arrogance of a "new generation of Americans," and weds all this to the ideology of a long-vanished frontier.

The America to which president spoke was a constellation of many attitudes and forces: a nation of 180 million people, a growing number of whom were white suburbanites living in quiet comfort on the edge of the older, urban areas, buying their goods in out-of-town shopping malls, and working in white-collar service-sector industries. While the income of middle-class Americans of working age continued to improve, that of the bottom 20 percent showed hardly any advance at all. There was conspicuous abundance, but there was equally conspicuous poverty: the rhetoric of the president possibly acknowledged this, but it tended to be forgotten amid the general euphoria, the sense of irresistible expansion and movement forwards toward a "new frontier." And it was only in the later 1960s that the seeds of discontent and dissension sowed by this conspicuous contrast between haves and have-nots began to be harvested.

In the meantime, in the 1960s, optimism and the promise of adventure were in the air. Responding to the sense of new frontiers to be conquered, many artists of the period, of every kind, were notable for their willingness to experiment, to confront and even challenge cultural and social norms. A decade is an artificial measure and, in this respect as in most others, "the sixties" had really begun in the middle to late 1950s: when the popular arts were revivified by a new sense of energy and power, and a lively avant-garde embarked on challenging conventional norms and forms. Happenings, festivals, multimedia performances became commonplace events. Readings of poetry and prose, often to jazz accompaniment, attracted dedicated audiences. There was a sense of risk, of venturing beyond the formalism, the preoccupation with craftsmanship of earlier decades. Writing became more open, rawer, alert to the possibility of change and the inclusion of random factors. There was a renewed emphasis on chance, difference, impermanency, a new willingness to see the new artistic object as shifting, discontinuous, part of the flux and variety of things. Modernism was, in effect, shading into postmodernism, with its resistance to finality or closure, to distinctions between "high" and "low" cultures, to grand explanations and master narratives—and to the belief that there is one, major or monolithic truth to be apprehended in art. With its preference for suspended judgments, its disbelief in hierarchies, mistrust of solutions, denouements and completions, the postmodernist impulse was a characteristic product of these times. It encouraged forms of writing that thrived on the edge that denied the authoritative in favor of the arbitrary and posited a random, unstructured world as well as an equally random, unstructured art. This was a different kind of new frontier, perhaps, from the one Kennedy anticipated. But it tapped a similar excitement: "this country might have been a pio neer land, once," declared the black poet Sonia Sanchez, "and it still is."

If one growing tendency of American writing of the 1960s was toward postmodernism, another was toward the political. Nowhere was this more notable than among African-American writers like Sanchez. The black arts movement, in particular, reacted to calls for "black power" and a new feeling of racial pride captured in the slogan "black is beautiful." Its attempt to define a "black aesthetic," what it meant to be a specifically black writer, encouraged analogous developments among other ethnic minorities and among women of all races. In conferences and workshops like the Second Black Writers' Conference at Fisk University in 1967, critics and writers worked with the issues of how literature might properly express and promote political causes. "The black arts and the black power concept," Larry Neal (1937—1981) wrote at the beginning of his essay "The Black Arts Movement" (1968), "both relate broadly to the African-American's desire for self determination and nationhood. Both concepts are nationalistic." And, just as African-American writers became intent on explaining and expressing their solidarity with their black brothers and sisters—the urban poor and dispossessed, the people of the newly independent African nations—so women writers, many of them, expressed a commitment to the new forms of feminism. "We can no longer ignore that voice within women that says, 'I want something more than my husband and my children and my home,'" wrote Betty Friedan (1921—2006) in *The Feminine Mystique* (1963). Following on from her, there was an exponential increase in writing about experiences and issues that vitally affected women—women's sexuality, the "feminine" role, childbirth, domestic politics, lesbianism—and a steady development of feminist criticism and theory, social history, and aesthetics. Not long after *The Feminine Mystique* was published, in 1965, Luis Valdez (1940—) combined Mexican-American literature with political purpose when he joined with the farm-workers' union led by César Chavez to form El Theater Campecino. This theater company mixed traditional Spanish and Mexican dramatic forms with agit-prop techniques to create dramatic sketches in support of union issues. The publication of *House Made of Dawn* by Scott Momaday in 1968, heralding the emergence of a major movement in native American writing, coincided with an upsurge in Indian protest: the symbolic seizing of Alcatraz and later armed conflict on reservations that helped generate revisionist histories like *Bury My Heart at Wounded Knee* (1971) by Dee Brown (1908—2002). Asian-Americans, too, gradually asserted their presence, first male writers such as Louis Chu (*Eat a Bowl of Tea*, 1961) and then later female writers like Chuang Hua (*Crossings*, 1968). In these works, a similar confluence of the personal and political was perceptible: the lives of Chinese men, who have left their wives and children for a better existence in America (*Eat a Bowl of Tea*), the lives of women struggling with the racial and cultural constraints imposed on them by an ancient culture (*Crossings*).

Both the impulse toward more openly political forms of writing, and the postmodern inclination toward the absurd, received a push from events that took place not long after President Kennedy took office. Indeed, if his inauguration acted as a catalyst for the optimism of the early 1960s, then his assassination in Dallas in November 1963 served as a focus for energies of another kind. The belief in the radical change persisted, but it was now continued within a harsher, more abrasive, and confrontational sense of the social realities. The divisions and discontent that had been always there—in a society still painfully split between rich and poor, white and colored, suburbanite and ghetto-dweller—now came to the surface; the violence that brought the president's life to an end was echoed in the national life, at home and abroad. The protest became more widespread and exacerbated, and the uneasiness burgeoned into open revolt. The civil rights movement, for example, grew more militant. Instead of merely boycotting segregated businesses and services, black and white activists began to use them, challenging the authorities to enforce iniquitous segregationist laws. Confrontations occurred in several southern townships between civil rights workers and white authorities. In August 1963 there was a massive demonstration in Washington, D.C. involving over a quarter of a million people, who heard Martin Luther King, the movement's inspiring leader, talking of his dream of a multiracial society. The demonstration was notably and triumphantly peaceful but, in this respect, it marked the end of an era. Within a few years, King himself had been assassinated and the ghettos of Los Angeles, Detroit, New York, Washington, and many other cities were aflame. During the late 1960s it seemed as if rioting in the streets of the cities had become an annual event, as black people expressed their anger with a social and economic order that tended to deprive them of their basic rights. At the same time, the nation's universities were the scene of almost equally violent confrontations, as students expressed their resistance to local university authorities and the power of the state.

For university students, as for many other protest groups of the time, the central issue was the Vietnam War. In the summer of 1964, President Lyndon Johnson persuaded Congress to give him almost unlimited powers to wage war against what was perceived as the communist threat from North Vietnam. American troops were committed to a massive land war against an indigenous guerrilla movement; the American military was involved in saturation bombing and what was euphemistically known as "defoliation"—that is, destruction of the forests, the vegetation, and plant life of a country situated about 12,000 miles from Washington; and American policy was, effectively, to bleed the nation's human and economic resources in support of what was little more than a puppet government in South Vietnam. By 1967, millions of Americans were beginning to feel that the war was not only useless but also obscene, and took to the streets in protest: these included novelists like Norman Mailer, and poets like Robert Lowell and Allen Ginsberg. Simultaneously with this, in response to what looked like the obscenity of the official culture, a vigorous alternative culture developed. Much of this alternative culture was especially political in its direction. Young man buries their draft cards; and, when the Democratic Party met in Chicago in 1968 to nominate their candidate for president, young people upstaged the proceedings by engaging in pitched battles with the police in the streets. But much of it, too, had to do with styles of life and styles of art. Hair was worn unconventionally long, skirts unconventionally short; hallucinogenic drugs, psychedelic art, and hugely amplified rock concerts all became part of an instinctive strategy for challenging standard versions of social reality, accepted notions of behavior and gender. The analytical mode was supplanted by the expressive, the intellectual by the imaginative; artists as a whole went further toward embracing a sense of the provisional, a fluid, unstructured reality; and artistic eclecticism became the norm, as writers in general hit upon unexpected aesthetic mixtures—mingling fantasy and commitment, myth and social protest, and high and popular art.

One of the paradoxes of the year 1968 was that it witnessed alternative culture at its zenith and the election of Richard Nixon, self-proclaimed spokesman for the "silent majority" of white, middle-class Americans, to the office of president. To the extent that "the sixties" have become a convenient label for a particular frame of mind—radical, experimental, subversive, and even confrontational—they did not end in 1970 any more than they began in 1960. Many aspects of the alternative culture survived well into the next decade; and some, like the feminist and ecological movements, effectively became part of the cultural mainstream. Nevertheless, the election of such an un-alternative, un-radical president as Nixon, and his reelection in 1972, did signal a shift in the national mood that was gradually confirmed in the 1970s and beyond. The Vietnam War was brought to an ignominious end, removing one of major sources of confrontation and revolt. Black Americans remained economically dispossessed, but the civil rights movement did increase their electoral power, and so gave them the opportunity of expressing their dissatisfaction through the ballot box rather than taking to the streets. The children of the postwar "baby boom," who had fueled the fires of apparent revolution, began to enter the workforce and take on the responsibilities of jobs, homes, and families. And, while the United States continued to prosper—the gross national product had risen to 974 billion in 1970—there were worrying signs of possible economic crisis. Inflation was worse than in most western European countries; the balance of payments deficit began to grow to frightening proportions; while the dollar steadily lost its purchasing power. As the economic situation grew harsher, especially after the oil crisis of the early 1970s, more and more Americans narrowed their horizons, devoting their attention and energies to the accumulation and preservation of personal wealth. One commentator christened the 1970s "the me decade"; another referred to the culture of narcissism. And these significant tendencies did not alter with the resignation of Nixon. The rhetoric of Reagan might have sounded similar, at times, to that of Kennedy—when, for instance, he talked about building a shining city upon a hill or declared that the best years of America were yet to come. But this rhetoric occurred within structures of belief and assumptions that were quite different from those of the assassinated president. For Reagan, the crucial appeal was to the past, the mythical American past of stable, familial, and to an extent pastoral values, that, as he saw it, it was the duty of Americans to recover; and to this predominantly backward-looking impulse was added a strong sense of personal responsibility, a feeling that each American should look after himself or herself, which found little room for accommodating the communal vision of an earlier decade.

Reagan might have appealed to the past. Later, in the 1990s, Bill Clinton might have tried to claim some of the spirit of the 1960s for himself, with his talk of being part of a raw, new postwar generation, his declaration of belief in a place called hope, and, not least, his use of an old movie showing him, as a boy, shaking hands with John Kennedy. The two President George Bushes, father and son, might suggest in turn a warier and more conservative America. What all these presidents have in common, however, is what they have presided over: a dissolution of the old social and cultural markets. Many of the great nation-states have disintegrated: notably, the sinister "other" of Cold War America, the Union of Soviet Socialist Republics. Along with them the great narratives, the meta-narratives used once to explain historical movement, have lost plausibility. The myth of Plymouth Rock, for example, of America as the exclusive domain for Europeans seeking religious and political freedom, has far less resonance in a world characterized by transnational drift and an American nation that is more than ever multicultural. So does the classic iconography of the United States as a melting pot, in which all cultures, all nationalities are resolving into one, which brings in the most significant series of markers that have now disappeared. American popular culture has become internationally dominant. In the global market place it is America that is the biggest item on sale. In a postcolonial world, our imaginations have been colonized by the United States. At the same time, and crucially, the United States itself has been internationalized. It has become, not a melting pot, but a mosaic of different cultures—what one American writer, Ishmael Reed, has called "the first universal nation."

"The world is here," Reed declared in an essay called, appropriately enough, "America: The Multinational Society" (1988). And the world is here, in the United States, for three seminal reasons. In the first place, particular ethnic groups that have been there for centuries have gained in presence and prominence. The national census of 1990, for instance, reported 1,959,234 native Americans living in a total population of over 248 million Americans. The figure was almost fourfold increase on the number of 523,591 native Americans in the 1960 census, which in turn built upon the population nadir of around 250,000 in 1900. The huge rise in the native American population was down to a consistently high birth rate and improved medical care, but also due to the increased number of people who claimed native American ancestry. Whether or not, as some cultural commentators have claimed, ethnicity is a matter of consciousness rather than cultural difference, it is clear that the consciousness of ethnicity has secured the status and significance of certain ethnic groups in the United States. Many more Americans are proud, eager to define themselves as native American. Many Mexican-Americans, in turn, have lived in a cultural borderland for two centuries, what they call *la frontera*, thanks to Spanish conquest and then American annexation. Along with certain other ethnic groups, notably those from Cuba, Dominica, and Puerto Rico, Mexican-Americans have effected a sea change in American culture and transformed the demographic destiny of the nation.

"American literature, especially in the twentieth century, and notably in the last twenty years," Toni Morrison wrote in 1992, "has been shaped by its encounter with the immigrant," which leads to the second, seminal reason why the United States has become "the first universal nation." Along with immigrants from the Hispanic world, those from the third world generally have been changing the character and destiny of the United States, especially after legislation in the 1960s first abolished national-origin quotas (which tended to favor northern Europeans) and then expanded immigration from countries such as China and India. Almost nine million legal immigrants came to America during the 1980s, along with two million undocumented immigrants. They accounted for 29 percent of the population growth from 226.5 million during the decade. From 1990 to 1997 another 7.5 million foreign-born individuals entered the United States legally, accounting for 29.2 percent of the population. By the middle of the twenty-first century, it has been calculated, "nonwhite" and third world ethnic groups will outnumber whites in the United Sates. Revealing the central dynamic of western life, and in some sense global life, today, which is marked by the powerful shaping force of shifting, multicultural populations, America has witnessed the disappearance of the boundary between the "center" and the "margins." And with white Americans moving, it seems, inexorably into a minority, it has lost any claim it may have had, or any pretence of one, to a Eurocentric character and an exclusive destiny.

Not that everyone would agree. The attacks by al-Qaeda terrorists on September 11, 2001 left almost three thousand people dead, the World Trade Center in New York City destroyed, and Americans rightly feeling that they were seriously threatened. The American government, led by President George W. Bush, responded to this by launching a "war on terror," first invading Afghanistan, which had harbored al-Qaeda terrorists, and then embarking on a lengthy diplomatic campaign to associate Iraq with international terrorism. In particular, it was claimed that Iraq possessed "weapons of mass destruction" that endangered the security of the United Sates and its allies. The diplomatic campaign was followed by a military one, which began on March 20, 2003 with the invasion of Iraq by a multinational force led by troops from the United States and United Kingdom. The military operation was swiftly finished, with the coalition declaring on April 15 that the invasion was effectively over and, later, Bush making what became known as his "mission accomplished" speech. What followed the operation, however, was continued chaos and conflict. Saddam Hussein was certainly removed from power, his totalitarian regime toppled. But the cost was high, with civil war and sustained acts of terrorism leaving five thousand members of the coalition army and up to seven hundred thousand Iraqis dead by the beginning of 2009. A vast majority of Americans and the international community came to believe that the Iraq War was a mistake; most intelligence experts agreed that it had only increased terrorism. The situation was exacerbated by the failure to discover any weapons of mass destruction in Iraq and by a series of human rights abuse in coalition detention centers, including the now notorious ones of Abu

Ghraib and Guantanamo Bay. If the mission of the war was to bring peace and prosperity to Iraq, it certainly failed. If it was to demonstrate a continued belief, at least in some quarters, in the special destiny of America, then it succeeded—but at an enormously high cost to the national reputation. The gap between the promise and performance of the mission was measured by two events. On April 9, 2003 a statue of Hussein was torn down by crowds in Baghdad to mark the fall of the city. Exactly six years later, tens of thousands of Iraqis gathering in Baghdad to demand the immediate departure of coalition forces, burned an effigy of George W. Bush.

By the time of the second event, Bush had ceased to be in power. The war, an economic crisis that came to be known as the Great Recession, a gathering sense that the nation had lost its way—all contributed to a remarkable event: the election of the first African-American, Barack Obama, to the office of president. Obama was born in Kenya, raised in Indonesia and then in Hawaii; and the "experience of a variety of cultures in a climate of mutual respect," he has said, became "an important part" of his "worldview." That worldview, after he was elected to the senate, made him one of the few major politicians initially opposed the Iraq War. During and after the presidential campaign, it also prompted him to stress the importance of reducing energy dependence and extending healthcare. Whether Obama will fulfill his stated ambitions as President—a rapid withdrawal of troops from Iraq, a reduction in carbon emissions, a radical increase in energy sources, and the realization of a universal healthcare system—remain to be seen. What is clear, however, is that like Franklin D. Roosevelt in the 1930s, Obama has restored the international reputation of the United States and reignited America's belief in itself. And his agenda, if exceptionalist, is so only in the sense that he embraces the idea of the United States as the first universal nation. What the story of the last ten years has told us is that there is still a deep division of opinion about the place and destiny of America, its position either as a crusade with a special mission, a manifest destiny to be realized at home and abroad, or as crossroads of culture, part of an international community of nations. In his inauguration speech, Obama referred to the "patchwork heritage" of America and called it a "strength, not a weakness." "We are shaped by every language and culture," "drawn from every end of this earth," he added. It is this notion of mosaic of cultures that has now reasserted itself, recapturing the center ground from the idea of mission, an exclusive destiny. But both ideas still command loyalty, and will presumably continue to struggle for supremacy, as Americans continue to engage in the task of reinventing themselves—or in what Obama, in his inauguration speech, called "the work of remaking America."

The consequence of all this for literature in America is debatable. Given that writers are responding on some level to their own unique encounters with history, they are in any event not easy, perhaps impossible, to summarize. For some, there has been a notable shift away from public affairs and commitment and toward introspection, the cult of the personal. Writers, quite a few of them, have turned away from immediate history, the pressures of the times, and devoted their imaginations to the vagaries of consciousness, the deeper forms of myth, ritual, and fantasy, the imagery figured and the language articulated by the isolated mind. For others, particularly many women writers and writers from "ethnic" or "nonwhite" cultures, the engagement with history remains pressing, even painful, although the terms in which that engagement is expressed may vary from the literal, the direct, as in the new journalism and forms of social realism, to the resonantly abstract, the figurative, or the archaic. Writers may devote themselves, say, to the interrogation and alteration of verbal structures, in the belief that what we see and think is shaped by such structures; our social life being grounded in language, in order to change society it is language that must be changed. Or they may respond to what Clifford Geertz has called "the international hodgepodge of postmodern culture" by creating an art of palpable discontinuity: yoking together wildly incongruous elements, mixing voices and genres, pursuing the inconsistent, the divergent and indeterminate. They may be inclined to the use of fabulation, magic, or dreams in the conviction that consciousness shapes history—or the simpler assumption that only a literature of the strange, the fantastic, can begin to recover the strangeness of contemporary America. Or they may turn to the oral or other traditions of one of the ancient cultures that inform American history: not to legitimate that culture (the time for that, if there ever was one, has long gone) but to explore the meaning of those traditions for all American society.

What surely all these, and other, forms of writing in contemporary America share is their condition: their presence in a permeable space where nations and cultures meet. It is a luminal space, the space of postmodernity, post-postmodernity or radicalized modernity, marked by dissolution and dispersal, mobility and fragmentation, the heterogeneous and the hybrid—all on a global scale. Representing different cultures, living between them, and responding to their diverse origins and experiences, all these writers effectively challenge the notion of common heritage and fixed boundaries. Of course, in doing so, they challenge the assumptions so central to the grand narrative of the American state. The country they discover and describe in their works does have the order, absolute contours of the American Eden. It is a place with fluid boundaries, where rival, overlapping, and ultimately interdependent cultural histories meet, conflict, and perhaps converge. American writers are still, as much as ever, concerned with the possibles and variables of American life, the material and mental contours of the American landscape, the imperatives of America history, and the inspiration of the American dream. But the possibles of American life have multiplied; the contours of American landscape have assumed a more elusive, enigmatic character; the imperatives of American history are more plural, more polyglot than ever before; and the American dream now is inspired by what seems a process of accelerated transformation, insistent reinvention. Responding to these changes, American writers have changed. What has happened may be measured in a small but significant shifting of words: American writing is now writing in America. The point is simple but fundamental. Nationality, at the scene of writing, is less determined and determining than it ever was previously, more open to other stories and histories. The scene of writing is one that is now genuinely transnational. In the postmodern period, American literature, with its unique thinking of the world from the perspective of pluralism and globalization and the innovative ever-changing various techniques and hybridization of all sorts of forms in textual structure to represent the uncertain reality and history, has exerted great influence on world literature in the 21st century.

Postmodernism

The postmodernist thought is the product of the postmodern society (or the post-industrial society, the information society, the late capitalism). It was gestated in the womb of its modernist mother in the 1930s, tore itself out of it after World War Ⅱ and became a cultural specter being praised and blamed at the same time and wandering in the whole field of western culture. Postmodernism formally appeared in the late 1950s and the early 1960s, engendered into an overwhelming momentum, and shocked the thinking circles in the 1970s and the 1980s.

Postmodernism deems that in the world today the important functions of such various phenomena as instability, indeterminacy, discontinuity, disorder, rupture, sudden changes, etc. have been more and more recognized and paid great attention to. In the circumstances, a new concept to look on the world has begun to go deep into people's consciousness. It opposes the practice of using the single, fixed logic, formula, principle, and the universally applicable law to explain and rule the world, advocates changes and innovations, emphasizes openness and pluralism, acknowledges and tolerates differences. The era nowadays has already given up the effort to constitute the unified and universally applicable patterns. Some new categories such as openness, polysemousness, polyphony, indeterminacy, possibility, unpredictableness, etc. have entered postmodern languages. In the postmodern era, thorough pluralism has become a universal basic concept; the postmodern pluralism is the nature of all fields of knowledge and all aspects of social life. The basic experiences in the postmodern times are the inalienable right of the totally different formations of knowledge, the designs of life, and the ways of thinking and behavior; the old pattern that everything revolves round one sun has been no longer effective; even truth, justice, humanity, and reason are all plural. The direct conclusion of the principles of pluralism is that it opposes any attempt at unification; that the postmodern thinking actively maintains the diversity and richness of things; that it firmly argues against any ambition for hegemony to impose one's own choice on others and make the alien things submit to one's own will; that it respects and acknowledges all the choices of social conceptions, ways of life, and cultural forms. The basic postmodernist contents "as the tenets of science and art had already existed in the first half of the twentieth century, most of them merely rested on a kind of proposition, manifesto or design, or they were merely special phenomena in a certain field. But today they have already begun to become the reality of our life roundly and thoroughly." In the sense of time, postmodernist thought might be understood as the continuity and development of modernism. But "in some problems, there are fundamental differences between postmodernism and modernism: postmodernism opposes any dream for oneness, negates all universally applicable and ever-unchanging principles, formulas, and laws, and gives up all the patterns for unification. Then, in this sense, postmodernist thought is the criticism and transcending of modernism."

Postmodernism is a social thought that is completely different from the movement of modernization since Renaissance. The appearance of postmodernism in the humanities and the social sciences signals the birth of another novel academic paradigm: "Rather, a radically new and different cultural movement is coalescing in a broad-gauged re-conceptualization of how we experience and explain the world around us. In its extreme formulations, postmodernism is revolutionary; it goes to the very core of what constitutes social science and radically dismisses it. In its more moderate proclamations, postmodernism encourages substantive re-definition and innovation. Postmodernism proposes to set itself up outside the modern paradigm, not to judge modernity by its own criteria but rather to contemplate and deconstruct it." Modernity stresses reason, democracy, and freedom. It cries up the progress of science and technology, equality and universal fraternity in the modern times. But all that modernity has created makes people doubt its original faiths. Postmodernists conclude that modernity is no longer a force of emancipation; on the contrary, it is the source of enslavement, oppression and repression. Postmodernists take a spurning attitude towards all the theories of modernity. They equally treat various concepts of modernity without discrimination and destroy them all, regarding them as the things of logos-centrism, foundationalism, and essentialism, as all-embracing things, and as the things narrated by meta-narrative. Having compared the system of modern thoughts with premodern things, postmodernists hold that, just as ancient people created myths, magic, alchemy, and primitive worship, modern people themselves have created modernity as a new myth. Postmodernism has abandoned all kinds of authorities, centers, foundations, and essences about modernity and caused delegitimation of all codes. The philosophical foundation of modernism is seeking the present metaphysics, a never-changing truth, the noumenon and epistemology of the ultimate value. But postmodernism "opposes not only the discourse considering that man has the natural essence of the mirror type but also the discourse holding that the world has identity, consistency, wholeness, and centricity; argues against not only the hierarchical division between different disciplines but also the quest for a certain first discipline." Postmodernism has abolished the antitheses and gaps established by modernity between this shore and the other shore, transience and eternity, center and margin, depth and surface, phenomenon and essence, subject and object, etc. It has actually cancelled the dimensions of knowledge such as foundation, center, essence, and noumenon. It wants to break through the whole well-organized and orderly world constructed by modernity and make the whole world go into the dimensions of pluralism, seemingness, transience, disorder, anarchism, ambiguity, and indeterminacy.

Postmodernist Fiction

The writing of fiction as a literary form reached its peak in the period of critical realism in the late 19th century, having established a pattern that everybody could imitate: a work should narrate a vivid and interesting story, portray one character or several characters, with these characters often falling into a kind of psychological or social contradictions and conflicts; along with the development of the plot the contradictions and conflicts would be solved in a certain way. The writing method of this sort of fiction takes characters as its core and the plot of the story can only unfold round the characters. The characters, especially protagonists, must have their own looks, personalities, behavior, and conduct, even their language is different from the common run, and they must live in given circumstances. In its narrative, the realistic fiction takes imitating or reproducing the objective reality as the basic principle; the unfolding of plots and the development of events are arranged according to the time sequence of reality, being shown in linear narrative and causal logic; the circumstances in which the characters are and the descriptions of their activities are confined in the conventional geometrical space. This kind of structure of time and space tightly fetters the reader in the everyday reality and he or she can only see the seeming phenomena of life but is unable to understand the deep meaning of the existence hidden behind them. The realistic fiction has definite intentions and themes of writing. The stories that it narrates aim at showing a certain determinate and concrete concept of value, moral principle or truth of life, trying to lead the reader to draw a specific moral conclusion and to realize the goal of moralization. The semantic meaning of this sort of fiction is onefold and transparent.

Like the other fields of human studies in which new thoughts constantly emerge, literature and art as the products of human society in given historical periods are also continually developing and innovating. From the end of the 19th century, the concepts of values and aesthetics of realistic literature were challenged forcefully by the methods of modernist literature such as symbolism, expressionism, surrealism, stream-of-consciousness, etc. The appearance of modernism brings with it the fundamental changes of the notions of fiction, the techniques of writing, the contents of thought, the forms of expression, artistic artifices, and styles. Modernist fictionists think that the reality does not mean only people and things in the superficial and objective world but also includes man's inner world and that man's subconscious and unconscious activities are a reality which is more important and more essential than that of the outside world. Therefore, the essential task of fiction is to represent man's innermost activities covered by the seeming phenomena of everyday life. Thus, in the modernist fiction, the description of outside circumstances and the things that take place in it is reduced to the minimum limit, and a majority of space is used to represent man's experience, recept and reflection of the outside, disorderly and absurd reality, and goes deep into man's subconsciousness and unconsciousness, probing into man's innermost concealed secret and revealing man's despair and the sense of crisis, the absurdity of world and the meaninglessness of life, etc. In consequence, modernist fiction abandons the integrality and dramaticness of story plots and the protagonists and characters in it do not have vivid personalities any more. The characters are observed from different points of view and from different situations in which they are put. They appear to be dim and fragmented. Because in the modernist fiction man's inner world is not restricted by realistic time and space, imaginations, reminiscences, associations, hallucinations, and dreams can move about freely and quickly and can go boundlessly to many faraway places, disordering and reversing the sequence of realistic events, making the past, the present, and the future intervein with each other arbitrarily. Thus, modernist fiction overthrows the principle of representation (imitating the reality) and the mode of representation (narrating a story) of realistic fiction and makes inside innovations in the structures, techniques, and language of fiction. It, however, does not touch the totality, closeness, and oneness of fiction as a literary form. Instead, it reserves the outside boundary between it and other literary forms and genres, still pays attention to the purity of its genre, and does its utmost to preserve the pureness and elegance of literary language and artistic artifices. Modernist fiction tries hard to express a certain metaphysical meaning or a suggestion that provides this meaning. Once they are extensively imitated and used, the techniques and forms of modernist fiction that are regarded as innovations quickly become new criteria and ossified modes that can no longer play any new designs. Consequently, the assertion claiming that "The fiction has died" is heard: "I believe that the genre of fiction, if it is not yet irretrievably exhausted, has certainly entered its last phase, the scarcity of possible subjects being such that writers must make up for it by the exquisite quality of the other elements that compose the body of a fiction."

Postmodernist fiction restores the vitality of "the literature of exhaustion" with new forms and techniques. As the art of the postmodern mass society, postmodernist fiction has destroyed the metaphysical conventions of modernist art, broken its close and self-contained aesthetic forms, and advocates thorough pluralism in thinking patterns, writing techniques, artistic genres, and language games. Postmodernists think that "reality is brought out by language, that is, a false language brings out a false reality. The narrative manner of traditional fiction (including realistic and modernist fiction) is one of the makers of the false reality: the fact itself that it fabricates a story to 'reflect' is a false reality, thus leading the reader into the double falsehood. The task of fiction is debunking this kind of beguilement and displaying the falsehood of reality and the falsehood of invented stories before the readers, thus urging them to think" Postmodernist fiction, however, not only subverts the internal formation and structure of traditional fiction but also shows its doubts about the fictional form and narrative itself. Postmodernist metafiction is the reflection, deconstruction, and subversion of fiction as a literary form and narrative itself. Though it reserves the appearance and outline of fiction, metafiction tells the reader how this story is fabricated while "telling" this story. It is a fiction about fiction. It overthrows the concept of pure fiction, destroys the narrative conventions of traditional fiction (e.g. linear narrative, causal logic, etc.), blurs the dividing line between it and other literary genres, adopts a great deal of representational techniques of other literary genres. In metafiction, the time crosses the past, the present, and the future and the names and identities of characters are all uncertain. In the postmodernist fiction there is not any objective or transcendental meaning; the so-called meaning is only produced in the differences of man-made language signs, namely, the effect produced by the permutation and combination of signs. Therefore, the writing of invented texts is only a language game. Any text is open and incomplete. It depends on other texts (on its differentiation from and relation with them) and especially on the reader's interpretation. It is the reader's interpretation that gives a certain meaning to the combination and permutation of signs. Postmodernist fiction transcends the dividing lines between belles-lettres and popular literature and between high literature and light literature, thus turning the literature as the privilege of the high-browed intellectuals into the literature of the reading public and showing a tendency towards popularization. In addition, in the postmodernist fiction, the artistic techniques of modernist fiction such as the interior monologue of stream-of-consciousness, symbolism, free association, the disorder of time and space, etc. have already dropped back to the secondary position though they have not yet been completely abandoned; the more frequently-used forms of expression are metafiction, language games, the tendency towards popularization, parody, collage, montage, labyrinth, black humor, etc. Such characteristics as the language subject, fragmented narrative, shifting signifiers, writing zero, etc. have also appeared in the postmodernist fiction.

Metafiction

A postmodernist writer deconstructs the traditional fictional form and narrative itself. First of all, he does this by means of metafiction. In order to explore the relation between fiction and reality, metafiction intentionally and systematically stresses its position as a man-made product. This sort of fiction provides a kind of criticism of its own structure and methods. While narrating stories, metafiction not only examines the basic structure of narrative itself but also explores the possible fictiveness of the world outside of literary work. Postmodernist writers pay close attention to the theoretical problem of fictional structure. Their works usually have the characteristic of self-reflection and at the same time show their inclination to doubt the fictional form. Every important feature of metafiction is used to inquire into the theory of writing and the practice of fictional production.

Since the 1960s, people have been extremely interested in how to reflect, how to describe, and how to spread the knowledge of their social experiences. Metafiction attempts to find the answers to these questions through its self-exploration of its own form. The writers of metafiction adopt the traditional simile that sees the world as a book, and often use contemporary theories of philosophy, linguistics, and literature to reconstruct fiction. These theories consider that we as individuals are not in the position of the selves but play all sorts of roles. Therefore, to study the characters in fiction can provide a useful pattern to understand the subjective structure of the world outside of fiction. Our knowledge of this world is spread through language, and the fiction as a literary genre (a world completely constructed with language) becomes a useful pattern to know the structure of realistic world.

People realize that, to the smallest pieces of material construction, every process of observation will cause a great stir; people also realize that it is impossible to describe a natural world because the observer always changes what he is observing. However, what metafiction is concerned about is more complicated than this because metafiction thinks that man cannot describe anything. The writers of metafiction have been aware of an essential dilemma: if he or she attempts to describe a world, he or she will soon realize that the world cannot be described. They consider that they can only describe the theory and the language about that world in the invented work of literature—fiction.

In the writing of metafiction, these writers use a kind of metalanguage that is not the language to describe the non-language events, situations, or objects but the language used to depict another sort of language. Along with the continuous growth of the self-consciousness about society and culture, the knowledge of the independence of language and experience is also continuously growing. The viewpoint that language only passively reflects a coherent and meaningful objective world can no longer hold water. Language is regarded as an independent and self-contained system. It can produce meaning by itself. The relation between language and realistic world is complicated, indeterminate, and controlled by convention. The writers of metafiction probe in their works the relation between this language system and the world outside of fiction. Consequently, they make their works constantly manifest the literary language that they consciously use and the habitual practice of writing fiction, clearly and definitely showing their features of artificial products and revealing the disjointedness between the sense of crisis, the sense of alienation, and the sense of oppression, and the traditional literary form (for instance, realism) which is no longer applicable to the representation of postmodern experience. Thus, metafiction has transformed the passive value of old habitual practice into the basis of the potential and constructive social criticism. In fact, it indicates that, just like using it to directly reflect the supposed human nature existing as an entity outside of the system of expression, using the artistic mirror to reflect its own language or its descriptive structure can achieve the same effect.

Metafiction is also usually based on essential, sustained opposite principles. While constructing the mirages of fiction (like the traditional realistic works), metafiction also reveals the nature of these mirages, making the readers realize that they are not copies of real life but only stories invented by the writer. This is clearly shown by the fact that in metafiction a story can be provided with several endings. If we define metafiction by using common language, metafiction is the fiction that comments on the writing of fiction itself while writing fiction. The two processes are closely combined, thus breaking the obvious dividing line between writing and criticism and merging them into the concepts of interpretation and decomposition.

According to the views of metafiction, both reality and history are transient. In the realistic fiction there are completely invented plots, the coherent narration by time sequence, the omniscient and omnipotent writer or narrator, the reasonable relation between the characters' behavior and their identities, and a kind of causal relation between the detailed description on the surface layer and the scientific laws on the deep layer. The writers of metafiction consider that the realistic fiction is a fictional form that is identical with the orderly social reality but the present world is no longer a permanent reality but a series of constructions, a non-perpetual structure. Consequently, the traditional form of fiction is no longer applicable for representing this reality and a kind of meta-language should be used to construct a fictional form that can be suitable for this reality.

Metafiction attaches importance to the examination of the fictional form itself. Its method of deconstruction not only helps the fictionist and the reader better understand the narrative structure of fiction but also offers an extremely clear pattern to understand the human experience of the contemporary world. For the writers of metafiction, the contemporary world is a composed product, a combination of techniques and a systematic network of signs that depend on each other in existence.

Modernist writers describe the struggle for individual independence as a conflict between the existing social system and the traditional conventions. This conflict or struggle inevitably leads to individual alienation and common spiritual death. The power structure of contemporary society tends to become more complicated, more diverse, more covert, and more mysterious so that postmodernist writers meet with greater difficulties when they recognize and represent rebellious objects. The method that the writers of metafiction use to solve the problem is to move their attention from the description of the outside objective world to the exploration of the techniques of expression of fiction itself. Its purpose is to examine the relation between the fictional form and the reality. In the final analysis, however, metafiction limits its rebellion within the range of the fictional form itself.

In order to analyze another kind of language, namely, the language of the traditional fiction, metafiction pays close attention to the habitual practice of fiction and exposes the process of its formation. For example, John Fowles uses the habitual practice of the omniscient and omnipotent writer in his novel *The French Lieutenant's Woman* (1969). Metafiction also often uses the form of parody that is written through the imitation of another work in order to comment on the mode of fiction. For example, John Gardner's novel *Grendel* (1971) recounts and comments on the ancient story *Beowulf* from the monster's narrative angle. John Hawkes' fiction *The Lime Twig* (1961) forms both a sample of popular thrillers and the criticism of it at the same time.

Among all the types of experimental fictions, metafiction does not appear very radical because metafiction only reveals the habitual practice of traditional fiction, neither ignoring it nor abandoning it. The traditional writing techniques provide a kind of control, a kind of standard, or background for metafiction. On this basis, the writers of metafiction put to good use of their experimental techniques. They often use anti-traditional techniques to weaken (not abandon) the omniscient and omnipotent writers or narrators, the complete endings and the definite explanations, and defamiliarize the traditional techniques and structures through the imitation of another language. Though some readers have become estranged from this kind of language as well as from the habitual practice and thought, this estrangement has been done on a basis that the readers are extremely familiar with them. Therefore, metafiction can be understood through the old structure. This sort of work not only makes itself welcome to the readers but also makes the readers participate in the construction of the meaning of works. Metafiction does not abandon the realistic world; its purpose is to look for a fictional form that is closely related with and understandable to the contemporary readers and to reexamine the habitual practice of the traditional fiction through its self-reflection. Metafiction reveals for us how literary works construct their imaginative worlds and by doing this helps us understand that the reality in which we live every day is similarly constructed and similarly written down.

Metafiction can be defined as the fiction about fiction and it can also be subdivided into the fiction about how this fiction becomes a fiction, the fiction about a previous fiction, and the fiction similar with other texts.

Terms of Postmodernist Literature

There are some important literary terms of postmodernist literature such as black humor, collage, montage, parody, hybridization, carnivalization, labyrinth, language games and the readers' interpretation, anti-genre, indeterminacy, immanence, just name a few frequently mentioned ones.

Black Humor Though very deeply influenced by existentialist philosophy, black humor as a postmodernist technique of expression, regarding the world as absurd and unreasonable and giving a smile after feeling extremely pessimistic, does not advocate the ways to save the world as existentialism does—to participate, to choose, or to cry and protest, or to struggle to resist, or to lament and sigh mournfully because doing like that can only make the absurdity more chaotic and more unendurable. To black humor fictionists, the absurdity of existence can only be accepted because it is an unchangeable part of the world. They indifferently consider that absurdity is a part of the world that is a farce in nature. They no longer make an effort to replace the value with the value of mission and responsibility or bemoan the state of the universe and pity the fate of mankind. But instead, they continue, by using language, to play the game in which existence does not put forth a card with reason. The writing characteristics of black humor generally manifest themselves as the following: comically and even absurdly dealing with intrinsically tragic subjects, representing the single-dimension character and the waste land background, constructing loose and usually disjointed structures without paying attention to time, confusing facts, and invention to reveal the unreliability of reality, stressing techniques, and formal designs, coldly looking on the despairing, fantastic, rude, and cruel events, telling the story with mockingly questioning-God tone and often with a laughter having no intention to punish the evil and praise the good. The origin of these is the writer's doubt about traditional philosophy and science.

Collage Imitating the method of newsreels adopted by John Dos Passos, some postmodernist fictionists combine together other texts such as fragments of some literary works, common sayings in everyday life, abstracts from newspapers and magazines, news reports, etc. and make these seemingly totally irrelevant fragments form an entity whose elements are related to each other, thus having broken the solidified formal structure of traditional fiction, caused a strong shock upon the reader's aesthetic habit, and produced the effect that the conventional narrative manner could not achieve. In the postmodernist fiction, the scattered and fragmented materials are everything. They will never give a certain combination of meanings or the final solution but can only give the reader a sense of moving combination in the eternal and present reading experience. This thorough pileup of fragmented images opposes the combination in any form. Barthelme thinks, "The principle of collage is the central principle of all the arts in all the media of dissemination in the 20th century." Again he explains, "The key point of collage lies in that the unsimilar things are glued together, which can create a reality when it is at best. This new reality, when it is at best, may be or suggest a comment upon the other reality from which it originates, or, not only these". *Snow White* is like a continuous gather-together of fragments which are loosely organized round the fairy tale about Snow White by means of collage of fragments.

Parody Parody is one of the important writing techniques used by many postmodernist fictionists. This is the most intentional and analytical literary method. Through its destructive imitation, this method exerts itself to stress the weakness, affectation, and the lack of self-consciousness of the target of its imitation. The so-called target of its imitation can be a work and the common style of some writers as well. Parody imitates the contents or the style of a serious literary work or a literary genre and makes this imitation very funny through the incoordination between the form, style, and absurd subjects of the work or the genre. It mocks a given work but its way of mocking is to use a joking and funny method and genre to deal with a lofty subject. The essence of parody is a phenomenon of genre—an exaggerative imitation of a writer or the forms and characteristics of a genre, whose mark is its inconformity in genre, structure, or theme. The obvious function of parody is satire. Its way of satirizing is to indirectly attack its target through the way of genre. Parody cites or indirectly mentions the work that it ridicules and uses the typical method of the latter in a way to abolish or subvert it. Critics have seen that the intentional and distorting imitation of a certain pattern may produce a very original work.

Montage If collage is an unconscious hodgepodge that is accidentally pieced together, montage, another expressive means of postmodernism, is a conscious combination. Like collage, montage also represents discontinuity—a time concept in the postmodern times. The characteristic of the postmodern times is a sort of schizophrenia or a rupture of the chain of signs. Because in the mind of a schizophrenic, the organization of syntax and time has completely disappeared and there are only the pure signifiers left, that is to say, in the minds of postmodern people, the time concepts of the past and the future have completely disappeared and only the eternal present is left. The method of montage links up the pictures and scenes that are not related to each other in contents and forms and on the different levels of time and space or rearranges and reorganizes different genres, the sentences in different styles and characteristics, and contents. It uses the artifices such as pre-narration, flashback, insertion, reiteration, close-up, the contrast between still and moving scenes, etc. to strengthen the stimulation of the reader's sense organs and acquire strong artistic effect.

Labyrinth Fredric Jameson claims, "If modernist architecture tells you how to read and interpret and how to live a life, then postmodernist works are the labyrinths that you can never read and interpret." Labyrinth refers to the intricate and dazzling structure without giving a way out that a postmodernist writer builds in his fiction. It is not like a detective fiction that is complicated and confusing but everything in it will certainly become clear and solved at last. What rules labyrinth is chaos or absence. It is like the image with no meaning or the bamboo fish trap with no fish. John Barth, Vladimir Nabokov, and Thomas Pynchon are all adept at building labyrinths. A theme that appears again and again in Pynchon's works is the essential disorder or disintegration of the western world. Pynchon metaphorically introduces entropy, an important concept in thermodynamics and information theory, into literary writing. In thermodynamics in physics, in a closed thermodynamic system having no material and energy to exchange with the outside world, the movements of molecules will become more and more disordered, finally reach the limit of disorder and form the state of heat balance with the same temperature. Entropy is a measure unit of the extent of this disorder. That is to say, in an isolated thermodynamic system, entropy will become bigger and bigger. Entropy is also a measure unit of the extent of disorder in information theory. According to the theory of heat death, the universe is an enormous closed system. Following the second law of thermodynamics, it is going towards disorder, decline, and death. In his works, Pynchon, using this view as a metaphor, regards the world in which he lives as a closed system and points out the inherent disorder, corruption in the western society and its fate: it will inevitably die in the end. Entropy indicates that all kinds of mechanisms and orders in the human society will finally go towards heat death, that is, towards chaos and disorder. The more orderly a mechanism or an institution or a system is, the greater its tendency towards heat death is, because the existing institutions and organizations in the human society will certainly exert strict controlling function upon it. The tighter the organizations are, the more complicated the information and meanings are and the more easily they will cause heat death and go towards its opposite side: order will change into disorder and civilization will be finally controlled by chaos.

Hybridization Hybridization, or the mutant replication of genres, includes parody, travesty, and pastiche. Hassan thinks, "The 'de-definition,' deformation, of cultural genres engenders equivocal modes: 'paracriticism,' 'factual discourse,' 'new journalism,' 'non-fiction fiction,' and a promiscuous category of 'para-literature' or 'threshold literature,' at once young and very old. Cliché and plagiarism, parody and pastiche, pop and kitsch enrich re-presentation. In this view image or replica may be as valid as its model…may even bring an '*augment d'etre*.' This makes for a different concept of tradition, one in which continuity and discontinuity, high and low culture, mingle, not to imitate but to expand the past in the present. In that plural present, all styles are dialectically available in an interplay between the Now and the Not Now, the Same and the Other. Thus, in postmodernism, Heidegger's concept of 'equitemporality' becomes really a dialectic of equitemporality, an intertemporality, a new relation between historical elements, without any suppression of the past in favor of the present..." To put it simpler, hybridization is a sort of variant imitation of genres including the funny and humorous imitations of poems and the mixed stew of various imitated works. Postmodernists have enriched the intention and extension of prototypes and enhanced the vitality of original texts (original works and prototypes) by means of decayed and plagiarized subjects, clumsy imitation and piecing together, the interveining and reversion of time sequence, the displacement of places and spaces, the appearance of the higher language together with the lower language, and the convergence of serious and popular subjects. Hybridization oversteps the dividing line between traditional disciplines and academic rules. It makes readers not know what to turn to, compels them to exist constantly in the specific language contents, refuses all their expectations of the preceding things, and makes them fall into the all-sided disorder of the inner world via the language world as medium from the outside physical world.

Carnivalization Carnivalization, a term borrowed by Hassan from the Russian literary theorist Mikhail Bakhtin, riotously embraces indeterminacy, fragmentation, decanonization, selflessness, irony, and hybridization, all of which were mentioned before. The term also conveys the comic or absurdist ethos of postmodernism, anticipated in the "heteroglossia" of Rabelais and Laurence Sterne, jocose prepostmodernists. Carnivalization further means "polyphony," the sense of fragmentation caused by the centrifugal power of language, the "gay relativity" of things, perspectivism and performance, participation in the wild disorder of life, the immanence of laughter. Indeed, what Bakhtin calls fiction or carnival—that is, antisystem—might stand for postmodernism itself, or at least for its ludic and subversive elements that promise renewal. For in carnival "the true feast of time, the feast of becoming, change, and renewal," human beings, then as now, discover "the peculiar logic of the 'inside out' (*a l'envers*), of the 'turnabout,' ...of numerous parodies and travesties, humiliations, profanations, comic crownings and uncrownings. A second life." Carnivalization removes all kinds of differences and dividing lines, makes all participants both actors (or actresses) and audience. Carnivalization makes man have the hallucination that he is the real master or dominator of the world. In the game, in the confusion, in the madness, and in the rebellion against traditional reason, carnivalization swallows everything, reconstructs everything, and acculturates everything.

Language Games and the Readers' Interpretation In the postmodern world, the thinking activities of thinkers and literary critics are all basically on the level of language. Their language statements are a sort of language structures that are purely controlled by the logic of language itself and are not identical with the realistic existence and the objective social reality. To postmodernist writers, everything is indeterminate, there is not any transcendental and objective meaning, and therefore they can only place their feelings on writing itself. Writing is nothing but a process through which a writer's introspection is symbolized. In other words, writing is a sort of information that refers to itself, expecting to gradually establish its own meaning in the process of exploring itself. Value originates from invention; meaning is generated in the differences of language symbols, that is, meaning is the effect produced by the permutation and combination of signs. Therefore, writing (especially the writing of invented texts) is only a language game. Jean-Francois Lyotard, French famous philosopher, thinks that in each discourse with a different nature people can design and determine language games by using optional game rules that explain the nature and usage of the discourse. But these game rules themselves cannot provide their own legitimacy for themselves and they can only be the products of the contract type between game players. Rules are the keys that games can be used. Any of their changes will change the nature of games. Like games, the speaking of any discourse has the implications of confrontation and competition and therefore has a characteristic that constantly gets rid of the stale and brings forth the fresh. Roland Barthes, French famous literary critic, thinks that a postmodernist writer is not a person who uses language as a tool to manifest his own ideas, express his own feelings, or represent his own imaginations but a person who thinks over language, a thinker-linguist (in other words, a person who is neither a complete thinker nor a complete linguist). The contemporary writing has already freed itself out of the dimension of expressing meaning and only refers to itself. Like playing games, writing reveals itself in its continually going beyond its own rules and violating its own limitations.

According to a very important idea in the theory of discourse, the language philosophy of postmodernism, language symbols have increasingly lost their ability to express meaning, that is, they can no longer hit meaning itself, and our written and spoken discourses including writing itself all have been lost in the endless chain of signifiers. This means that any postmodern text does not have a unified core of meaning. The meaning of a text does not come from the writer's creation but from the reader's interpretation of the text. Anybody can give his own interpretation of the text. The postmodern reader, taking a critical and creative attitude and exploring the implications or the overtones of the text through the subjective construction of meaning, has finally rewritten the original text. Barthes thinks that, in the process of writing of a postmodernist writer, firstly, the subject (the writer) experiences the courses of deconstruction and reconstruction. Secondly, on the subconscious level, he thirsts for his reader's understanding and helping, and longs for establishing a kind of mechanism of the dialogue type between him and the reader. Barthes regards a literary work as a process of production and reproduction and changes the reader from a consumer into a producer who participates in the process of production and reproduction. The meaning of a work is not decided by the writer but created by the reader who redisplays the productive process of the text and participates in this process. The reading manner of postmodernist fiction attaches importance to aesthetic delight instead of aesthetic joyfulness, emphasizes digging out infinite plural meaning in the endless movement of signifiers of texts, stresses symbolic thinking, active participation, direct experience, and sudden realization, and dedicates itself to the breakthrough of the subconscious activities in rational and visual thinking . In the postmodern times, the reading activity is no longer the activity to grasp the writer's original intentions but has changed into the activity to look for and explain the logic of texts, trace the activities of dismantling and recombining texts for the value of language itself, thus finding out the multiplicity of meaning and the infinitely various interpretations of the meaning of texts.

Anti-genre In the eyes of Charles Newman, American famous literary theorist and critic, postmodernist writers are a generation who bravely subvert the old orders and undertake the play of dispelling as their profession. They dissolve the identity of the propositions such as emancipation and liberty and replace it with a plural, centerless, and centrifugal structure. Having separated themselves from the influence of traditional writers of the old generation, they are going along the road that the literary paradigm is thoroughly innovated. Consequently, being opposite with the serious fiction of the old generation, postmodernist writers are forced into a lane that their works are not only different from serious fiction but also different from pastime fiction. On the one hand, they try to break away from the influence of the old generation and on the other, they make an effort to take the differentiation engendered from an ordinary but low-grade common denominator as their strategy for continuous development. In order to satirize the pastime fiction or the classic fiction, they intentionally write the completely contrary works whose characteristics are not established on some remains that they have destroyed but on the success of their opposition to the stylization of the pastime fiction. Anti-genre has become a dominant pattern in our times. Like the refined language in the past, traditional genres are also regarded as the adversaries. The writing of fiction has become a bold risk. Now that the boundaries do not exist any more, any writing can be named fiction. Thus, fiction is bound to invade and occupy the fields of other genres and appears to be hybrid. At the plural present, all the genres have appeared in the interweaving of the present and the non-present, and of identity and difference. Barthelme's short stories "The Glass Mountain" and "Kierkegaard Unfair to Schlegel" (1970) are the products of this anti-genre pattern of writing.

The form of the short story "The Glass Mountain" is very strange. It is constructed with the phrases, sentences, and paragraphs that are arranged in the order of serial numbers from 1 to 100. It is a reversely writing of a Scandinavian story "The Princess on the Glass Mountain." Though the hero in Barthelme's short story also woos the princess and has climbed up the top of the mountain with the help of a hawk, he lifts the princess and throws her down from the mountain to his acquaintances, letting them treat her the way they like with his heart at rest. The short story suddenly ends with the words like codes: "100. Even many hawks seem not to be believable, not a bit, not a second." Having rewritten the traditional story with a postmodern city as its background, Barthelme has disturbed the true and false values of the traditional story. He does not use the classic plots to show the existence of some lasting human values and concerns but instead he insults the classic plots to display how unable the traditional narrative is when it deals with the postmodern conditions. On the one hand, Barthelme's hero runs after his objective but on the other, he dismantles it and finally acquires nothing. Here is no honor and dignity. Barthelme has not only weakened the traditional values but also broken the conventions of fictional writing with his fiction appearing to be the gather-together of language fragments from 1 to 100. This sort of anti-genre writing has generated two results. Firstly, what the writer has given prominence to is techniques instead of contents, appearance instead of depth, and artificiality instead of credibility, and thus the writer has debased characterizing, imitation, hallucination and the like that traditional narrative concerns itself about and also broken the usual reading structure. Secondly, these phrases, sentences, and paragraphs with serial numbers indicate that traditional genres having become conventions have turned to be so dull, so empty, and so easy to reproduce that they can be written with numerals to some extent. Like a group of codes, the last concluding sentence means to suggest: traditional creeds and structures are unable to deal with postmodern experiences. The hawk's function lies in that it is an absurd mechanical god descending to help the hero detach himself from his real difficult position and realize his ideal. Thus, he has proved the ineffectiveness and incredibility of old narrative forms and contents. Barthelme's "The Glass Mountain" has become an allegory that dismantles the transcendental signified that is symbolized by the princess.

The short story "Kierkegaard Unfair to Schlegel" goes on in the form of questions and answers, appearing in the disordered state, and seems to be pieced with scattered fragments. The short story begins with the answerer's narration about a European girl whom he met in a train. Then, the answerer tells the reader that he participates in politics, criticizes the government, and then turns to discuss the function of irony: to make fun of the special ways that people choose to deal with boredom, with which the writer introduces Kierkegaard's theoretical explanation of the concept of irony. He thinks that an irony aiming at the whole of existence can generate poetry and estrangement. Thus, irony becomes an infinite and absolute negation and the essence of irony is poetry. Therefore, Kierkegaard describes Schlegel's novel *Lucinde* as a book written with poems and thinks that Schlegel has built an esse that is superior to and able to replace the historical esse. The answerer, however, thinks that the relation between Schlegel's novel and the esse is not the one that Kierkegaard has explained. Kierkegaard only fixes his eyes on the prescriptive aspect of Schlegel's novel—a text that tells us how to live but ignores the other aspects, for instance, its different objects to different persons. Therefore, the answerer thinks that Kierkegarrd is unfair to Schlegel. Obviously, the fiction here has entered the field of literary criticism and lost its own field with its strong theoretical coloring.

Indeterminacy   Ihab Hassan thinks that indeterminacy is the first essential characteristic of postmodernism. It includes all kinds of ambiguities, ruptures, and displacements that affect knowledge and society. Indeterminacy has permeated all the thoughts and actions of the people in the postmodern society and formed the most basal situation of the world that people actually face. Hassan gives a specific explanation of indeterminacy. He thinks that indeterminacy is a category consisting of different concepts that help delineate: ambiguity, discontinuity, heterodoxy, pluralism, randomness, revolt, perversion, and deformation. Deformation alone subsumes a dozen current terms of unmaking: disintegration, deconstruction, decenterment, displacement, discontinuity, decomposition, detotalization, delegitimation, etc.—let alone more technical terms referring to the rhetoric of irony, rupture, silence. It is just indeterminacy that reveals the spirit and nature of the postmodern times. Through all these signs a vast will moves to unmake and affect the body politic, the body cognitive, the erotic body, and the individual psyche—the entire realm of discourse in the West. Only in literature, all of our ideas about writers, readers, reading, writing, texts, schools, critical theories, and literature itself are suddenly queried. Barthelme himself asserts like this: "My song of songs is the principle of indeterminacy."His novel *Snow White* embodies this indeterminacy in portraying the images of characters.

Immanence Postmodernism has two most essential features: one is indetermanacy and the other is immanence. Immanence "refers, without religious echo, to the growing capacity of mind to generalize itself through symbols. Everywhere now we witness problematic diffusions, dispersals, dissemination; we experience the extension of our senses...through new media and technologies. Languages, apt or mendacious, reconstitute the universe—from quasars to quarks and back, from the lettered unconscious to black holes in space—reconstitute it an immanent semiotic system. The language animal has emerged, his/her measure the intertextuality of all life. A patina of thought, of signifiers, of 'connections,' now lies on everything the mind touches in its gnostic (noo)sphere, which physicists, biologists, and semioticians...explore. The pervasive irony of their explorations is also the reflexive irony of mind meeting itself at every dark turn. Yet in a consuming society such immanence can become more vacuous than fatidic. They become... pervasively 'obscene,' a 'collective vertigo of neutralization, a forward escape into the obscenity of pure and empty form." Immanence indicates the effort of a postmodern individual to realize self-expansion, self-increase, and self-multiplication in virtue of all kinds of discourses or signs. Immanence stresses personification, the semiotic respect of nature, the society, the world, and knowledge. Everything in the world is the projection of man's immanence and finally shows itself in the form of signs. Immanence means that postmodernism no longer has transcendental meanings and it is no longer interested in transcendent values such as spirit, value, ultimate concern, truth, the beautiful, the good, and the like. On the contrary, it is an inward shrink to the subject and an inherent adaptation to the circumstances, the reality, and the creation. Postmodernism becomes intoxicated with the pleasure produced by the language signs in trivial circumstances.

As a general artistic, social, cultural, and philosophical phenomenon, "postmodrnism has veered towards open, playful, provisional (open in time as well as in structure or space), disjunctive or indeterminate forms, a discourse of ironies and fragments, a 'white ideology' of absences and fractures, a desire of diffractions, an invocation of complex, articulate silences. Postmodernism has veered towards pervasive procedures, ubiquitous interactions, immanent codes, media languages." It is startling that when people are looking for the legitimated basis of a new authority in the postmodern world that has already appeared the authority itself has already self-disintegrated! Everything is all right but everything is meaningless. For postmodernism, philosophy does not exist in explaining or changing the world but in inherently adapting itself in this indeterminate world.

Writing Zero   Roland Barthes thinks that in literature the function of writing activity "is not only to transmit or express but also impose a thing outside of language upon the reader" ; a writer's writing "is a way to ponder literature instead of a way to extend literature." He adds, "From Flaubert to our times, the whole literature has become a problem of language." Writers no longer pay attention to concepts, ideas, and contents but they pay close attention to media, language, forms, and the aspects of style. Literature shows solicitude for language itself instead of social life. Writing has become an intransitive action: unlike classicism that writes about a specific subject for a given purpose, writing itself becomes a purpose and a passion. People try to develop a neutral and non-emotional writing to realize writing zero, which means to realize a pure writing without considering a writer's social and political missions. Barthes thinks that writing zero is an indicative writing in a straightforward manner, a writing without moods that is not commanding, nor imperative as he says that "This neutral writing lies in the boundless ocean of all kinds of voices and judgments but does not get involved in it... Thus, we can say that this is a completely unexcited writing or a pure writing," literature becomes the problem of language and "the utopia of language," and the writer inevitably becomes "a prisoner of his own myth of forms." The writer's position as the subject and his consciousness of social participation are confined in the cage of language. The main characteristics of Barthes' concept of writing zero are stressing the forms and disputing the subject.

Bibliography

Barth, John. "The Literature of Exhaustion." *The Friday Book: Essays and Other Nonfiction*. Baltimore: The Johns Hopkins University Press, 1997.

Barthelme, Donald. *Snow White*. Trans. Zhou Rongsheng and Wang Baihua. Harbin: Harbin Publishing House, 1994.

Barthes, Roland. *The Pleasure of the Text*, 1973. *From Modernism to Postmodernism*. Ed. Liu Mingjiu. Beijing: China Social Science Press, 1994.

——. *The Noise of Language*, 1984. *From Modernism to Postmodernism*. Ed. Liu Mingjiu. Beijing: China Social Science Press, 1994.

——. *Elements of Semiology*. Beijing: Sanlian Bookshop, 1988.

Chen, Shidan. *A Study of American Postmodernist Fiction*. Tianjin: Nankai University Press, 2010. 1–13.

Fiedler, Leslie. *Cross the Border—Close the Gap*. New York: Stein and Day, 1972. *From Modernism to Postmodernism*. Ed. Liu Mingjiu. Beijing: China Social Science Press, 1994.

Gasset, J.O.Y. *The Dehumanization of Art and Other Writings on Art and Culture*. New York: Doubleday, 1956.

Gray, Richard. *A History of American Literature*, Second Edition. Malden, UK: Wiley-Blackwell, 2012. 519–531.

Hassan, Ihab. *The Postmodern Turn: Essays in Postmodern Theory and Culture*. Columbus: Ohio State University Press, 1987.

Hawkes, Terence. *Structuralism and Semiotics*. Shanghai: Shanghai Translations Press, 1987.

Jameson, Fredric. *The Theory of Postmodernism and Culture*. Tran. Tang Xiaobing. Beijing: Beijing University Press, 1997.

Kitler, Friedrich. "The Being of Postmodern Art." *Texts in March*, 1984. Zhang Guofeng. "From 'Modern' to 'Postmodern.'" *From Modernism to Postmodernism*. Ed. Liu Mingjiu. Beijing: China Social Science Press, 1994.

Newman, Charles. *The Postmodern Aura: The Act of Fiction in an Age of Inflation*. Evanston: Northwestern University Press, 1985.

Rosenau, P.M. *Post-modernism and the Social Sciences: Insights, Inroads, and Intrusions*. Princeton, N.J.: Princeton University Press, 1992.

Wang Yuechuan. *Study on Culture of Postmodernism*. Beijing: Peking University Press, 1996.

Welsch, Wolfgang. "*Our Postmodern* Modernity." Trans. Zhang Guofeng. *Postmodernism*. Beijing: Social Science Documents Press, 1999.

Yu Baofa. "Metafiction." *A Handbook of New Disciplines and New Methods of Literature*. Eds. Lin Xianghua et al. Shanghai: Shanghai Literature Press, 1987.

Zhang, Guofeng. "From 'Modern' to 'Postmodern.' " *From Modernism to Postmodernism*. Ed. Liu Mingjiu. Beijing: China Social Science Press, 1994.

Zhao, Yiheng. "The Criteria to Judge Postmodernist Fiction." *A Study of Foreign Literatures*. Beijing: The Book and Newspaper Information Center of Renmin University of China, 1994.

Robert Lowell

His Life and Writing Career

His Life

Robert Traill Spence Lowe Ⅳ (1917—1977) was an American poet, one of the founders of the confessional poetry movement. He was appointed the sixth Poet Laureate Consultant in Poetry to the Library of Congress and won many prizes including the Pulitzer Prize, the National Book Award, and the National Book Critics Circle Award.

Lowell was born to Commander Robert Traill Spencer Lowell Ⅲ and Charlotte (née Winslow) on March 1, 1917 in Boston, Massachusetts, two distinguished families. His father was a naval officer. His mother was a descendant of William Samuel Johnson, a signer of the United States Constitution.

Many distinguished poets played an important role in Lowell's poetry career. Richard Eberhart influenced Lowell so much that Lowell decided to be a poet in the future. Lowell attended Harvard University for two years. At Harvard College, Lowell asked Robert Frost for feedback on a long poem he'd written on the Crusades. Allen Tate offered Lowell a lot of guidance. At that time, Lowell converted to Catholicism, a religion he shared with Tate. Then, Lowell transferred to Kenyon College to study with poet and critic John Crowe Ransom. Lowell studied with and befriended fellow students Peter Taylor, Robie Macauley, and Randall Jarrell. In 1940 Lowell graduated from Kenyon College with a degree in classics, and pursued a master's degree in English literature at Louisiana State University under critics Cleanth Brooks and Robert Penn Warren. Before finishing graduate school, Lowell moved to New York, where he became an editor for a Catholic publishing house.

Lowell's nickname "Cal" originated from tyrannical Roman emperor Caligula because he had a tendency for violence and bullying other children when he was young. Lowell wrote to President Roosevelt and refused to fight in World War Ⅱ in 1943. Because of his conscientious objector stance, Lowell served several months at the federal prison in Danbury, Connecticut. Before that he was held in a prison in New York City which he later wrote about in the poem "Memories of West Street and Lepke" from his book *Life Studies*. In 1944, Lowell's first book, *The Land of Unlikeness* was published, followed by *Lord Weary's Castle* two years later. During 1947,

Lowell was poetry consultant to the Library of Congress. During 1949 he served on the committee for the first Bollingen Prize. In the 1950s, Lowel traveled in Europe and taught at Kenyon college, the University of Iowa, Indiana University, the University of Cincinnati, and Boston University, forming great influence on many writers. At the University of Iowa, Lowell taught in the famous Iowa Writers' Workshop and Paul Engle, Robie Macauley, and Anthony Hecht became his fellow colleagues. Among his many students were poets W. D. Snodgrass, Sylvia Plath, and Anne Sexton, and critic Helen Vendler. Lowell also published three books of verse, won two prestigious awards, and had his first child, Harriet Winslow. For the whole of the 1960s, Lowell lived in New York City, worked as a poet-librettist for the Metropolitan and New York City operas, published poetry and plays, received more awards and a lifelong appointment at Harvard, and taught at Yale University. Lowell also participated actively in the civil rights movement and opposed the US involvement in Vietnam. His participation in the October 1967 peace march in Washington D.C. caused his later arrest. In 1967, Lowell was introduced in an article of *Time* magazine and he was wellknown as the most public, well-known American poet of his generation. From 1970 to 1976, Lowell lived in England and taught at Essex University for two years. In 1973, Lowell's tenth volume of poetry, *The Dolphin*, won the Pulitzer Prize. Still more awards followed for books and lifetime achievement.

Lowell had three marriages. Lowell married the novelist Jean Stafford in 1940 and their tumultuous marriage ended in 1948. In 1949 Lowell married the writer Elizabeth Hardwick with whom he had a daughter, Harriet. But their marriage still could not escape the fate of failure. In 1972, he was divorced from Elizabeth Hardwick and then married writer Caroline Blackwood, with whom he had already had a child, Sheridan, in 1971. Lowell also became the stepfather to Blackwood's young daughter, Ivana. Elizabeth Bishop and Randall Jarrell had been Lowell's best friends. Lowell had a close friendship with the poet Elizabeth Bishop that lasted from 1947 until Lowell's death in 1977. Both writers influenced one another's work by means of critiques of their poetry respectively. And, the friendship between Lowell and Randall Jarrell began from the time when they met at Kenyon College in 1937 until Jarrell's death in 1965. Lowell continuously sought out Jarrell's input about his poems before he published them and publicly appreciated Jarrell's influence over his writing.

Lowell suffered from manic depression and was hospitalized many times throughout his adult life for this mental illness. However, his manic depression and mental illness produced some of his most important poetry, particularly his book *Life Studies*. Lowell died in 1977, having suffered a heart attack in a taxi in New York City on his way to see his ex-wife, Elizabeth Hardwick. By the time he died at the age of sixty, Lowell was considered one of the most important writers in English in the latter half of the twentieth century. He was buried in Stark Cemetery, Dunbarton, New Hampshire.

His Writing Career

Lowell's first book of poems, *Land of Unlikeness*, appeared in 1944, and his next book, *Lord Weary's Castle*, came out in 1946. It contained thirty-five poems, five among which were slightly revised from *Land of Unlikeness*. *Lord Weary's Castle* received critics' attention and was awarded the Pulitzer Prize in 1947. "Mr. Edwards and the Spider" and "The Quaker Graveyard in Nantucket" are the better-known poems in the volume. Lowell adopted formal and ornate style to illustrate the theme of violence and theology, especially in "The Quaker Graveyard."

In 1951, Lowell published The Mills of the Kavanaughs. It was an epic poem but failed to receive high praise from critics and readers. However, Lowell revived his reputation with his most influential book, *Life Studies* (1959), whicn won him the National Book Award for poetry in 1960. *Life Studies* introduces many of the stylistic and thematic elements that would characterize what many called "confessional" poetry. The poems were largely free-verse, colloquial, and autobiographical; among their subjects was the poet's psychological turmoil. Many of the poems in *Life Studies* documented Lowell's family life and personal problems, and Lowell adopted the language much more informal than that he had used in his first three books. *Life Studies* signaled a turning point in Lowell's career, and even in American poetry in general. These poems were labeled "confessional" by M. L. Rosenthal and thereby, Lowell was grouped together with other influential confessional poets like Lowell's former students W. D. Snodgrass, Sylvia Plath, and Anne Sexton.

The poems in *Imitations* (1961) were different from Lowell's previous works. It was a volume of loose translations of poems by Rilke, Montale, Baudelaire, Pasternak, and Rimbaud. The 1962 Bollingen Poetry Translation Prize was awarded to Lowell for his contribution to the translation of these classical and modern European poems. However, critical response to *Imitations* was mixed and sometimes hostile. The poet Michael Hofmann thought *Life Studies* was Lowell's best book, *Imitations* was Lowell's most "pivotal book," because *Imitations* was full of "international style," as Lowell explained in the book's introduction that his translations should be regarded as "imitations" rather than strict translations since he translated the originals in comparatively free way and he would rather think of authors of the originals as people in modern and American context.

His next book *For the Union Dead* (1964) was widely praised. *For the Union Dead* began with a description of the decaying South Boston Aquarium, focused on a memorial at the Statehouse for Colonel Robert Gould Shaw and black army regiment in the Civil War. The poems in *For the Union Dead* were not notably "confessional" and more emphasized the interplay of past and present, the social and the political. *Life Studies* focused on Lowell's emotionally personal life and family history, while *For the Union Dead* dealt with the spiritual hollowness of modern society. In the poems, Lowell showed individual's alienation and isolation which technologically advanced society brought them. Lowell's mental illness was obvious in *Life Studies* but rare in *For the Union Dead*. Lowell wrote about a number of world historical figures in poems like "Caligula," "Jonathan Edwards in Western Massachusetts," and "Lady Raleigh's Lament." The subject matter in *For the Union Dead* was much broader than it was in *Life Studies*.

Lowell's *The Old Glory* was produced Off-Broadway in New York City in 1964 and was published in 1965 (with a revised edition following in 1968). It was three one-act plays including "Endecott the Red Cross," "My Kinsman, Major Molineux," and "Benito Cereno." Among them the first two were adapted by Nathaniel Hawthorne's short stories, and the third was adapted by Herman Melville's novella. *The Old Glory* won five Obie Awards in 1965, one of which was an award for "Best American Play."

In 1967, Lowell published his next book of poems, *Near the Ocean*. Lowell's writing style changed again. His verse returned more formal and metered. The loose translations (including verse approximations of Dante, Juvenal, and Horace) again appeared in *Near the Ocean*. The contemporary American politics overtly entered into Lowell's work, which was shown in his best known poem "Waking Early Sunday Morning."

Notebook 1967—1968 was published as a verse journal and later was republished in a revised and expanded edition, titled *Notebook*. In *Notebook 1967—1968* Lowell wrote his sonnets in blank verse with a definitive pentameter and a small handful included rhyme. Some poems in *Notebook* were originally published in his previous works. "In the Cage" originated from *Lord Weary's Castle*; "Caligula" and "Night-Sweat" from *For the Union Dead*; "1958" and "To Theodore Roethke: 1908—1963" from *Near the Ocean*. In addition, Lowell's source materials for the poems derived from a number of other writers including Jesse Glenn Gray's "The Warrior," Simone Weil's "Half a Century Gone," Herbert Marcuse, Aijaz Ahmad, R. P. Blackmur, Plutarch, Stonewall Jackson, and Ralph Waldo Emerson.

Lowell liked sonnet form so much that he reworked and revised many of the poems from *Notebook* and used them as the foundation for his next three volumes of verse: *History* (1973), *For Lizzie and Harriet* (1973), and *The Dolphin* (1973). *Notebook 1967—1968* is a combination of polished verse and spontaneous expression. Actually, in his later life Lowell wrote and revised extensively, expressing his strong sense of personal history and literary tradition, uncovering the problems in his private life and the world around him. *History* basically concerned world history from antiquity till the mid-20th century except that some poems dealt with Lowell's friends, peers, and family. *For Lizzie and Harriet* described the breakdown of Lowell's second marriage in the voices of his daughter, Harriet, and his second wife. *The Dolphin* was reputed works and won the 1974 Pulitzer Prize. It addressed such actual events in Lowell's life as an extramarital affair, the birth of a child out of wedlock, divorce, and remarriage, including poems about his daughter, his ex-wife, and his new wife Caroline Blackwood. *The Dolphin* also featured a self-conscious depiction of the poem. It reflected Lowell's emotional candor and the confessional nature of his verse. Derek Walcott and William Meredith praised *Notebook* and *The Dolphin* upon their publication. Meredith thought that Robert Lowell's *Notebook 1967—1968* was a beautiful and major work. Michael Hofmann, William Logan, and Richard Tillinghast praised the sonnets in reviews of Lowell's *Collected Poems*. The negative reviews mainly came from A. O. Scott and Marjorie Perloff, the latter of whom called the sonnet poems "trivial and catty," considering them to be Lowell's least important volumes.

In 1977, Lowell published his last volume of poetry, *Day by Day*. *Day by Day* was awarded that year's National Book Critics Circle Award for poetry. Anthony Hecht praised highly the poetry and thought "it was a very touching, moving, gentle book, tinged with a sense of [Lowell's] own pain and the pain [he'd] given to others." In *Day by Day*, Lowell reflects on his life, his past relationships, and his own mortality. "Epilogue" is the best-known poem from this collection in which Lowell reflects upon the "confessional" school of poetry. *Day by Day* more focused on personal life and ignored ambitious metaphors and political engagement. Vendler praised some of Lowell's descriptions, particularly his descriptions of impotence, depression, and old age and she wrote, "Now [Lowell] has ended [his career], in *Day by Day*, as a writer of disarming openness, exposing shame and uncertainty, offering almost no purchase to interpretation, and in his journal-keeping, abandoning conventional structure, whether rhetorical or logical. The poems drift from one focus to another; they avoid the histrionic; they sigh more often than they expostulate. They acknowledge exhaustion; they expect death."

Although changes in artistic forms in his poetry were diverse, Lowell had been engaged in demonstrating connected theme, expressing his personal torment and the contemporary and historical struggles of the nation. Obviously, his body of work was unified and related between the past and present periods. Lowell became a distinguished poet in that in his work he combined formal techniques and personal concerns, showed completely the conflict between the public and private selves, and reflected his superior talent in crafting work.

He had published 18 major works (poetry, drama, and translation) such as *Land of Unlikeness* (1944), *Lord Weary's Castle* (1946), *The Mills of the Kavanaughs* (1951), *Life Studies* (1959), *Phaedra* (translation) (1961), *Imitations* (1961), *For the Union Dead* (1964), *The Old Glory* (1965), *Near the Ocean* (1967), *The Voyage & Other Versions of Poems of Baudelaire* (1969), *Prometheus Bound* (translation) (1969), *Notebooks, 1967—1968* (1969), *History* (1973), *For Lizzie and Harriet* (1973), *The Dolphin* (1973), *Selected Poems* (1976), and *Day by Day* (1977).

Analyses of and Comments on His Representative Poems

Robert Lowell and the Confessional Poetry

In 1959, M. L. Rosenthal first used the term "confessional" in a review of Robert Lowell's *Life Studies* entitled "Poetry as Confession." *Life Studies* was the first book in the confessional mode. In the poems, Lowell alludes to his struggles with mental illness and his experiences in a mental hospital. The "confessional poetry" was associated with several poets including Robert Lowell, Sylvia Plath, John Berryman, Anne Sexton, Allen Ginsberg, and W. D. Snodgrass. They redefined American poetry in the generation following World War II. Some key texts of the American confessional school of poetry include Lowell's *Life Studies*, Plath's *Ariel*, Berryman's *The Dream Songs*, Snodgrass' *Heart's Needle*, and Sexton's *To Bedlam and Part Way Back*.

Confessional poetry is the poetry of the personal or "I." This style of writing appeared in the late 1950s and early 1960s. Lowell's book *Life Studies* was a highly personal account in which his life and familial ties were represented. Lowell's work influenced greatly his students —Plath and Sexton. The confessional poetry dealt with total new subjects such as people's feelings about death, trauma, depression, and relationships. Sexton in particular was interested in the psychological aspect of poetry, having started writing at the suggestion of her therapist. The confessional poets recorded their emotions in their poems, in the meanwhile, they used corresponding poetic craft and construction to stress the theme of poems, most of which were often written in an autobiographical manner. The confessional poets maintained a high level of craftsmanship through their careful attention to and use of prosody.

The confessional poets pioneered a type of writing, and it changed the landscape of American poetry forever. The generations of writers absorbed the tradition of confessional poetry, and they started to focus on their personal experience. Marie Howe and Sharon Olds are two contemporary representative poets who were greatly influenced by the confessional poetry. Confessional free verse poetry became the popular approach in the second half of the 20th-century American poetry. One of the most prominent, consciously confessional poets to emerge in the 1980s was Sharon Olds whose focus was on taboo sexual subject.

For the Union Dead (1964)

Contents Summary

For the Union Dead is a book of poems by Robert Lowell that was published by Farrar, Straus & Giroux in 1964. It was Lowell's sixth book. Lowell originally wrote the poem "For the Union Dead" for the Boston Arts Festival in 1960.

For the Union Dead refers to the 1928 poem "Ode to the Confederate Dead" by Lowell's former teacher and mentor Allen Tate. *For the Union Dead* contemplates the legacy of the Civil War, embodied in the memorial to Colonel Robert Shaw, a white soldier who died while commanding an all-black regiment. To many northerners, Shaw symbolized union idealism: one hundred years after his death, Lowell contrasts Shaw's heroism with contemporary forms of self-interest and greed in "For the Union Dead."

In the poem, Lowell's visit to the park leads to a series of associations. Lowell sees construction of the underground parking garage beneath the Common, and he remembers his childhood and the changes of Boston. It reminds him of the Robert Gould Shaw Memorial, especially the history associated with the memorial including Colonel Robert Gould Shaw and the all-black 54th Massachusetts Volunteer Infantry. Besides, Civil Rights Movement which was controversial and the images of black and white school-children on television came into his mind.

The opening stanza describes the old South Boston Aquarium: "broken" and "boarded" windows; "lost" weather vane's scales; "airy" and "dry" fish tanks. The ruined, broken, and bare scenery emphasizes a sense of loss and dilapidation and evokes melancholy mood.

The next two stanzas suggest that the past was far from ideal. The speaker remembers a childhood visit to the aquarium. The "burst the bubbles" brings him delight and fish in the tanks are trapped and submissive. The kingdom of fish is literally heading "dark downward" as they swim away from the aquarium light. More broadly, like the fish kingdom, the kingdom of humans is getting worse, darker, and nobler. "For the Union Dead" addresses the mood of American society as it regresses from idealism to despair.

Then, the poem describes the "new barbed and galvanized fence on the Boston Common." The Boston Common symbolizes a public area for people to gather usually while the new barbed and galvanized fence is a menacing border between people and preventing people from enjoying together. Lowell portrayed bulldozers as "dinosaur[s]" and "the underground garage" as an "underworld." Thus, modern construction tools evoke a prehistoric, animalistic world, a savage and hellish world.

The poem's central figure is a memorial to Colonel Robert Gould Shaw, who led the 54th Massachusetts Volunteer Regiment on an attack on Fort Wagner, South Carolina during the Civil War. The monument commemorates the honorable moments in that Boston's past. "For the Union Dead" portrays the threat of contemporary existence to the monument. The monument symbolizes the idealism displayed by the soldiers for a just cause while contemporary society struggles for more parking spaces, destroying the idealism.

"For the Union Dead" also contrasts Boston's present with its past. Lowell presents deep appreciation and respect for the soldiers' heroism and sacrifice. However, a few generations later, the city's attitude toward the soldiers changed a lot. The stern images of Colonel Shaw presented in the poem suggest Shaw's discomfort with the public role others claim for him.

Themes

Shaw displayed some particular heroism. Shaw's self-sacrifice seems incomprehensible to the contemporary age. New England is full of "small town New England greens," "white churches," and the monument. New England's present is becoming increasingly different from its past. "For the Union Dead" idealizes Shaw's sacrifice, also points out that Shaw's noble actions are not appreciated by people in modern society.

A series of apocalyptic images of twentieth-century life are shown in "For the Union Dead." The ditch of "The ditch is nearer" is just the place where Shaw and the black soldiers were hastily buried. The television set presents images of civil rights strife: civil rights activists faced various difficulties and African-American schoolchildren encountered great hostility in their life.

"For the Union Dead" reflects paradox in Colonel Shaw's idealism and reality. Shaw thinks that the power that he chooses life and die is "lovely." It is full of love, because he, like Christ, desires to sacrifice himself. In addition, the "peculiar power" is strange to humans in that Colonel Shaw cannot save his life and only die for his idealism. The "peculiar power" is particular to humankind in that Colonel Shaw realizes that he risks his life although he behaves like a hero.

"For the Union Dead" also reflects devolution of humankind. According to "For the Union Dead," technology works to make humans turn into beasts. Technology blurs the boundaries between the kingdom of "fish and reptile" and that of humans. "For the Union Dead" is full of fear that technology devolves humankind. "Dinosaur steam shovels" and "cars nose" are inanimate technological products. Modern technology including atomic bombs, "Space is nearer," and "the blast" puts humankind closer to the point of extinction.

"For the Union Dead" concerns a public subject: the Civil War's tortured legacy. At the beginning, Lowell recalls his visiting the South Boston Aquarium. Then, he gradually addresses various public events and places: a memorial to the union dead, William James' comments, and a photograph of Hiroshima. In the poem, Lowell introduces personal anecdote which guides readers to reflect on the larger societal, cultural, and historical forces at work.

Literary Techniques

"For the Union Dead" is written in free-verse quatrains. Each stanza consists of four lines whose lengths are different from each other. In the poem Lowell does not adhere to a metrical or rhyming pattern.

Skunk Hour (1958)

Contents Summary

"Skunk Hour" was the final poem in *Life Studies* (1959), but it was the first to be completed. Lowell began work on the poem in August 1957, and the poem was first published in the January 1958 issue of the *Partisan Review*.

"Skunk Hour" is one of Robert Lowell's most frequently anthologized poems. It was published in his groundbreaking book of poems, *Life Studies*, and is regarded as a key early example of confessional poetry.

In general, the speaker in the poem reflects on a town in Maine. An elderly, wealthy woman seems to have a ton of property, but is alone at that time. Lowell describes the millionaire, the depressed and poor town decorator, and the pretty sad place. Then the speaker shifts the focus to himself. He remembers his driving through the town one night, his sight and feeling at that time. It all seems pretty gloomy, depressed, and crazy. As the poem progresses, it gets pretty bleak.

Specifically, first, an heiress in Nautilus Island in Maine doesn't get out much. She still gets by colder weather in her simple cottage. Her sheep graze on her property, her son's occupation is noble, and her farmer holds a seat in local government. She doesn't live a luxurious life and she's old and weak. She wants to be left alone during her prosperous golden years. She buys all the houses that are blocking her sea view and then gets rid of them. The millionaire who lived in Nautilus Island over the summer is gone now. He seems to be from L. L. Bean (a Maine company) and his nice boat is sold to the lobstermen. It is fall of year, and the leaves on Blue Hill turned red. The local shoe-repair shop owner is decorating his store with orange things for fall, and he doesn't make a lot of money but he prefers to settle down.

The speaker is driving his old car (a Ford Tudor) up Blue Hill, looking for parked cars with lovers but finding bleak graveyard. A love song from one of the cars causes him to feel terrible. The speaker realizes that his own agony lies in himself. Nobody's in the private hell or in the hill except that only "skunks" are looking for something to eat. The skunks walk under the night shadows of this big, Gothic-looking church in the main part of the town. A mother skunk with her babies is walking around in a garbage can, get some sour cream, and will not scare.

Themes

The speaker's madness is demonstrated in "Skunk Hour" in some sense. The sentence his "mind's not right" is an evidence of his madness. In the poem, we learn that he's feeling a little down in the dumps and is tired as he's driving around at night. Actually, He becomes more disturbed at night; he's restless, searching for something he never finds.

Isolation is another theme of "Skunk Hour." The speaker of "Skunk Hour" is stuck on an island, so his human interaction is limited to people there. Although he knows a lot of folks from the outside, he doesn't actually know them very well. He is isolated from outside actually. He tried to change the situation, driving around in the town at night to look for signs of human life, and find nothing but skunks. Class issues and envy are the reasons for our speaker's feelings of loneliness and madness.

Home is what Lowell tries to explore in "Skunk Hour." In Nautilus Island the speaker doesn't feel "at home" although he lives there year-round. He tells us others come here only for summer and he doesn't feel more comfortable and easier there. The speaker used to feel at home there, but now that the mystery person has left, he's feeling too lonely to feel homey.

"Skunk Hour" is a play on "witching hour" and the skunks are like "witches." At "witching hour," witches do all their weird stuff actively. The skunks' behavior is strange and disturbing. They accompany the speaker's madness. The skunks can be considered as the eyes of a mentally ill man. They take on a stranger, darker light.

Literary Techniques

This poem is told through the lens of the mentally ill. Therefore, the words and phrases in this poem have shifting, sneaky, and double meanings. For example, "Spartan" describes something simple or severe but it also tracks back to ancient Greece. "A red fox stain" describes red leaves of fall in Blue Hill, but it also makes us think of a bloodstain. The nets containing fish reminds us of the stockings.

The stanzas in the poem are six lines apiece and there's definitely some rhyming. But, all through the poem the rhyme scheme is not perfect harmonious. In some stanzas (the fourth stanza) Lowell sticks to a perfectly predictable pattern: a-b-c-b-c-a. But none of the other stanzas follow that pattern exactly. Most of the time each end word (the last word in a line) has a rhyming match within the stanza, but when and where the match comes varies throughout the poem.

Bibliography

Ruby, M.K., ed. *Poetry for Students, Vol. 7*. Detroit: Gale, 2000. 65–72.

http://en.wikipedia.org/wiki/Confessional_poetry 2013-02-17

http://www.shmoop.com/skunk-hour 2013-02-15

Charles Olson

His Life and Writing Career

His Life

Charles Olson (1910—1970) was a second generation American modernist poet and was recognized as a major shaper of a postmodern American poetry, the chief successor to Ezra Pound and William Carlos Williams. Critics commonly regarded him as a representative figure of Black Mountain Poets which included Robert Creeley, Robert Duncan, Edward Dorn, and Joel Oppenheimer among others. Many postmodern groups, such as the poets of the language school, regarded Olson as a primary and precedent figure.

Olson was born to Karl Joseph and Mary Hines Olson on December 27, 1910 and grew up in Worcester, Massachusetts. His father was a Swedish letter carrier and his mother was a Catholic Irish-American. At Classical High School in Worcester, Olson was a distinguished orator and took the third place in the National Oratorical Contest, winning a tour of Europe as a prize. In Europe he met Irish poet William Butler Yeats. From 1928 to 1933, he attended Wesleyan University in Middletown, Connecticut, earning his bachelor's degree and master's degree in literature and American studies. His thesis for MA was "The Growth of Herman Melville, Prose Writer and Poetic Thinker." Then, he began teaching English at Clark University in Worcester as an instructor for two years. In 1936, he went on a swordfishing cruise and the sea drew him to Melville and to the old fishing town of Gloucester, a city that became inseparable from his life and his poetic career ever after. In the same year, Olson attended Harvard University as a doctoral candidate, first in English and American literature, then in new American civilization program. He studied with Frederick Merk and F. O. Mattthiessen. However, Olson only completed his coursework for a Ph.D. and failed to earn his degree because he didn't submit his dissertation. In 1939 and 1948 he received two Guggenheim fellowships for his studies of Herman Melville.

In 1941, Olson moved to New York and became a publicity director for the American Civil Liberties Union. He lived with Constance Wilcock in a common-law marriage in 1942, having one child, Katherine. In September, Olson and his wife moved to Washington, D. C., where he became assistant chief of the foreign language section of the Office of War Information (OWI), the forerunner of the US Information Agency. Olson was strongly interested in politics and the Franklin D. Roosevelt revolution. He was active in the Franklin D. Roosevelt campaign, "Everyone for Roosevelt." In 1945, Roosevelt died and an era of liberalism in Washington came to an end. Olson left politics and he moved to Key West, Florida, dedicated himself to poetry. In 1946 he defended Ezra Pound against charges of treason, and during the following two years Olson visited Ezra Pound at St. Elizabeths psychiatric hospital in Washington D.C regularly.

Between 1947 and 1951 Olson lectured at the University of Washington in Seattle, American University in Washington, D. C., and Black Mountain College, in western North Carolina. During these years, he established his intellectual relationships with many people. Especially, in 1951, as a visiting professor, Olson came to Black Mountain College, an innovative arts school. He met thinker Buckminster Fuller, choreographer Merce Cunningham, painters Franz Kline and Josef Albers, and poets Robert Duncan and Robert Creeley. Olson became the rector of Black Mountain College. From 1951 to 1956, he raised a literary movement known as Black Mountain poetry. Many students and fellow poets admired him for his verse experiments, and his theories on history and myth. At Black Mountain College, Olson separated from Connie Wilcock and lived with Betty Kaiser in a common-law marriage. Betty Kaiser was a Black Mountain music student.

Olson left Black Mountain College in 1957. He settled down in Gloucester and lived in poverty with his second wife, Betty Kaise, and their son, Charles Peter Olson. From 1963 to 1965 he taught American poetry and mythology at the State University of New York at Buffalo. But Olson's second wife was killed in a car accident in January 1964. His wife's death haunted him deeply and he resigned from the State University of New York at last. In 1969 he was invited to teach at the University of Connecticut, but after several sessions he was obliged to give up his work due to his liver. Olson's life was marred by alcoholism, which led to his early death from liver cancer. In the last years of his life, he was extremely isolated and worked hard. He died in New York Hospital on January 10, 1970, two weeks past his fifty-ninth birthday, while in the process of completing *The Maximus Poems*. Although Olson aroused many controversies from critics circle in his life, his reputation as an innovator and thinker was acknowledged widely.

His Writing Career

Olson's literary output was prolific, including his poetry and prose works that expounded his theories about writing. His achievements in literary history includes his epic series, *The Maximus Poems* (1953—1975), the theoretical manifesto "Projective Verse" (1950), essays such as "Human Universe" (1951), his study of Herman Melville, myth and America, *Call Me Ishmael* (1947), his energetic letters, as well as his acknowledged influence on an entire generation of poets.

Olson's first book, *Call Me Ishmael* (1947), a study of Herman Melville's novel *Moby-Dick*, was evolved from his master's thesis at Wesleyan. Melville's *Moby-Dick* was perceived as a new myth of the West. Ishmael, the lone survivor of the tale, was the counter to the egocentric and imperial Ahab. Ishmael was full of curiosity and interested in the life around him. Olson tried to show Ishmael's careful scrutiny of life.

In 1950, Olson published his essay "Projective Verse" in *Poetry New York*, a manifesto for the postmodernist poetry movement in America. It was first published as a pamphlet, and then was quoted extensively in William Carlos Williams' *Autobiography* (1951). The essay introduces his ideas of "composition by field" through projective or open verse. Actually, Olson continually represented the views of Ezra Pound and William Carlos Williams. Pound asked poets to "compose in the sequence of the musical phrase, not in sequence of a metronome," and William Carlos Williams proposed that a poem should be approached as a "field of action." Composition by field differs from the traditional method of poetic composition, and the latter depends on received form and measure. Olson argues that a received structure including rhyme, meter, and sense is no longer regarded as a propulsive force by a poet and the breath should be a poet's central concern.

Olson argues that simile and description should not play a major role in the construction of a poem, and syntax should be shaped by sound rather than sense, with nuances of breath and motion to be conveyed to the reader through typographical means. As Nicholas Everett pointed out in *Charles Olson's Life and Career*, "Projective Verse" aims to transfer energy from the world to the reader without artificial interference, syntax is shaped by sound, not sense; sense is conveyed by direct movement from one perception to another, not rational argument; and the reader's rendition directed by freely varied spacing between words and lines on the page. Olson argued that poetic language must be spontaneous, expressing what is actually seen and felt, rather than following traditional rules of logic and order. He put forward his projective mode in poem writing. In brief, a poetic meter was based on the poet's breathing and an open construction was based on sound and the linking of perceptions rather than syntax and logic. He favored that meter was not based on syllable, stress, foot, or line but using only the unit of the breath. In the projective poem, the flow and mingling of words in the poet's mind were projected onto paper. In "Projective Verse," Olson expounded his "objectivism" (Ishmael's selfless scrutiny of life), meaning that poet was mere object for writing poetry, and human subjects are cast among the flowers and animals of everyday life. Olson argued that human had no privilege as the observer of nature. Surrounding nature was important, regarded as resources and implements of poems.

His first book of poetry, *In Cold Hell, in Thicket* was published in 1953. Olson went to the Yucatan Peninsula, studying Mayan temples and artifacts. Olson's research into Mayan hieroglyphs was recorded in letters to the poet Robert Creeley, collected in *Mayan Letters* (1953). Many short poems followed the publication of "Projective Verse," variously collected in *In Cold Hell, in Thicket* (1953), *The Distances* (1960), *Archaeologist of Morning* (1970), and *The Collected Poems of Charles Olson* (1987). These poems dealt with subjects like war, death, and the nature of history. *The Distances* (1960), his second collection, is less formally innovative but more ambitious in treating personal dreams and universal myths. Olson's shorter verse, poems such as "Only the Red Fox, Only the Crow," "Other Than," "An Ode on Nativity," "Love," and "The Ring Of" manifested a sincere, original, emotionally powerful voice.

Human Universe and Other Essays was published in 1965. It concerns most Olson's reviews and speculations on objectivism and explores animistic roots in non-western thought. In "Human Universe," Olson illustrated in detail Mayan myth and its reflection in contemporary poetry; in "The Gate and the Center," Olson argued that human migration played an important role in human history, and the individual came into being when western alienation from nature appeared.

Olson spent many years in writing *The Maximus Poems*. *The Maximus Poems* was published gradually with the completion of each part. In 1953 *The Maximus Poems 1—10* was published, *Maximus 11—22* followed in 1956. The first volume of the work appeared in 1960 as *The Maximus Poems*. The second volume, *Maximus* was issued in 1968, and the final volume, *The Maximus Poems: Volume Three*, appeared posthumously in 1975. Olson's epic remained unfinished at the poet's death. *The Maximus Poems* explored social, historical, and political concerns. The long poem dealt with the origins of America and its long and ancient cultural background, which even dated back to Mesopotamia. Olson explored the present western civilizations by means of ancient myths, cultural morphologies, and archetypal events.

Maximus explored American history in the broadest sense and reflected also an epic of place, Massachusetts and specifically the city of Gloucester where Olson had settled. Dogtown, the wild, rock-strewn centre of Cape Ann, next to Gloucester is important in *The Maximus Poems*. Maximus, as speaker of *The Maximus Poems*, represented Maximus of Tyre, an itinerant Greek philosopher, and Olson himself. In the first volume, *The Maximus Poems*, Maximus, dismayed by the culture of contemporary Gloucester, examined its origins in the European settlement of America. Olson told the history how Cape Ann became the Plymouth Bay colony and then Massachusetts. Olson demonstrated how British investors controlled a small community of fishermen, and then controlled America. In the second volume, *The Maximus Poems,* IV, V, VI, (1968), Olson employed ancient myths and religious texts, and scrutinized certain documentary details of Gloucester's past. Olson used the cascade of words, numbers, and documents to map the phases of western migration, the origins of Gloucester, and the growth and decay of American culture. *The Maximus Poems, Volume Three* followed the logic of the preceding books, Olson imagined a new Gloucester in which material and commercial values were abandoned and spiritual and communal values were restored. *The Maximus Poems* reflected modern Gloucester by means of the rise and fall of civilizations elsewhere. Many myths in everyday life were scattered in the elegiac or contentious, but elegant poems. The minutiae of the town revealed the grand cosmic design. *The Maximus Poems* bears a memory, a "history of time."

Olson's papers are deposited in the Olson Archive of the University of Connecticut and the Humanities Research Center at the University of Texas, Austin. Other works by Olson are *Causal*

Mythology (1969), *The Fiery Hunt and Other Plays* (1977), and *The Post Office: A Memoir of His Father* (1974). Olson's reading list for poets is in *A Bibliography on America for Ed Dorn* (1964), *Selected Writings* (1966), and *Additional Prose* (1974). *The Special View of History* (1970) and *Muthologos: The Collected Lectures and Interviews* contain his works on history. *Charles Olson and Ezra Pound: An Encounter at St. Elizabeths* (1975) reprints his notes on Pound.

Analyses of and Comments on His Representative Poems

Charles Olson and the Black Mountain Poetry

The Black Mountain poets were American avant-garde or postmodern poets, and they were loosely associated with Black Mountain College, near Asheville, North Carolina, during the 1950s. Black Mountain College, founded in 1933, became an experiment in community education. Many avant-garde musicians, artists, and writers came to the college and grew up around the poets Robert Creeley, Robert Duncan, and Charles Olson while they were teaching at Black Mountain College. These poets emulated the freer style of William Carlos Williams and refused the poetic tradition espoused by T. S. Eliot. Charles Olson was the core of the Black Mountain poets.

Charles Olson's essay "Projective Verse" (1950) became the Black Mountain poets' manifesto, on which these poets based their poems' approach. Olson believed that a poem's essential energy is translated through the poet to the reader. This theory of projective verse called for poets to return to an organic basis for their form, to a poetic line controlled by the physiology of the poet's breathing instead of by preset meter. The essay stressed the reader's share in the creative process and called for the use of colloquial language. Robert Creeley argued that form is never more than the extension of content. Robert Duncan liked to use lyric, magical language in his poems. Much of the group's early work was published in the magazine *Origin*. Dissatisfied with the lack of critical material in that magazine, Creeley and Olson established the *Black Mountain Review*. It featured the work of William Carlos Williams, Paul Blackburn, Denise Levertov, Allen Ginsberg, and Gary Snyder.

Olson owed much to Pound. He urged an open form that would allow for poetry to be a process of discovery. Olson's call influenced many writers, who were dedicated to undermining the orthodox insistence on predetermined, closed form. Some of the Black Mountain poets are often considered to have contributed to the San Francisco Renaissance.

Maximus to Gloucester, Letter 27 [withheld] (1968)

Contents Smmary

The poem was published in *The Maximus Poems* in 1968. At the very beginning, Olson takes his readers into his personal background, sharing childhood experiences that he is reminiscing now. In his memory, readers can sense "the land falling off to the left where my father shot his scabby golf" and "the summer darkness until no flies could be seen." These vivid images are so familiar to common readers that they can immediately create a sense of carefreeness and recall their own happy and easygoing early life as if they were reliving it for the moment. Meanwhile, Olson's analysis of his pastimes is profound and deep, which can naturally suggest that his early experiences must have been of great significance to his later life. The fact that Gloucester wasn't over-crowded with technology when he was growing up in it foreshadows his whole thinking of "changes."

In the second part of his memory, Olson recollects the specific details of his parents' daily life. He remembers that "she laughing, so sure, as round as her face, Hines pink and apple" and he is "a man for kicks." The details help Olson convey his inner feelings of his parents, indicating the value of his parents in his life. Besides, this particular memory has "the geography of it," the geography of Polis. Again, the nostalgic feeling reminds the readers of the time when the major technologies were not applied in the city.

The first two stanzas in the poem are in two bunches and then the lines begin to scatter around the page. Olson's purpose in spacing out the rest of his poem and scattering his words around the page may have been to reflect the idea of change and how different the new Polis is than the old one. This juxtaposition is important because it relates back to the idea of "breath" that Olson had mentioned in his projective verse. Instead of focusing on punctuation of a poem, Olson preferred to emphasize the significance of breath when reading a poem and how readers should read a poem exactly how the author intended.

Finally Olson ends his poems by "compelling Gloucester to yield to change." This is where Olson contradicts his previous assertions about moving forward. It's as if he wants to move forward but yet doesn't want the change that he sees occurring, which brings us back to the idea that he wants positive change to happen. So in this poem, Olson combines his lyric, historic, and aesthetic concerns.

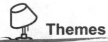

Themes

In the poem "Maximus to Gloucester, Letter 27 [withheld]," Charles Olson suggests that the city of Polis is in desperate need of change but not "bad change," rather "good change." It is addressed not to individuals, but to the people of a city.

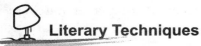

Literary Techniques

Olson uses different literary techniques throughout his poem such as imagery, simile, and metaphor to create a nostalgic setting for the readers to follow all the way to the end. Thus, the subtext of the poem is quite complex and well-hidden in the several lines of his stanzas.

The Kingfishers (1949)

Contents Summary

The poem was published in 1949 and then collected in Olson's first book of poetry, *In Cold Hell, in Thicket* (1953).

As Olson's first long poem, "The Kingfishers" is so crucial to understanding every aspect of Olson's early life and thought. It provides an insight into Olson's apprenticeship and purposes. The understanding of this poem can remove obstacles in the path of further study of Olson. "The Kingfishers," a lyrical meditation on the ruins of an Aztec burial ground, is one of Olson's finest poems concerns Aztec religion, modern Mexico, archaeology, and world events. In "The Kingfishers," Olson breaks away from his European heritage and believes the Indian cultures of the New World.

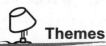

Themes

The poem has the shades of thrill and enigama around itself, which provokes a sense of horror, uncertainty, and yearning. The poet seems to have a mixted feeling about changes. The year of its composition reflects the strong sense of conflicts in the poet's mind: 1949. It is the same year as Mao's forces triumphed in China; It was just four years after the throwing of the nuclear bombs on Hiroshima and Nagasaki, when the outcomes of the disasters were just appearing. Again, it was just four years after the gates of Auschwitz camp were broken open and the unfathomable lies and the miserable sufferings in this unadulterated hell were disclosed. Obviously, Olson was greatly influenced by these events and ideas. For example, Olson's "La lumiere de l'aurore est devant. Nous nous devant nous lever et agir" is from Mao, which means "The light of dawn is before us. We must arise and act."

The unpredictable and unavoidable changes all over the world give the poem a stirring voice. The opening line "What does not change / is the will to change" reminds the readers of the philosophy of Heraklitus. It seems to be telling the readers "all is change, stasis is Thanatos (a death wish; Death as a personification or as a philosophical notion)", or simply "All is flux, nothing is stationary." In the poem, one phrase follows the other, producing different effects, for example, hectoring and bursting through the dead silence and complacency often associated with this Cold War moment in US history. The poet seems to have resolved to get rid of all the conformity, wiping everything that intends to stay in history, especially in literary history. One thought is overlaid on another, a veritable palimpsest. Everything contributes to the tendency of change. The rhetorical power is echoing and reproducing Ezra Pound's manifesto "Make it new." Hence, a poetics of dynamic movement.

Beyond the strong desire to change, the poem should also be noted for its complicated attidude toward history. The use of references implies the attractions and profoundity of human cultural histories. For example, the lines "the priests rush in among the people," "of green feathers feet, beaks and eyes / of gold" reminds the readers of Prescott's *History of the Conquest of Mexico*. The line "I thought of the E on the stone" goes to Frank O'Hara. Then comes "Si j'ai du goût, ce n'est guère / Que pour la terre et les pierres" ("I only find within my bones / A taste for eating earth and stones"), a couplet from Rimbaud's *Season in Hell* ("Alchemy of the Word"). Thus, Rimbaud, Heraklitus, Mao, Prescott, and Delphi are not only stones with which a new world might be built, but also the weights of a still not satisfactory world. The dillema provokes the poet's uncertainty about where to go: "shall you uncover honey / where maggots are? / I hunt among stones."

Literary Techniques

The poem takes on a radical new mode of poetic expression including the tenets of modernism and objectivism, which Charles Olson explained shortly after in his essay of 1950, "Projective Verse." "The Kingfishers" is a most striking application of his projective verse. The poem proceeds through a succession of widely varying stanzaic units instead of the traditional formalities such as rhyme, regular meters, symmetrical stanzas, and the normal pattern of argument. The design of the poem inspires rich imagination. The changing lengths and the layout of the sentences makes the poem a bracing test of nonlinear reading, using a scattered ideogram layout to facilitate the display of changes.

Olson is not seeking a place within the "modern movement," but rather, because what does not change "is the will to change," he is creating the ground for a new and different future, a postmodern turn and he is acknowledging the crisis in western culture in the wake of the war. The poet is calling his doubts about the current world: "The kingfishers! / who cares / for their feathers / now?"

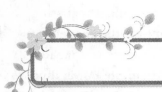

Bibliography

http://charlesolson.uconn.edu/Personal_and_Professional_Life/biography.htm 2013-02-12
http://www.anb.org/articles/16/16-02171.html 2013-02-13
http://www.english.illinois.edu/maps/poets/m_r/olson/life.htm 2013-02-15

Joseph Heller

His Life and Writing Career

His Life

Joseph Heller (1923—1999) was born in Coney Island in Brooklyn, New York, the son of poor Jewish parents, Lena and Isaac Donald Heller, from Russia. Even as a child, he loved to write; as a teenager, he wrote a story about the Russian invasion of Finland and sent it to *New York Daily News*, which rejected it. At least one scholar suggests that he knew that he wanted to become a writer, after recalling that he received a children's version of the *Iliad* when he was ten. After graduating from Abraham Lincoln High School in 1941, Heller spent the next year working as a blacksmith's apprentice, a messenger boy, and a filing clerk. In 1942, at age 19, he joined the US Army Air Corps. Two years later he was sent to the Italian front, where he flew 60 combat missions as a B-25 bombardier. His unit was the 488th Bombardment Squadron, 340th Bomb Group, the 12th Air Force. Heller later remembered the war as "fun in the beginning... You got the feeling that there was something glorious about it." On his return home he "felt like a hero... People think it quite remarkable that I was in combat in an airplane and I flew sixty missions even though I tell them that the missions were largely milk runs."

After the war, Heller studied English at the University of Southern California and New York University on the G.I. Bill. In 1949, he received his MA in English from Columbia University. Following his graduation, he spent a year as a Fulbright scholar at St. Catherine's Society in Oxford University. After returning home, he taught composition at the Pennsylvania State University for two years. He also taught fiction and dramatic writing at Yale. He then briefly worked for Time, Inc., before taking a job as a copywriter at a small advertising agency, where he worked alongside future novelist Mary Higgins Clark. At home, Heller wrote. He was first published in 1948, when *The Atlantic* ran one of his short stories. That first story nearly won the "Atlantic First." Heller did not begin work on a story until he had envisioned both a first and last line. The first sentence usually appeared to him "independent of any conscious preparation." In most cases, the sentence did not inspire a second sentence. At times, he would be able to write several pages before giving up on that hook. Usually, within an hour or so of receiving his inspiration, Heller would have mapped out a basic plot and characters for the story. When he was ready to begin writing, he focused on one paragraph at a time, until he had three or four handwritten pages, which he then spent several hours reworking. Heller maintained that he did not "have a philosophy of life, or a need to organize its progression. My books are not constructed to say anything." Only when he was almost one-third finished with the novel would he gain a clear vision of what it should be about. At that point, with the idea solidified, he would rewrite all that he had finished and then continue to the end of the story. The finished version of the novel would often not begin or end with the sentences he had originally envisioned, although he usually tried to include the original opening sentence somewhere in the text.

On Sunday, December 13, 1981, Heller was diagnosed with Guillain-Barré syndrome, a debilitating syndrome that was to leave him temporarily paralyzed. He was admitted to the Intensive Care Unit of Mount Sinai Medical Hospital the same day, and remained there, bedridden, until his condition had improved enough to permit his transfer to the Rusk Institute of Rehabilitation Medicine, which occurred on January 26, 1982. His illness and recovery are recounted at great length in the autobiographical *No Laughing Matter*, which contains alternating chapters by Heller and his good friend Speed Vogel. The book reveals the assistance and companionship Heller received during this period from a number of his prominent friends— Mel Brooks, Mario Puzo, Dustin Hoffman, and George Mandel among them. Heller eventually made a substantial recovery. He later married Valerie Humphries, one of the nurses who helped him get better.

His Writing Career

Joseph Heller is a popular and respected writer whose first and best-known novel, *Catch-22* (1961), is considered a major work of the post-World-War-II era. He began his writing career as the author of short stories and the novel *Catch-22* in 1961. After he won his acclaim with his first novel, he continued to finish other works, *Something Happened* (1974), *New Haven* (1967), *Good as Gold* (1979), *God Knows* (1984), *Poetics* (1987), *Picture This* (1988), and *Portrait of an Artist* (1999). Heller's works are characterized by a satirical sense of the absurd, speaking out against the military-industrial complex and those organized institutions which seem to manipulate people's lives in the name of reason or morality. Heller's tragicomic vision of modern life, found in all of his novels, focuses on the erosion of humanistic values and highlights the ways in which language obscures and confuses reality. In addition, Heller's use of anachronism reflects the disordered nature of contemporary existence. His protagonists are antiheroes who search for meaning in their lives and struggle to avoid being overwhelmed by such institutions as the military, big business, government, and religion. While Heller's later novels have received mixed reviews, *Catch-22* continues to be highly regarded as a trenchant satire of the big business of modern warfare. Presenting existence as absurd and fragmented, this irreverent, witty novel satirizes capitalism and the military bureaucracy. Heller's tragicomic vision of modern life, found in all of his novels, focuses on the erosion of humanistic values and highlights the ways in which language obscures and confuses reality. In addition, Heller's use of anachronism reflects the disordered nature of contemporary existence.

Catch-22 is most often interpreted as an antiwar protest novel that foreshadowed the widespread resistance to the Vietnam War that erupted in the late 1960s. Heller's penchant for anachronism, evident in all of his novels, reflects the disordered nature of contemporary existence. *Catch-22* is like no other novel. It has its own rationale, its own extraordinary character. It moves back and forth from hilarity to horror. It is outrageously funny and strangely affecting. It is totally original. This novel is a microcosm of the twentieth-century world as it might look to someone dangerously sane. It is a novel that lives and moves and grows with astonishing power and vitality—a masterpiece of our time. Joseph Heller's manic, bleak, blackly humorous, and brilliant novel has become a classic of American literature. It is a brilliant satirical critique of a number of modern social phenomena. It is generally referred to as an antiwar novel, but Heller's criticisms extend beyond the absurdity of war to capitalism itself and the social relations that arise from it. To be sure, his analysis is at times confused, and is often directed at surface elements while neglecting more fundamental issues. Nonetheless, *Catch-22* stands as a strong protest against the conditions of modern society.

Shortly after *Catch-22* was published, Heller thought of an idea for his next novel, which would become *Something Happened*, but did not act on it for two years. In the meantime he focused on scripts, completing the final screenplay for the movie adaptation of Helen Gurley Brown's *Sex and the Single Girl*, as well as a television comedy script that eventually aired as part of "McHale's Navy." He also completed a play in only six weeks, but spent a great deal of time working with the producers as it was brought to the stage. In 1969, Heller wrote a play called *We Bombed in New Haven*. It delivered an anti-war message while discussing the Vietnam War. It was originally produced by the Repertory Company of the Yale Drama School, with Stacey Keach in the starring role. After a slight revision, it was published by Alfred A. Knopf and then debuted on Broadway, starring Jason Robards. Heller's follow-up novel, *Something Happened*, was finally published in 1974. Critics were enthusiastic about the book, and both its hardcover and paperback editions reached number one on the *New York Times* bestseller list. Heller wrote another five novels, each of which took him several years to complete. One of them, *Closing Time*, revisited many of the characters from *Catch-22* as they adjusted to post-war New York. All of the novels sold respectably well, but could not duplicate the success of his debut. Told by an interviewer that he had never produced anything else as good as *Catch-22*, Heller famously responded, "Who has?"

Analysis of and Comment on His Representative Novel

Catch-22 (1961)

 Plot Summary

The setting of *Catch-22* is the island of Pianosa, the base of the Twenty-seventh Air Force. *Catch-22* concerns a World War II bombardier named Yossarian who believes his foolish, ambitious, mean-spirited commanding officers are more dangerous than the enemy. In order to avoid flying more missions, Yossarian retreats to a hospital with a mysterious liver complaint, sabotages his plane, and tries to get himself declared insane. Variously defined throughout the novel, Catch-22 refers to the ways in which bureaucracies control the people who work for them. The term first appears when Yossarian asks to be declared insane. In this instance, Catch-22 demands that anyone who is insane must be excused from flying missions. The catch is that one must ask to be excused; anyone who does so is showing rational fear in the face of clear and present danger, is therefore sane, and must continue to fly. In its final, most ominous form, Catch-22 declares they have the right to do anything we cannot stop them from doing. Although most critics identify Yossarian as a coward and an antihero, they also sympathize with his urgent need to protect himself from this brutal universal law. Some critics have questioned the moral status of Yossarian's actions, noting in particular that he seems to be motivated merely by self-preservation and that the enemy he refuses to fight is led by Adolf Hitler. Other, however, contend that while *Catch-22* is ostensibly a war novel, World War II and Air Force base where most of the novel's action takes place function primarily as a microcosm that demonstrates the disintegration of language and human value in a bureaucratic state.

The novel follows Captain John Yossarian, a US Army Air Forces B-25 bombardier. Most of the events in the book occur while the fictional 256th squadron is based on the island of Pianosa, in the Mediterranean Sea west of Italy. The novel looks into the experiences of Yossarian and the other airmen in the camp, and their attempts to keep their sanity in order to fulfill their service requirements, so that they can return home. The phrase "Catch-22," "a problematic situation for which the only solution is denied by a circumstance inherent in the problem or by a rule," has entered the English language. *Catch-22* tells many stories, but its central figure is a bombardier named Yossarian. The war has come to seem to Yossarian quite crazy. Men went mad and were rewarded with medals. All over the world, boys on every side of the bomb line were laying down their lives for what they had been told was their country; and no one seemed to mind, least of all the boys who were laying down their young lives. Yossarian minds very much: "He had decided to live forever or die in the attempt, and his only mission each time he went up was to come down alive. Yossarian is a rational man trying not to be killed in a wholly irrational world, forced to resort to even more irrational behavior than that of his superiors in order to survive. He is an expert malingerer; he performs minor acts of sabotage on his own plane; he takes every possible form of evasive action. But he cannot succeed against the appalling Colonel Cathcart, who continually raises the number of missions the men have to fly before they can be sent home, solely to get a reputation as a tough leader of men. Whatever Yossarian does, there is always a Catch-22 "says they have a right to do anything we cannot stop them from doing." It is an unwritten law which is ruthlessly enforced.

 Themes

Like many 1960s' novels, *Catch-22* is about the anarchic, individualistic human spirit and also its systematic denaturing, by society, corporate capitalism, and the military machine, as well as by mortal weakness and the threat of danger and death. But it also acquires a metaphorical and indeed metaphysical dimension; war is the general human condition, and Pianosa and the Eternal City are the landscapes in which we live. Since the world denatures us, or renders us inhuman or inanimate, the subject itself requires, in part, a similarly denatured tone: a comic method that, for much of the time, itself renders all things impersonal, inhuman, and cruel. Human beings are eccentrics, or nothing more than the sum of their rules. Since the world is absurd, language renders itself to us in the form of absurdities; and logic only in the form of contradiction or paradox.

Heller creates an artistic world which is higher and also is based on the reality with the symbolization of "Catch-22," expressing the westerners' bewilderment towards human's situation. The artistic world created by Heller belongs to a postmodernist art which advocates a thorough pluralism in thinking modes. In this sense, *Catch-22* is one of the postmodernist novels. The postmodernist novel is no longer the novel in the traditional sense, but is a rethinking, deconstruction and subversion of the novel form and narrative itself. Since its appearance, this kind of new novel has rethought, deconstructed, even self-mockingly imitated and analyzed the novel form and narrative and has become more and more popular. The postmodernist novelists claim that reality is made by language, and the false language makes the false reality. So in *Catch-22*, the mad and absurd social reality is made by a chaos and formless language.

Although *Catch-22* deserts the writing techniques of the traditional novel, it neither lacks of the writing methods nor the forms. In fact, its narration and structure are both under the author's control. This novel not only intensifies the mad and absurd theme, but also establishes the mad and absurd measures. *Catch-22* is an antiwar novel. This novel, for obvious and tragic reasons, is one of the dominant and shaping literary forms of the troubled twentieth century. It has not only played its part in defining the historical story of the century, but also shaped the techniques, the flavor, and the artistic essence of the postmodernist novel. War had shattered older notions of art, of form and representation; it had transformed notions of reality, the rules of perception, and the structures of artistic expression. It fragmented, hardened, postmodernized the voice of fiction, increased its sense of extremity, of irony, of tragedy, passing its critical lesson on into the history of postmodern fiction, and the whole literary and cultural tradition.

Critical appreciation of *Catch-22* was a bit slow in developing because the character of the novel was misunderstood. The book was presumed to be about World War II in particular and war in general, whereas Heller has said that he was inspired by the civilian situation in this country in the 1950s, and that *Catch-22* certainly has more meaning in regard to the Vietnam War than World War II. Heller has even bluntly insisted that *Catch-22* is not about World War II. Moreover, as critics to the issues of war, they have tended to argue that the theme of *Catch-22* is the absurdity, irrationality, and nightmare of a disordered universe, a universe in which fantasy and the grotesque are indistinguishable. The novel's chaotic surface has been seen as imitative form, a fictional texture expressing Heller's deepest intuition that the universe is absurd, irrational, and nightmarish. Though others have recognized the inadequacy, indeed the inaccuracy of this view, much more needs to be said about what Heller was really trying to do in *Catch-22* and how well he has in fact done it.

Heller's book hardly seems an act of literary propaganda, as so many of these earlier books do, nor is it a dramatic action in the tradition of Crane, Dreiser, and Steinbeck. *Catch-22* continues the tradition of literary protest. Like the books cited above, Heller's novel is informed by a militantly liberal point of view. A close friend once said that Heller is an ultra-liberal, and Heller himself has remarked that *Catch-22* is a liberal book. Asked to name the major American novelists of the early twentieth century, Heller cited Faulkner and Steinbeck—the choice of Steinbeck surely suggesting Heller's sympathies with the social protest tradition. What Heller does in *Catch-22* is to address traditional social problems from the usual point of view but by means of quite modern—even modernist—literary techniques.

Heller goes beyond his liberal predecessors to show that the enemy is not just the corporations and their authorities (in this case the military and its commanding officers). Humanity exists behind the absurdity, and this is what the book gradually discloses. Meantime, as the number of missions demanded of him rises and rises, and the frequency of death and the intensity of pain increases, Ocarina, deciding to live forever or at least die trying, tries to resist the universal victimization. This involves a struggle of identity, a quarrel with the contract, a battle with the language, as he increasingly defines himself in conflict and revolt. Language spawns counter-language, logic counter-logic, giving the narrative its growing order and structure, deepening its distinctive comic linguistic register. By the end of the book much of what has been first stated as absurd farce is recreated as tragedy. The characters that die in battle are no longer unknown. The victims are also the culprits, the culprits also the victims. The Roman scenes are a harrowing of hell; Heller has said they are conscious echo of Dostoevsky's dark passages. The deaths of men are the results of the corrupt ambitions of their officers; and Ocarina too has the death of comrades on his conscience.

Literary Techniques

Black Humor *Catch-22* is considered one of the typical novels of black humor, regarding the world as absurd and unreasonable and giving a smile after feeling extremely pessimistic, comically and even absurdly dealing with intrinsically tragic subjects, representing the single-dimension character and the waste land background, constructing loose and usually disjointed structures without paying attention to time, confusing facts and invention to reveal the unreliability of reality, stressing techniques and formal designs, coldly looking on the despairing, fantastic, rude, and cruel events, telling the story with mockingly questioning-God tone and often with a laughter having no intention to punish the evil and praise the good. *Catch-22* voices the anxious, absurd, outrageous reaction of a generation to a dark conflict that had taken American soldiers and airmen to Europe, and concludes not only in the defeat of totalitarianism, but in a victory on behalf of the world of our glossy, often alienating, and postmodern affluence. And the book is not just a satire on war but a story of that age of burgeoning affluence and all it brings with it—the grim period of arctic hostilities called the Cold War, the affluent society, and finally the postmodern phase of confident, narcissistic, consumptive late capitalism in which Heller's elderly survivors of wartime, have ended up. The book owes much to the tradition of surrealism and grotesquerie, but it is not simply a novel of war as grotesque farce, nor a surreal burst of laughter in the face of chaos, meaninglessness, cruelty, or a journey into the fantastic unconscious. It also possesses a vivid satirical energy and a distinctive rage, and a pained moral aspiration. The plot that starts in festive disorder and misrule, in the realm of the carnivalesque, gradually makes its way toward an individual search for meaning and order. Those characters who see it as a just cause or a defence of American values are themselves absurd innocents, and objects of satire; the ones who do succeed are the ambitious, the cynical, the depraved, the self-seeking, the corrupt, and the mad. Society no longer possesses a controlling meaning or a historical ideal. Italy is no repository of civilization but a version of the modern damnation. The world seems lacking in all divine intention and possesses no significant historical ideal. Madness prevails, the crazy is everywhere, and each individual bears his or her own crazed intention— though some of them, like Ocarina, are also the wise or the holy fools. The war is a mechanism for the violation of the body and a weapon for displaying the eternal human vulnerability. But most of the real danger comes not from enemy fire—however much the absurdity and the pathos of this is explored—but from the manipulations and corruptions of one's own comrades and superiors, and from the abstract military machine itself, which creates that world boiling in chaos where everything was in the proper order to which Ocarina wakes in his tent every morning.

Formlessness, Repetition, and Tonal Structure　The plot structure of this fiction enables the readers to see clearly the plot arrangement of this novel, including formlessness, repetition, and tonal structure. Heller presents his story in such a way that at certain points it is literally impossible to determine the order of events. But Heller was trying to match form and content. At the same time Heller fashions a fictional world in which he introduces numerous repetitions without undue awkwardness. Heller speaks of the novel's recurring and cyclical structure. These three features about the novel's structure are all fit together to advance Heller's radical protest against the modern social order. The structural complexity of *Catch-22* thus embodies the novel's theme more thoroughly.

Bibliography

Aldridge, John W. "The Deceits of Black Humor." *Harper's, Vol. 258, No. 1546*. New York City: Harper's Magazine Foundation, 1979.

Billson, Maecus K. Ⅲ, "The Un-minderbinding of Ocarina: Genesis Inverted in *Catch-22*." *Arizona Quarterly, Vol. 36, No. 4*. Tucson: The University of Arizona, 1980.

Cockburn, Alex. "A Review of *Catch-22*." *New Left Review, No. 18*. London: New Left Review, 1963.

Dickstein, Morris. "Black Humor and History: The Early Sixties." *Gates of Eden: American Culture in the Sixties, 1977*, Reprint by Penguin Books, 1989.

Heller, Joseph. *Catch-22*. New York: Everyman's Library, 1995.

Hicks, Granville. "Medals for Madness." *Saturday Review, Vol. XLIV, No. 40*. New York: McCall Corporation, 1961.

Kiley, Frederick and Walter McDonald. *A "Catch-22" Casebook*. New York: Crowell, 1973.

Lindberg, Gary. "Playing for Real." *The Confidence Man in American Literature*. Oxford: Oxford University Press, 1982.

Mailer, Norman. "Some Children of the Goddess." *Contemporary American Novelists*. Illinois: Southern Illinois University Press, 1964.

Meller, James M. "Heller's 'Catch-22'." *The Exploded Form: The Modernist Novel in America*. Urbana, Chicago, and London: University of Illinois Press, 1980.

Merrill, Robert. "The Structure and Meaning of Catch-22." *Studies in American Fiction, Vol.14, No.2*. Boston: Northeastern University's English Department, 1986.

Mitchell, Julian. "Under Mad Gods." *Spectator, Vol. 208, No. 6990*. London: The Spectator Ltd., 1962.

Nagel, James. *Critical Essays on Joseph Heller*. Boston: G. K. Hall, 1984.

http://en.wikipedia.org/wiki/Joseph_Heller 2013-2-15

Kurt Vonnegut

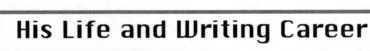

His Life and Writing Career

His Life

Kurt Vonnegut, Jr. (1922—2007) was an American novelist known for works blending satire, black comedy, and science fiction, such as *Slaughterhouse-Five* (1969), *Cat's Cradle* (1963), and *Breakfast of Champions* (1973). He was known for his humanist beliefs as well as being honorary president of the American Humanist Association.

Kurt Vonnegut was born to fifth-generation German-American parents (Kurt Vonnegut, Sr., and Edith née Lieber), son and grandson in the Indianapolis firm Vonnegut & Bohn. He attended Cornell University, where he served as assistant managing editor and associate editor for the student newspaper, the *Cornell Daily Sun*, and majored in chemistry. While attending Cornell, he was a member of the Delta Upsilon Fraternity, following in the footsteps of his father. While at Cornell, Vonnegut enlisted in the US Army. The army sent him to the Carnegie Institute of Technology and the University of Tennessee to study mechanical engineering. On May 14, 1944, Mothers' Day, his mother committed suicide.

Kurt Vonnegut's experience as a soldier and prisoner of war(POW) had a profound influence on his later work. As a private with the 106th Infantry Division, Vonnegut, along with five other battalion scouts, wandered behind enemy lines for several days. They were cut off from their battalion and captured by Wehrmacht troops on December 14, 1944. Imprisoned in Dresden, Vonnegut was chosen as a leader of the POWs because he spoke some German. After insulting some German soldiers that were guarding him he was beaten and had his position as leader taken away. While a prisoner, he witnessed the fire bombing of Dresden in February 1945 which destroyed most of the city.

Vonnegut was one of a group of American prisoners of war to survive the attack in an underground slaughterhouse meat locker used by the Germans as an ad hoc detention facility. The Germans called the building *Schlachthof Fünf* (Slaughterhouse-Five) which the Allied POWs adopted as the name for their prison. Vonnegut said the aftermath of the attack was "utter destruction" and "carnage unfathomable." This experience was the inspiration for his famous novel, *Slaughterhouse-Five*, and is a central theme in at least six of his other books. In *Slaughterhouse-Five* he recalls that the remains of the city resembled the surface of the moon, and that the Germans put the surviving POWs to work, breaking into basements and bomb shelters to gather bodies for mass burial, while German civilians cursed and threw rocks at them. Vonnegut eventually remarked, "There were too many corpses to bury. So instead the Germans sent in troops with flamethrowers. All these civilians' remains were burned to ashes."

Vonnegut was repatriated by Red Army troops in May 1945 at the Saxony-Czechoslovakian border. Upon returning to America, he was awarded a Purple Heart for what he called a "ludicrously negligible wound," later writing in *Timequake* that he was given the decoration after suffering a case of "frostbite."

After the war, Vonnegut attended the University of Chicago as a graduate student in anthropology and also worked at the City News Bureau of Chicago. Vonnegut admitted that he was a poor anthropology student, with one professor remarking that some of the students were going to be professional anthropologists and he was not one of them. According to Vonnegut in *Bagombo Snuff Box*, the university rejected his first thesis on the necessity of accounting for the similarities between Cubist painters and the leaders of late 19th century native American uprisings, saying it was "unprofessional." He left Chicago to work in Schenectady, New York, in public relations for General Electric, where his brother Bernard worked in the research department. The University of Chicago later accepted his novel *Cat's Cradle* as his thesis, citing its anthropological content and awarded him the MA degree in 1971.

In the mid 1950s, Vonnegut worked very briefly for *Sports Illustrated* magazine, where he was assigned to write a piece on a racehorse that had jumped a fence and attempted to run away. He refused and left. On the verge of abandoning writing, Vonnegut was offered a teaching job at the University of Iowa Writers' Workshop. While he was there, *Cat's Cradle* became a best-seller, and he began *Slaughterhouse-Five*, now considered one of the best American novels of the 20th century, appearing on the 100 best lists of *Time* magazine and the Modern Library.

The author's name appears in print as "Kurt Vonnegut, Jr." throughout the first half of his published writing career; beginning with the 1976 publication of *Slapstick*, he dropped the "Jr." and was simply billed as Kurt Vonnegut. His elder brother, Bernard Vonnegut, was an atmospheric scientist at the University at Albany, SUNY, who discovered that silver iodide could be used for cloud seeding, the process of artificially stimulating precipitation.

On November 11, 1999, the asteroid 25399 Vonnegut was named in Vonnegut's honor. On January 31, 2001, a fire destroyed the top story of his home. Vonnegut suffered smoke inhalation and was hospitalized in critical condition for four days. He survived, but his personal archives were destroyed. After leaving the hospital, he recuperated in Northampton, Massachusetts.

Vonnegut smoked unfiltered Pall Mall cigarettes, a habit he referred to as a "classy way to commit suicide."

Vonnegut died on April 11, 2007, in Manhattan, following a fall at his Manhattan home several weeks earlier which resulted in irreversible brain injuries.

His Writing Career

Vonnegut's first short story, "Report on the Barnhouse Effect" appeared in the February 11, 1950 edition of *Collier's* (it has since been reprinted in his short story collection, *Welcome to the Monkey House*). His first novel was the dystopian novel *Player Piano* (1952), in which human workers have been largely replaced by machines. He continued to write short stories before his second novel, *The Sirens of Titan*, was published in 1959. Through the 1960s, the form of his work changed from the relatively orthodox structure of *Cat's Cradle* (which in 1971 earned him a master's degree) to the acclaimed, semi-autobiographical *Slaughterhouse-Five*, given a more experimental structure by using time travel as a plot device.

These structural experiments were continued in *Breakfast of Champions* (1973), which included many rough illustrations, lengthy non-sequiturs and an appearance by the author himself, as a *deus ex machina*.

"This is a very bad book you're writing," I said to myself.
"I know," I said.
"You're afraid you'll kill yourself the way your mother did," I said.
"I know," I said.

Deadeye Dick (1982), although mostly set in the mid-twentieth century, foreshadows the turbulent times of contemporary America; it ends prophetically with the lines "You want to know something? We are still in the Dark Ages. The Dark Ages—they haven't ended yet." The novel explores themes of social isolation and alienation that are particularly relevant in the postmodern world. Society is seen as openly hostile or indifferent at best and popular culture as superficial and excessively materialistic.

Vonnegut attempted suicide in 1984 and later wrote about this in several essays. *Breakfast of Champions* became one of his best-selling novels. It includes, in addition to the author himself, several of Vonnegut's recurring characters. One of them, science fiction author Kilgore Trout, plays a major role and interacts with the author's character.

In much of his work, Vonnegut's own voice is apparent, often filtered through the character of science fiction author Kilgore Trout (whose name is based on that of real-life science fiction writer Theodore Sturgeon), characterized by wild leaps of imagination and a deep cynicism, tempered by humanism. In the foreword to *Breakfast of Champions*, Vonnegut wrote that as a child, he saw men with locomotor ataxia, and it struck him that these men walked like broken machines; it followed that healthy people were working machines, suggesting that humans are helpless prisoners of determinism. Vonnegut also explored this theme in *Slaughterhouse-Five*, in which protagonist Billy Pilgrim "has come unstuck in time" and has so little control over his own life that he cannot even predict which part of it he will be living through from minute to minute. Vonnegut's well-known phrase "So it goes," used ironically in reference to death, also originated in *Slaughterhouse-Five* and became a slogan for anti-Vietnam War protestors in the 1960s. "Its combination of simplicity, irony, and rue is very much in the Vonnegut vein."

With the publication of his novel *Timequake* in 1997, Vonnegut announced his retirement from writing fiction. He continued to write for the magazine *In These Times*, where he was a senior editor, until his death in 2007, focusing on subjects ranging from contemporary US politics to simple observational pieces on topics such as a trip to the post office. In 2005, many of his essays were collected in a new best-selling book titled *A Man Without a Country*, which he insisted would be his last contribution to letters.

The April 2008 issue of *Playboy* featured the first published excerpt from *Armageddon in Retrospect*, the first posthumous collection of Vonnegut's work. The book itself was published in the same month. It included never before published short stories by the writer and a letter that was written to his family during WWII when Vonnegut was captured as a prisoner of war. The book also contains drawings that Vonnegut himself drew and a speech he wrote shortly before his death. The introduction of the book was written by his son, Mark Vonnegut.

Vonnegut was deeply influenced by early socialist labor leaders, especially Indiana natives powers Hapgood and Eugene V. Debs, and he frequently quotes them in his work. He named characters after both Debs (Eugene Debs Hartke in *Hocus Pocus* and Eugene Debs Metzger in *Deadeye Dick*) and Russian communist leader Leon Trotsky (Leon Trotsky Trout in *Galápagos*). He was a lifetime member of the American Civil Liberties Union and was featured in a print advertisement for them.

Vonnegut frequently addressed moral and political issues but rarely dealt with specific political figures until after his retirement from fiction. (Although the downfall of Walter Starbuck, a minor Nixon administration bureaucrat who is the narrator and main character in *Jailbird* (1979), would not have occurred but for the Watergate scandal, the focus is not on the administration.) His collection *God Bless You, Dr. Kevorkian* referenced controversial assisted suicide proponent Jack Kevorkian.

With his columns for *In These Times*, he began a blistering attack on the Bush administration and the Iraq war. "By saying that our leaders are power-drunk chimpanzees, am I in danger of wrecking the morale of our soldiers fighting and dying in the Middle East?" he wrote. "Their morale, like so many bodies, is already shot to pieces. They are being treated, as I never was, like toys a rich kid got for Christmas." *In These Times* quoted him as saying "The only difference between Hitler and Bush is that Hitler was elected."

In *A Man Without a Country*, he wrote that "George W. Bush has gathered around him upper-crust C-students who know no history or geography." He did not regard the 2004 election with much optimism; speaking of Bush and John Kerry, he said that "no matter which one wins, we will have a Skull and Bones President at a time when entire vertebrate species, because of how we have poisoned the topsoil, the waters and the atmosphere, are becoming, hey presto, nothing but skulls and bones."

Vonnegut was descended from a family of German freethinkers, who were skeptical of "conventional religious beliefs." His great-grandfather Clemens Vonnegut had authored a free thought book entitled *Instruction in Morals*, as well as an address for his own funeral in which he denied the existence of God, an afterlife, and Christian doctrines about sin and salvation. Kurt Vonnegut reproduced his great-grandfather's funeral address in his book *Palm Sunday* (1981), and identified these free thought views as his "ancestral religion," declaring it a mystery as to how it was passed on to him.

Vonnegut described himself variously as a skeptic, freethinker, humanist, Unitarian universalist, agnostic, and atheist. He disbelieved in the supernatural, considered religious doctrine to be "so much arbitrary, clearly invented balderdash," and believed people were motivated by loneliness to join religions.

Vonnegut considered humanism to be a modern-day form of free thought, and advocated it in various writings, speeches, and interviews. His ties to organized humanism included membership as a Humanist Laureate in the Council for Secular Humanism's International Academy of Humanism. In 1992, the American Humanist Association(AHA) named him the Humanist of the Year. Vonnegut went on to serve as honorary president of the American Humanist Association, having taken over the position from his late colleague Isaac Asimov, and serving until his own death in 2007. In a letter to AHA members, Vonnegut wrote: "I am a humanist, which means, in part, that I have tried to behave decently without expectations of rewards or punishments after I am dead."

Vonnegut's views on religion were unconventional and nuanced. While rejecting the divinity of Jesus, he was nevertheless an ardent admirer, and believed that Jesus' Beatitudes informed his own humanist outlook. While he often identified himself as an agnostic or atheist, he also frequently spoke of God and despite describing free thought, humanism, and agnosticism as his "ancestral religion," and despite being a Unitarian, he also spoke of himself as being irreligious. In a press release by the American Humanist Association he was claimed to have been "completely secular."

He had published 14 novels such as *Player Piano* (1952), *The Sirens of Titan* (1959), *Mother Night* (1961), *Cat's Cradle* (1963), *God Bless You, Mr. Rosewater; or, Pearls Before Swine* (1965), *Slaughterhouse-Five; or, The Children's Crusade* (1969), *Breakfast of Champions; or, Goodbye Blue Monday* (1973), *Slapstick; or, Lonesome No More* (1976), *Jailbird* (1979), *Deadeye Dick* (1982), *Galápagos* (1985), *Bluebeard* (1987), *Hocus Pocus* (1990), and *Timequake* (1997).

Analysis of and Comment on His Representative Novel

Slaughterhouse-Five (1969)

Plot Summary

The narrator opens with an elaborate hyperbole of a subtitle for the book, explaining that he is a veteran living in easy circumstances, who witnessed the bombing of Dresden, Germany as a prisoner of war and survived to tell the tale in the manner of the planet of Tralfamadore where the flying saucers come from. He went back to Dresden with a war buddy years later. He ends the first chapter saying that his war novel, his novel of looking back is over since there is nothing intelligent one can say about a massacre.

He then tells the story of Billy Pilgrim, who is unstuck in time—he uncontrollably gets flung around the scenes of his life. He was a prisoner of war, became an optometrist, and married a rich girl who died of carbon monoxide poisoning. He was the only survivor of a plane crash. He was abducted and kept in a zoo on the planet Tralfamadore, where he was mated with movie star Montana Wildhack.

With every mention of death in the book, the narrator says, "So it goes," Tralfamadorians believe that time exists all at once and not moment-by-moment like beads on a string. So a person is never dead, because he is still alive in the past. Billy's daughter Barbara is furious at him for trying to tell people his crazy notions.

He wandered behind enemy lines with a fat, sadistic soldier named Roland Weary and two scouts, who ditched them. Weary got so mad at Billy for this that he beat him and when they were captured by German soldiers, he convinced many others that it was Billy's fault when he died. Pre-capture, Billy also traveled to, among other places, his mother's nursing home, where she asked him weakly how she got old, and to the YMCA where his father taught him to swim by throwing him into the deep end. He also goes back to the night of his abduction.

Everyone at the prison camp was shocked to see how weak the Americans were. Billy was delirious, and he flipped out and was hospitalized. Edgar Derby, an older soldier who would be shot for plundering a teapot, stayed with him. Paul Lazzaro, a weak, hateful man, told Billy he had sworn to avenge Roland Weary by shooting him. Billy was not worried; he had seen when he would die. He traveled in time to his second hospitalization during his last year of optometry school. There he met Eliot Rosewater, who introduced him to the science fiction works of Kilgore Trout.

While there, Billy traveled back to Tralfamadore. When he told the crowd at the zoo to fear the power of Earthlings, they thought he was stupid; they knew it would be them, experimenting with a new jet fuel, which would destroy the universe.

Billy and the other soldiers were transferred to Dresden, which was a beautiful city. Billy traveled to the airplane crash, where he mistook the people who rescued him for German soldiers. During surgery, he traveled back to Dresden. In Dresden, he worked at a factory that made malt syrup with vitamins, which everyone illegally spooned. They were kept in slaughterhouse number five. About a month later, the city was bombed, and the prisoners survived in an underground bunker.

At his eighteenth wedding anniversary party, to which he invited Trout after they met in an alley, Billy flipped out; the barbershop quartet reminded him of the Dresden guards.

Years later, in the hospital after the plane crash, Billy met Air Force Historian and war-hawk Bertram Copeland Rumfoord, who told him that the bombing of Dresden was necessary and had to be kept a secret because of all the American "bleeding hearts."

After the crash, Billy escaped to New York, where he snuck onto a radio show to preach his Tralfamadorian wisdom.

In the last chapter, the narrator tells of how he traveled back to Dresden, and how Billy and the other prisoners had been made to dig up corpses from the ruins.

Themes

Fate and Free Will and the Illogical Nature of Human Beings *Slaughterhouse-Five* explores fate and free will and the illogical nature of human beings. Protagonist Billy Pilgrim is unstuck in time, randomly experiencing the events of his life, with no idea of what part he next will visit (re-live)—so, his life does not end with death; he re-lives his death, before its time, an experience often mingled with his other experiences.

Billy Pilgrim says there is no free will; an assertion confirmed by a Tralfamadorian, who says, "I've visited thirty-one inhabited planets in the universe ... Only on Earth is there any talk of free will." The story's central concept: most of humanity is inconsequential; they do what they do, because they must.

To the Tralfamadorians, everything simultaneously exists, therefore, everyone is always alive. They, too, have wars and suffer tragedies (they destroy the universe whilst testing spaceship fuels), but, when Billy asks what they do about wars, they reply that they simply ignore them. The Tralfamadorians counter Vonnegut's true theme: life, as a human being, is only enjoyable with unknowns. Tralfamadorians do not make choices about what they do, but have power only over what they think (the subject of *Timequake*). Vonnegut expounds his position in chapter one, "that writing an anti-war book is like writing an anti-glacier book," both being futile endeavors, since both phenomena are unstoppable. This concept is difficult for Billy to accept, at first.

Vonnegut's other novels, e.g. *The Sirens of Titan*, suggest that the Tralfamadorians, in *Slaughterhouse-Five*, satirize fatalism. The Tralfamadorians represent the belief in war as inevitable. In their hapless destruction of the universe, Vonnegut does not sympathize with their philosophy. To human beings, Vonnegut says, ignoring a war is unacceptable when we have free will.

This human illogicality appears in the climax that occurs, not with the Dresden fire bombing, but with the summary execution of a man who committed a petty theft. Amid all that horror, death, and destruction, time is taken to punish one man. Yet, the time is taken, and Vonnegut takes the outside opinion of the bird asking, "Poo-tee-weet?" The same birdsong ends the novel *God Bless You, Mr. Rosewater*, as the protagonist gives away his fortune to the plaintiffs of hundreds of false paternity suits brought against him—a Dada observation of human absurdity.

Slaughterhouse Five is framed with chapters in the author's voice, about his experience of war, indicating the novel is intimately connected with his life and convictions. That established, Vonnegut withdraws from the unfolding of Billy Pilgrim's story, despite continual appearances as a minor character: in the POW camp latrine, the corpse mines of Dresden, when he mistakenly dials Billy's telephone number. These authorial appearances anchor Billy Pilgrim's life to reality, highlighting his existential struggle to fit in the human world.

Literary Techniques

Black Humor Like *Catch-22* by Joseph Heller, *Slaughterhouse-Five* is also considered a representative work of black humor. It is generally acknowledged that with the publication of novels of black humor such as *Catch-22* (1961), *Cat's Cradle* (1962), and *Slaughterhouse-Five* (1969) that American postmodernist literature formally appeared in the 1960s. The story in *Catch-22* continually employs the refrain "So it goes" when death, dying, and mortality occur, as a narrative transition to another subject, as a memento mori, as comic relief, and to explain the unexplained. It appears one hundred and sixteen times.

Metafiction As a postmodern metafictional novel, the first chapter of *Slaughterhouse-Five* is an author's preface about how he came to write *Slaughterhouse-Five*, apologizing, because the novel is "so short and jumbled and jangled," because "there is nothing intelligent to say about a massacre." As in *Mother Night* (1961), but more extensively, Vonnegut manipulates fiction and reality. The first sentence says: "All this happened, more or less," then appears in Billy Pilgrim's WWⅡ, then followed by the narrator's note: "That was I. That was me. That was the author of this book."

The story repeatedly refers to real and fictional novels and fiction; Billy reads *The Valley of the Dolls* (1966), and skims a Tralfamadorian novel, and participates in a radio talk show, part of a literary expert panel discussing "The Death of the Novel."

The narrator introduces *Slaughterhouse-Five* with the novel's genesis and ends discussing the beginning and the end of the novel. The story proper begins in chapter two, although there is no reason to presume that the first chapter is not fictional. This is a technique common to postmodern metafiction. The story purports to be a disjointed, discontinuous narrative, of Billy Pilgrim's point of view, of being unstuck in time. Vonnegut's writing usually contains such disorder.

The narrator reports that Billy Pilgrim experiences his life discontinuously, wherein he randomly experiences (re-lives) his birth, youth, old age, and death, not in (normal) linear order. There are two narrative threads, Billy's experience of war (itself interrupted with experiences from elsewhere in his life) is mostly linear; and his discontinuous pre-war and post-war lives. Billy's existential perspective was compromised in witnessing Dresden's destruction, although he had come unstuck in time before arriving to Dresden. *Slaughterhouse-Five* is told in short, declarative sentences that impress the sense of reading a report of facts.

The narrator begins the novel telling his connection to the Dresden bombing, why he is recording it, a self-description (of self and book), and of the fact that he believes it is a desperate attempt at scholarly work. He then segues to the story of Billy Pilgrim: "Listen: Billy Pilgrim has come unstuck in time," thus, the transition from the writer's perspective to that of the third-person, omniscient narrator.

Kilgore Trout, whom Billy Pilgrim meets, operating a newspaper delivery business, can be seen as Vonnegut's alter ego, though the two differ in some respects. For example, Trout's career as a science fiction novelist is checkered with thieving publishers, and the fictional author is unaware of his readership.

Slaughterhouse-Five is structured like a Tralfamadorian novel, the literature Billy Pilgrim encounters on Tralfamadore. The only Earth reading available to Billy is a popular novel, *Valley of the Dolls* (1966); asking his captors what they read, he is handed thin booklets with symbols. The Tralfamadorians tell him the symbols represent pleasing thoughts and events. When they are all simultaneously read, as do the Tralfamadorians, it creates an emotion in the reader's mind. Billy's time-tripping juxtaposes his life's events—war, wedding night, travel to father's funeral—mixing black humor, tragedy, and happiness in few paragraphs.

Bibliography

Chen, Shidan. *A Study of American Postmodernist Fiction*. Beijing: Foreign Language Teaching and Research Press, 2010.

Chen, Shidan. *Vonnegut's Art of Postmodernist Fiction*. Beijing: Foreign Language Teaching and Research Press, 2010.

http://en.wikipedia.org/wiki/Kurt_Vonnegut 2013-02-15

http://en.wikipedia.org/wiki/Slaughterhouse-Five 2013-02-15

John Barth

His Life and Writing Career

His Life

John Barth (1930—   ), called "Jack," was born in Cambridge, Maryland. Barth has an elder brother, Bill, and a twin sister, Jill. He briefly studied "elementary theory and advanced orchestration" at Juilliard before attending Johns Hopkins University, from which he received a BA in 1951 and an MA in 1952 (for which he wrote a thesis novel, *The Shirt of Nessus*). Barth was a professor at Pennsylvania State University from 1953 to 1965. During the "American high sixties," he moved to teach at University at Buffalo, the State University of New York from 1965 to 1973. In that period he came to know "the remarkable short fiction" of the Argentine Jorge Luis Borges, which inspired his collection *Lost in the Funhouse*. He then taught at Boston University (visiting professor, 1972—1973) and Johns Hopkins University (1973—1995) before retiring in 1995.

John Barth is the author of *Giles Goat-Boy* (1966), *The Sot-Weed Factor* (1960), and *Chimera* (1972), among many others. His short story collection *Lost in the Funhouse* (1968) and his essay "The Literature of Exhaustion" (1967) have been required reading on college campuses since the 1970s. Barth is widely considered to be among the most important American novelists of the 20th century and one of the foremost practitioners of postmodernism and metafiction. He was born in Cambridge on the eastern shore of Maryland, the grandson of nineteenth-century German immigrants on May 27, 1930. After graduating from high school, Barth briefly attended the Julliard School of Music before enrolling as a scholarship student at John Hopkins University. While an undergraduate, he published two stories in the student literary magazine and "Lilith and the Lion" in the *Hopkins Review*. He married Harriete Anne Strickland on January 11, 1950. He received his BA in creative writing from Hopkins and enrolled in the institution's graduate writing program in 1951. He received a BA in 1951 and an MA in 1952 in Johns Hopkins University. After the birth of his son John in 1952, Barth had to leave graduate school for financial reasons. He accepted a position as an instructor in the English Department at Pennsylvania State University in 1953, and the next year saw the birth of his second son, Daniel. Barth spent the first three months of 1955 writing the first part of *The Floating Opera*, the next three months revising it for his publisher, and the last three months of the year writing *The End of the Road* (1958). Once upon a time, Barth was the hippest writer in America. Nowadays many consider his concerns with the mythical story cycle and the mechanics of storytelling relics from the 1960s. While college students still read stories from *Lost in the Funhouse* in literature classes, his works do not seem to maintain the same kind of cultural resonance as, say, those of Thomas Pynchon or Don DeLillo. It doesn't help that Barth's novels are almost entirely unfilmable, rarely touch on current affairs, and don't trade in self-pity or ingratiating sarcasm or apocalyptic pessimism.

His Writing Career

Barth began his career with *The Floating Opera* (1956). He is also the author of *The End of the Road* (1958), *The Sot-Weed Factor* (1960), *Giles Goat-Boy* (1966), *Lost in the Funhouse: Fiction for Print, Tape, Live Voice* (1968), *Chimera* (1972), *Letters: A Novel* (1979), *Sabbatical: A Romance* (1982), *Tidewater Tales: A Novel* (1987), *The Last Voyage of Somebody the Sailor* (1991), *Once upon a Time: A Floating Opera* (1994), *On with the Story* (1996), *Coming Soon!!!: A Narrative* (2003), *The Book of Ten Nights and a Night: Eleven Stories* (2004), and *Where Three*

Roads Meet: Novellas (2005). *The Floating Opera* and *The End of the Road* are two short realist novels that deal wittily with controversial topics, suicide and abortion respectively. They are straightforward realistic tales; as Barth later remarked, they "didn't know they were novels." *The Sot-weed Factor*, was initially intended as the completing novel of a trilogy comprising his first two realist novels, but, as a consequence of Barth's maturation as a writer, it developed into a different project. The novel is significant as it marked Barth's discovery of postmodernism. Barth's next novel, *Giles Goat-Boy* (about 800 pages), is a speculative fiction based on the conceit of the university as universe. A boy raised as a goat discovers his humanity and becomes a savior in a story presented as a computer tape given to Barth, who denies that it is his work. In the course of the novel Giles carries out all the tasks prescribed by Joseph Campbell in "The Hero with a Thousand Faces." Barth kept a list of the tasks taped to his wall while he was writing the book. The short story collection *Lost in the Funhouse* and the novella collection *Chimera* are even more metafictional than their two predecessors, foregrounding the writing process and presenting achievements such as a seven-deep nested quotation. *Chimera* shared the US National Book Award for fiction. In the novel *Letters* (1979), Barth interacts with characters from his first six books. His 1994 *Once upon a Time: A Floating Opera* reuses stock characters, stock situations and formulas. Styles, approaches and artistic criteria Barth's work is characterized by a historical awareness of literary tradition and by the practice of rewriting typical of postmodernism. He said: "I don't know what my view of history is, but insofar as it involves some allowance for repetition and recurrence, reorchestration, and reprise [...] I would always want it to be more in the form of a thing circling out and out and becoming more inclusive each time." In Barth's postmodern sensibility, parody is a central device. Around 1972, in an interview, Barth declared that "The process [of making a novel] is the content, more or less."

Barth's fiction continues to maintain a precarious balance between postmodern self-consciousness and wordplay and the sympathetic characterization and "page-turning" plotting commonly associated with more traditional genres and subgenres of classic and contemporary storytelling. While writing these books, Barth was also pondering and discussing the theoretical problems of fiction writing. In 1967 he wrote a highly influential and some controversial essay considered a manifesto of postmodernism, "The Literature of Exhaustion" (first printed in *The Atlantic*, 1967). It depicts literary realism as a "used-up" tradition; Barth's description of his own work, which many thought illustrated a core trait of postmodernism, is "novels which imitate the form of a novel, by an author who imitates the role of author." The essay was widely considered a statement of "the death of the novel" (compare with Roland Barthes' "The Death of the Author"). Barth has since insisted that he was merely making clear that a particular stage in history was passing, and pointing to possible directions from there. He later (in 1980) wrote a follow-up essay, "The Literature of Replenishment," to clarify the point.

Barth's novel *The End of the Road* was published in 1958 and nominated for the National

Book Award. Barth's awards and honors include National Book Award nominations for *The Floating Opera* and *Lost in the Funhouse*, and the Award itself for *Chimera*. He also won a Brandeis University Creative Arts Award in 1965, a Rockefeller Foundation grant for 1965—1966, a National Institute of Arts and Letters grant in 1966, and an honorary LittD degree from Johns Hopkins in 1973. Barth is widely considered to be among the most important American novelists of the 20th century and one of the foremost practitioners of postmodernism and metafiction.

Analysis of and Comment on His Representative Novel

The Sot-Weed Factor (1960)

Plot Summary

The Sot-Weed Factor was initially intended as the completing novel of a trilogy comprising his first two realist novels, but, as a consequence of Barth's maturation as a writer, it developed into a different project. The novel is significant as it marked Barth's discovery of postmodernism. The novel is a satirical epic of the colonization of Maryland based on the life of an actual poet, Ebenezer Cooke, who wrote a poem of the same title. *The Sot-Weed Factor* (which means "tobacco salesman") introduces Barth's penchant for fancy wordplay, ontological tricks, historical parody, and existential games. The book is a bare-knuckled satire of humanity at large and the grandiose costume romance, done with meticulous skill in imitation of such eighteenth-century picaresque novelists as Fielding, Smollett, and Sterne.

The novel is set in the 1680s and 1690s in London and on the eastern shore of the colony of Maryland. It tells the story of an English poet named Ebenezer Cooke who is given the title "Poet Laureate of Maryland" by Charles Calvert. He undergoes many adventures on his journey to Maryland and while in Maryland, all the while striving to preserve his innocence (i.e. his virginity). The book takes its title from the grand poem that Cooke composes throughout the story, which was originally intended to sing the praises of Maryland, but ends up being a biting satire based on his disillusioning experiences. *The Sot-Weed Factor* was initially intended, with Barth's first two, as the concluding novel on a trilogy on nihilism, but the project took a different direction as a consequence of Barth's maturation as a writer. The novel takes its title from a poem of the same name published in London in 1708 and signed Ebenezer Cooke. "Sot-weed" is an old term for the tobacco plant. A "factor" is a middleman who buys something to resell it.

The novel parodies, mimics, recuperates, and rewrites the forms of the 18th century genre of the Bildungsroman (formation novel) and Künstlerroman (novel on the formation of an artist), and in particular Henry Fielding's *Tom Jones* (1749), Laurence Sterne's *Tristram Shandy* (1759— 1767), and Samuel Richardson's three epistolary novels. The narrative presents Ebenezer as a Künstlerroman hero. The novel is also a parody of the picaresque genre, in particular of *Tristram Shandy* and *Tom Jones*. *The Sot-Weed Factor* is ushered into a special category of literature: it is seemingly received into that hall of infamy, barred to the ordinary reader by the champions of prudishness, and thrown open only by future enlightened generations—the rogue's gallery inhabited by, for example, D. H. Lawrence and *Lady Chatterley's Lover* (1928), and Vladimir Nabokov and *Lolita* (1955). The first edition was written during four years, and published by Doubleday in 1960, consisting of about 800 pages. Barth revised the text for a new edition issue in 1967 by another publisher, dried off by 60 pages. In 1987, the revised edition was reissued by the original publisher, in the Doubleday Anchor Edition series, with an added foreword. The novel has been translated to several languages, including Italian, Japanese, and others. *Time* included it in its TIME 100 Best English-language Novels from 1923 to 2005.

In *The Sot-Weed Factor*, born in America, with a twin sister Anna, Ebenezer is raised in England towards the close of the seventeenth century and tutored by one Henry Burlingame III. Subconsciously in live with his sister, Ebenezer decides to become a poet and remain a virgin for the rest of his life, thus devoting himself to the sublimation of sex through words. He rejects the advances of the whore Joan Toast, offering her his pure love instead. Named Poet Laureate of Maryland by Lord Baltimore, the proprietor of the province, who happens to be Henry Burlingame in disguise, he sets out for America in order to sing the New World's praise in a long epic poem which he intends to call Marylandiad. Yet after his encounters with life in an American colony, he writes a satiric poem entitled *The Sot-Weed Factor* instead. Unbeknownst to him, Ebenezer has been followed by Joan Toast, who has fallen in love with him. She ultimately becomes his wife, after enduring every sort of physical illness and psychic humiliation imaginable. Through a string of unforeseen occurrences she can re-bestow on her husband the title to Malden, his father's former estate in Maryland, which Ebenezer, through inexperience and wrongheaded idealism, had lost shortly after his arrival in America. However, Joan insists that he first consummate their marriage despite the fact that she suffers from syphilis. Thus, Ebenezer loses his innocence, if not his health. When Joan Toast dies shortly after wedding, Ebenezer, disillusioned, lives out his life together with his twin sister Anna. Together they raise Anna's son, Henry Burlingame's child. Following his successful sexual union with Anna, Burlingame, the "anti-hero" of the novel, who is as many-faced in attitude and appearance as Ebenezer is single-minded and constant, disappears from history, civilization, and the novel's plot, although Barth's later novels will be haunted by his descendants. Ebenezer Cooke's *The Sot-Weed Factor* is published and later revised.

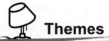

Themes

The Sot-Weed Factor pretends to "re-write" the satirical poem, first published in 1708, of one Ebenezer Cooke, poet Laureate of Maryland. Cooke and his poem in fact existed, and the sot-weed of the title is tobacco, in which the factor traded. Since it is only through words that the historical eighteenth-century Ebenezer Cooke can be revived, the fictional twentieth-century Ebenezer Cooke must pay the price for this revival by remaining within the realm of words, and becoming the plaything of Barth's fiction. This is not just the condition, but the principle of his existence. When Ebenezer, who has vowed to remain a virgin, eventually breaks his vow in order to consummate his marriage with the former whore Joan Toast, he and his author must both lay down their pens, for "pen" and "penis," both tools of productivity, cannot be employed at the same time. Thus, in *The Sot-Weed Factor*, Sigmund Freud's notion that literature is a sublimation of unfulfilled sexual desire is taken literally and consequently parodied; for whereas words flow seemingly without difficulty, sex is their ultimate "end." When physical and spiritual productivity become severed from one another, when, that is, one is but delimited by the other, then both are reduced to a quantitative measure, and values are leveled. This applies particularly the genre of Bildungsroman, since the idea of Bildung is dependent on individual advancement through conscious choice, the preference of one set of rules over another. *The Sot-Weed Factor* can indeed be described as Bildungsroman, a description of the character development of the protagonist Ebenezer Cooke, whose unfounded idealism, after being thwarted time and again by his harsh encounters with reality, is ultimately replaced with a pragmatic attitude toward life. Thus, Ebenezer seems to pursue the well-trodden path of the American youth's initiation into life, originating in innocence and terminating in experience.

Literary Techniques

The novel takes its title from a poem of the same name published in London in 1708 and signed Ebenezer Cooke. "Sot-weed" is an old term for the tobacco plant. A "factor" is a middleman who buys something to resell it. As Barth explained: "*The Sot-Weed Factor* began with the title and, of course, Ebenezer Cooke's original poem... Nobody knows where the real chap is buried; I made up a grave for Ebenezer because I wanted to write his epitaph."

Barth also made extensive use of the few pieces of information known at the time about the historical Cooke, his assumed father and grandfather, both called Andrew Cooke, and his sister, Anna.

The novel parodies, mimics, recuperates, and rewrites the forms of the 18th century genre of the Bildungsroman (formation novel) and Künstlerroman (novel on the formation of an artist), and in particular Fielding's *Tom Jones*, Sterne's *Tristram Shandy*, and Samuel Richardson's three epistolary novels. The narrative presents Ebenezer as a Künstlerroman hero. The novel is also a parody of the picaresque genre, in particular of *Tristram Shandy* and *Tom Jones*.

Bibliography

Betts, Richard A. "The Joke as Informing Principle in *The Sot-Weed Factor*." *College Literature 10, No.1*. Pennsylvania: West Chester University, 1983. 38–49.

Bowen, Zack. *A Reader's Guide to John Barth*. London: Greenwood Press, 1994.

Dippie, Brain. "'His Visage Wild; His Form Exotick': Indian Themes and Cultural Guilt in John Barth's *The Sot-Weed Factor*." *American Quarterly 21*. Baltimore: Johns Hopkins University Press, 1969. 113–121.

Diser, Philip. "The Historical Ebenezer Cooke." *Critique 10, No. 3*. London: Glasgow University, 1968. 48–59.

Fiedler, Leslie. "John Barth: An Eccentric Genius." *On Contemporary Literature*. Ed. Richard Kostelanetz. New York: Avon Books, 1964.

Gladsky, T. S. "*The Sot-Weed Factor* as Historiography." *Publication of the Arkansas Philological Association 7, No. 2*. Arkansas: Arkansas Philological Association, 1981. 37–47.

Kostelanetz, Richard. *The New American Arts*. New York: Horizon Press, 1965.

Miller, Russsell H. "*The Sot-Weed Factor*: A Contemporary Mock-Epic." *Critique: Studies in Modern Fiction 8, No. 2*. CA: Bolingbroke Society, Heldref Publications, 1965—1966. 88–100.

Puetz, Manfred. "John Barth's *The Sot-Weed Factor*: The Pitfalls of Mythopoesis." *Critical Essays on John Barth*. Ed. Joseph J. Waldmeir. Boston: G. K. Hall, 1980.

Ziegler, Heide. *John Barth*. New York: Methuen Co. Ltd, 1987.

http://en.wikipedia.org/wiki/John_Barth 2013-2-15

http://www.dave-edelman.com/barth/ 2013-2-15

Donald Barthelme

His Life and Writing Career

His Life

Donald Barthelme (1931—1989) was born on April 7 in Philadelphia in 1931. His parents had attended the University of Pennsylvania. His father was a noted architect, who was trained in the beaux arts tradition of meticulous draftsmanship, soon moved the family to Houston, where, much in advance of his time, he developed an interest in the modernism of Le Corbusier, Mies van der Rohe, and Alvar Aalto, who, Barthelme noted, were interested not only in aesthetics but in the possibility of improving human existence. Their influence, which Barthelme acknowledges as visually and spiritually important to him, was felt most immediately in the home his father designed for the family. Barthelme describes it as somewhat weird, although beautiful and similar to Mies van der Rohe's Tugendhat House. Barthelme was interested not only in aesthetics but in the possibility of improving human existence. Though he contends there is very little autobiography in his work, Barthelme acknowledges the influence of his mother, who he describes as a "wicked wit." Barthelme's association with contemporary painters and his interest in contemporary painting and literature did not so much serve to provide models for his own writing as a sense of the possibilities open to a writer. He received his education in Texas, where he attended the University of Houston as a journalism major and worked for the *Houston Post*. He founded the University of Houston *Forum*, a literary journal. In 1974—1975, Barthelme served as a distinguished visiting professor of English at the City College of the City University of New York. He has been placed in the front rank of postmodernist writers along with John Barth, John Hawkes, Thomas Pynchon, and Italo Calvino. Donald Barthelme died of cancer in Houston on July 23, 1989. He was 58 years old. Barthelme fondly recalled childhood visits with his grandfather, a rancher and lumber dealer in Galveston, whose home on the Guadalupe River not far from San Antonio the writer described as "a wonderful place to ride and hunt, talk to catfish and try to make the windmill run backward." With the appropriate changes, those encounters with the windmill at times appear to reflect the way in which much of his fiction is written.

In 1951, as a student, he wrote his first articles for the *Houston Post*. Two years later, Barthelme was drafted into the US Army, arriving in Korea on July 27, 1953, the day of the signing of the *Korean Armistice Agreement*, which ended the Korean War. He served briefly as the editor of an army newspaper before returning to the US and his job at the *Houston Post*. Once back, he continued his studies at the University of Houston, studying philosophy. Although he continued to take classes until 1957, he never received a degree. He spent much of his free time in Houston's black jazz clubs, listening to musical innovators such as Lionel Hampton and Peck Kelly, an experience that influenced his later writing.

Barthelme's relationship with his father was a struggle between a rebellious son and a demanding father. In later years they would have tremendous arguments about the kinds of literature in which Barthelme was interested and which he wrote. While in many ways his father was avant-garde in art and aesthetics, he did not approve of the post modern and deconstruction schools. Barthelme's attitude toward his father is delineated in the novels *The Dead Father* and

The King as he is pictured in the characters King Arthur and Lancelot. Barthelme's independence also shows in his moving away from the family's Roman Catholicism (his mother was especially devout), a separation that troubled Barthelme throughout his life as did the distance with his father. He seemed much closer to his mother and agreeable to her strictures.

Barthelme went on to teach for brief periods at Boston University, University at Buffalo, and the College of the City of New York, where he served as distinguished visiting professor from 1974 to 1975. His brothers Frederick (born in 1943) and Steven (born in 1947) are also respected fiction writers.

 ## His Writing Career

Barthelme would go on to write over a hundred more short stories, first collected in *City Life* (1970), *Sadness* (1972), *Amateurs* (1976), *Great Days* (1979), and *Overnight to Many Distant Cities* (1983). Many of these stories were later reprinted and slightly revised for the collections *Sixty Stories* (1981), *Forty Stories* (1987) and, posthumously, *Flying to America* (2007). Though primarily known for these stories, Barthelme also produced four novels characterized by the same fragmentary style: *Snow White* (1967), *The Dead Father* (1975), *Paradise* (1986), and *The King* (1990, posthumous). In 1971, he won the National Book Award in the juvenile literary category for his book *The Slightly Irregular Fire Engine*; *or the Hithering Thithering Djinn*, which he also illustrated. Donald Barthelme died of cancer in Houston on July 23, 1989.

In 1961, Barthelme became director of the Contemporary Arts Museum in Houston; he published his first short story the same year. His New Yorker publication, "L'Lapse," a parody of Michelangelo Antonioni's film L'Eclisse, followed in 1963. The magazine would go on to publish much of Barthelme's early output, including such now famous stories as "Me and Miss Mandible," the tale of a 35-year-old sent to elementary school by either a clerical error or failing at his job as an insurance adjuster and failing in his marriage, and "A Shower of Gold," in which a sculptor agrees to appear on the existentialist game show "Who Am I?" In 1964, Barthelme collected his early stories in *Come Back, Dr. Caligari*, for which he received considerable critical acclaim as an innovator of the short story form. His style (fictional and popular figures in absurd situations, e.g., the Batman-inspired "The Joker's Greatest Triumph"), spawned a number of imitators and would help to define the next several decades of short fiction.

Barthelme continued his success in the short story form with "Unspeakable Practices" and "Unnatural Acts" (1968). One widely anthologized story from this collection, "The Balloon," appears to reflect on Barthelme's own intentions as an artist. The narrator of the tale inflates a giant, irregular balloon over most of Manhattan, causing widely divergent reactions in the populace. Children play across its top, enjoying it quite literally on a surface level; adults attempt to read meaning into it, but are baffled by its ever-changing shape; the authorities attempt to destroy it, but fail. Only in the final paragraph does the reader learn that the narrator has inflated the balloon for purely personal reasons, and sees no intrinsic meaning in the balloon itself, a metaphor for the amorphous, uncertain nature of Barthelme's fiction. Other notable stories from this collection include "The Indian Uprising," a mad collage of a Comanche attack on a modern city, and "Robert Kennedy Saved From Drowning," a series of vignettes showing the difficulties of truly knowing a public figure; the latter story appeared in print only two months before the real Kennedy's 1968 assassination.

Barthelme also wrote the nonfictional *Guilty Pleasures* (1974). His other writings have been posthumously gathered into two collections, "The Teachings of Don B.: Satires," "Parodies," "Fables, Illustrated Stories," and "Plays of Donald Barthelme" (1992), and "Not-Knowing: The Essays" and "Interviews" (1997). With his daughter, he wrote the children's book *The Slightly Irregular Fire Engine*, which received the 1972 National Book Award in category children's books. He was also a director of PEN and the Author's Guild, and a member of the American Academy and Institute of Arts and Letters.

Analysis of and Comment on His Representative Novel

Snow White (1965)

Plot Summary

Snow White, published first in *The New Yorker* in 1965 and then in hard cover in a slightly different novel. The plot of *Snow White* follows the broad outline of the fairy tale of that name, and the characters are vaguely analogous to the characters in the fairy tale. A consideration of Barthelme's treatment of character and plot in *Snow White* will reveal how far Barthelme departs from the conventional treatment of these elements and how well *Snow White* operates within the formula that we have defined. *Snow White* opens with what can only be called a map: "She is a tall dark beauty containing a great many beauty spots: one above the breast, one above the belly, one above the knee, one above the ankle, one above the buttock, one on the back of the neck. All of these are on the left side, more or less in a row as you go up and down." What follows are six printer's bullets, set in a straight vertical line that leads to a single sentence: "The hair is black as ebony, the skin white as snow". Snow White, 22, is a college graduate. A section describing her education, which she later refers to as her training in "the finest graces and arts," reveals a conscious attempt to fashion herself in the image of a renaissance woman: "She studied *Modern Woman, Her Privileges and Responsibilities*: the nature and nurture of women and what they stand for, in evolution and in history, including householding, upbringing, peacekeeping, healing, and devotion, and how these contribute to the rehumanizing of today's world." And in typical Barthelme anticlimactic juxtaposition: "Then she studied *Classical guitar I*, utilizing the models and techniques of Sor, Tarrega, Segovia, etc." This is followed by: "Then she studied *English Romantic Poets II*: Shelley, Byron, Keats". "Then she studied *Theoretical Foundations of Psychology*: mind, consciousness, unconscious mind, personality, the self, interpersonal relations, psychosexual norms, social games, groups, adjustment, conflict, authority, individuation, integration, and mental health. Then she studied *Oil Painting I* ...," followed by a list of the 12 paints she was told to bring to the first class. It goes on: "*Personal Resources I and II*: self-evaluation, developing the courage to respond to the environment, opening and using the mind, individual experience, training, the use of time, mature redefinition of goals, action project," and, finally, "*Realism and Idealism in the Contemporary Italian Novel*" with a list of 17 Italian writers, and ending at a stroke with the fragment "Then she studied—" The eclecticism of all this reflects her superficiality. The original *Schneewittchen* or her Disney counterpart would never give a thought to being a renaissance woman. This is a setup for failure, not only of imagination, as she says, but a failure of quest.

These old and often funny juxtapositions of Barthelme's have a disjunctive function, quite the opposite of Hawthorn's embroidery of paranormal events onto history. Mentioned are the following: a horror film, a sexual advance, a dry martini garnished with a picked onion, a trout garnished with almonds, God, a Polish film, Snow White's reputation, and the name of an esoteric religious philosopher read by Snow White when she sulks in her room. Rather than flowing with the narrative, each of these stands apart, and with the appearance of a name like Teilhard de Chardin, impedes it. The jackdaw again, a glittering accretion. Snow White's seven housemates manufacture and distribute Chinese-style baby food with labels like *Baby Dow Shew*, bean curd stuffed with ground pike; *Baby Gai Goon*, chicken, bean sprouts and cabbage; and *Baby Pie Guat*, pork and oysters in soy sauce. Despite occasional ups and downs—"The grade of pork ears we are using in the Baby Ding Sam Dew is not capable of meeting US Govt. standards, or indeed, any standards"—the business has been lucrative: "It is amazing how many mothers will spring for an attractively packed jar of Baby dim Sum, a tasty-looking potlet of Baby Jing Shar Shew Bow. Heigh-ho." The recipes came from their father, who had always told them, "Try to be a man about whom nothing is known." Such a man was their father: "Nothing is known about whom nothing is known." Such a man was their father: "Nothing is known about him still. He gave us the recipes. He was not very interesting."

Themes

Love, sympathy, and satisfactoriness all have disappeared in the postmodern world. The seven wonder how life would be if they got into another line of work: "God know what. We do what we do without thinking. One tends the vats and washes the buildings and carries the money to the vault and never stops for a moment to consider that the whole process may be despicable." Before Snow White entered their lives, "There was equanimity for all. We washed the buildings, tended the vats, wended our way to the county cathouse once a week (heigh-ho). Like everybody else. We were simple bourgeois. We knew what to do." But everything has changed since the day came upon her wandering in the forest, hungry and distraught, and gave her food. "Now we do not know what to do. Snow White has added a dimension of confusion and misery to our lives. Whereas once we were simple bourgeois who knew what to do, now we are complex bourgeois who are at a loss. We do not like this complexity." It is on a Monday that Snow White "let[s] down her hair black as ebony form the window." She says, "This motif, the long hair streaming from the high window, is a very ancient one I believe, found in many cultures, in various forms. Now I recapitulate it, for the astonishment of the vulgar and the refreshment of my venereal life." The hair generates public reaction. Two old men remark, "You need a Paul or Paul-figure for that sort of activity. Probably Paul is even now standing in the wings, girding his pants for his entrance." Actually, Paul is in his bath, trying to get over a case of nerves caused by seeing the hair black as ebony on his way back from the Unemployment Office.

Snow White, meanwhile, becomes agitated by the 200 people watching her. She wishes she were on the beach at St. Tropez, "surrounded by brown boys without a penny. Here everyone has a penny. Here everyone worships the almighty penny." She laments: "O Jerusalem, Jerusalem! Thy daughters are burning with torpor and a sense of immense wasted potential, like one of those pipes you see in oil fields, burning off the natural gas that it isn't economically rational to ship somewhere!" Although this passage could be one of the targets of Barthelme's self-accusation, one joke too many, it does make the point that real men are in short supply for the daughters.

As more is revealed about Snow White—she's alternately bored, unpredictable, compulsive, narcissistic, and without "a pinch of emotion coloring the jet black of her jet-black eyes"—a fine tension is set up between what she's supposed to be and what she is here. Certainly, she's physically similar to the Disney version, and to the original *Schneewittchen* in the German tale of the Brothers Grimm collection. What happens in Barthelme's novel is that the *Schneewittchen* becomes the *doppelganger*, the ghostly double haunting and weaving a spell over her postmodern counterpart, who knows the old story and the role she's supposed to play. The contrarieties at work here—the impostor, her hoax and pretenses, and the other characters with their consciousness of self and awareness of the story on which they are based, each trying to play the role of their counterpart in the original—generate disharmony and greater tension. And they're all double minded. If only we make a little contrast between it and the original "Snow White" in *Grimm's Fairy Tales*, we can go beyond its own surface layer without depths and obtain such a new meaning: in the postmodern world, love, sympathy, and satisfactoriness all have disappeared and similarly morality and even logic do not exist any more.

Literary Techniques

Short-Short Story Barthelme's short stories are often exceptionally compact (a form sometimes called "short-short story," "flash fiction," or "sudden fiction"), often focusing only on incident rather than complete narratives. (He did, however, write some longer stories with more traditional narrative arcs.) At first, these stories contained short epiphanic moments. Later in his career, the stories were not consciously philosophical or symbolic. His fiction had its admirers and detractors, being hailed as profoundly disciplined or derided as meaningless and academic postmodernism. Barthelme's thoughts and works were largely the result of 20th-century angst as he read extensively, for example in Pascal, Husserl, Heidegger, Kierkegaard, Ionesco, Beckett, Sartre, and Camus.

Collage Barthelme's stories typically avoid traditional plot structures, relying instead on a steady accumulation of seemingly-unrelated details. By subverting the reader's expectations through constant nonsequiturs, Barthelme creates a hopelessly fragmented verbal collage reminiscent of such modernist works as T. S. Eliot's "The Waste Land" and James Joyce's *Ulysses*, whose linguistic experiments he often challenged. However, Barthelme's fundamental skepticism and irony distanced him from the modernists' belief in the power of art to reconstruct society, leading most critics to class him as a postmodernist writer. Literary critics have noted that Barthelme, like the French poet Stéphane Mallarmé, whom he admired, plays with the meanings of words, relying on poetic intuition to spark new connections of ideas buried in the expressions and conventional responses.

Illustrations Another Barthelme device was breaking up a tale with illustrations culled from mostly 19th century popular publications, collaged, and appended with ironic captions; Barthelme called his cutting up and pasting together pictures "a secret vice gone public." One of the pieces in the collection Guilty Pleasures, called "The Expedition," featured a full-page illustration of a collision between ships, with the caption "Not our fault!"

Accumulation of Seemingly-unrelated Details Barthelme's stories typically avoid traditional plot structures, relying instead on a steady accumulation of seemingly-unrelated details. He maintains words are not inert, but furiously busy. In that moment, fiction does not so much provide a compensatory or even distractive balance to the inadequacy of experience— sexual, marital, filial, even, it turns out, linguistic. Rather it immerses the reader directly in that experience. Accordingly readers have difficulty identifying in his work a narrative voice outside the action which connects it to a system of values or beliefs, even to a designated set of attitudes or feelings that would allow them to interpret a story or indicate how they are expected to react to it. His prescription for fiction cannot be read literally. What his fiction draws upon most of all is the ability of language to look both ways—transparently toward the world and self, apparently toward the mediating function of other words upon each other. What emerges as a defining element of Barthelme's fiction is a tendency which, like abstract painting, is significant for what it subtracts from conventional form. There is no linear development (beginning, middle, and end) either within his stories or from one collection to the next. Motivation remains unclear or, at best, arbitrary. Within the narrative there is no focus which allows for development, no clear indication of an agent whose purpose generates the action, an antagonist or natural force who opposes this purpose, a deepening or complication of the circumstances, and a final confrontation followed by a resolution which points up or explains the significance of what has happened. Irony is very much a tonal element in his fiction; but it is an element which itself proves subject to ironic challenge and which finally gives way to appreciation of the sensuous moment whose transient quality at once occasions pain and is a cause for celebration. For Barthelme, the joke occurs, if anywhere, in the disparity between the response the reader is prepared to make and the one the text actually invites.

Drawing upon Common Art Forms   Barthelme's fiction, especially in its approach to language, has much in common with the cultural tendency to draw upon common art forms— the Wild West show, the music hall tradition, the comic strip—that Pauline Kael points to in her celebrated essay "Trash, Art and the Movies." The enjoyment of these films, Kael argues, comes often despite the audience's knowledge of the actors and of the circumstances in which the films are made, often, in fact, as a result of the presence created by the actor in a series of roles in previous movies. Accordingly, she concludes, unlike pure art, movies may be enjoyed for many reasons that have little to do with the story or the subtleties of theme or character, and so are more open and unlimited. In Barthelme's fiction, the catalog neither nostalgically commemorates the objects or events that evoke a historical moment nor plays with the seemingly infinite elaborations of reality that present themselves to the literary imagination. Its intent, in fact, is not so much illustration or expansion at all as it is the celebration of reality through repetition. Unlike those found in Whitman, Barthelme's catalogs do not name things which, almost mystically, exist by virtue of an incantatory act that demonstrates a unity in time and space. That unity does inform Barthelme's enumeration, but it does not call things into being or magically summon their presence; it reminds the reader of their unique and unknowable nature.

Bibliography

Arnason, H. H. *History of Modern Art*. New York: Harry N. Abrams, 1986.

Barth, John. "Thinking Man's Minimalist: Honoring Barthelme." *The New York Times Book Review, Vol. 94*. New York: New York Times Co., 1989.

Bartheleme, Donald. "Not-Knowing." *Major Writers of Short Fiction: Stories and Commentarie*s. Ed. Ann Charters, Boston: Bedford Books of St. Martin's Press, 1993. 113–24.

——. *Snow White*. New York: Atheneum, 1972.

Bernhard, Thomas. *The President & Eve of Retirement*. Trans. Gitta Honegger. New York: Performing Arts Journal Publications, 1982.

Handke, Peter. *Kaspar and Other Plays*. Trans. Michael Roloff. New York: Farrar, Straus and Giroux, 1969.

Hern, Nicholas. *Peter Handke*. New York: Frederick Ungar Publishing Co., 1972.

Herzinger, Kim, ed. *The Teachings of Don B: Satires, Parodies, Fables, Illustrated Stories, and Plays of Donald Barthelme*. New York: Turtle Bay Books, 1992.

Hudgens, Michael Thomas. *Donald Barthelme Postmodernist American Writer*. New York: The Edwin Mellen Press, 2001.

Kael, Pauline. "Trash, Art, and the Movies." *Going Steady*. Boston: Little, Brown, 1970. 85–129.

McCaffery, Larry. "An Interview with Donald Barthelme." *Anything Can Happen: Interview with Contemporary American Novelists*. Eds. Thomas LeClair and McCaffery. Urbana: University of Illinois Press, 1983. 32–44.

O'Hara, J. D. "Donald Barthelme: The Art of Fiction LXVI." *The Paris Review*. New York: The Paris Review Fourdation, Inc., 1981. 180–210.

Schlueter, June. *The Plays and Novels of Peter Handke*. Pittsburgh: University of Pittsburgh Press, 1981.

Trachtenberg, Stanley. *Understanding Donald Barthelme*. Columbia: University of South Carolina Press, 1990.

Venturi, Robert. *Complexity and Contradiction in Architecture, 2nd Ed*. New York: Museum of Modern Art, 1977.

http://en.wikipedia.org/wiki/Donald_barthelme 2013-2-15

Thomas Pynchon

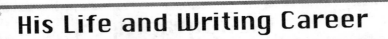

His Life and Writing Career

His Life

Perhaps the most acclaimed and the most elusive of the postmodernists, Thomas Pynchon (1937—   ) is generally regarded as a figure whose writing is unprecedented yet somehow entirely representative of the fiction of a particular age. It is often remarked that Pynchon is to postmodernism what James Joyce to modernism. Pynchon's work, *Gravity's Rainbow* (1973), which was a co-winner of the National Book Award, is regarded as the model for postmodern fictions and has spawned a vast industry of interpreters and devoted students, determined to pursue every lead in the text and decode every reference.

Thomas Ruggles Pynchon, Jr. was born on May 8, 1937, in Glen Cove, New York, one of three children of Thomas Ruggles Pynchon, Sr., and Katherine Frances Bennett Pynchon. The family moved when Pynchon was a child. His father became town supervisor of Oyster Bay, New York, and later an industrial surveyor. Pynchon graduated from Oyster Bay High School in 1953 at age 16 with distinction in English. He received a scholarship to Cornell University and took engineering and physics classes until he left school during his sophomore year, in 1955, for service in the navy. He returned to Cornell two years later and took classes in English, including a course taught by Vladimir Nabokov (who did not remember him). Pynchon was on the editorial staff of the *Cornell Writer*, which published his first short story, "The Small Rain," in 1959. He graduated with distinction that year.

Pynchon had several options after graduating, including pursuing a number of fellowships, teaching creative writing at Cornell, becoming a disk jockey, or working as a film critic for *Esquire*. He published many short stories, including "Mortality and Mercy in Vienna" in *Epoch* (1959), "Low-lands" in *New World Writing* (1960), and "Under the Rose" in *The Noble Savage* (1961). He also began work on his first novel, *V.* (1963), while in New York and in Seattle, where he worked writing technical documents for the Boeing Company until 1962. He finished *V.* in California and Mexico and in 1963. *V.* was published and won the William Faulkner Foundation Award for best first novel of the year. *V.* is a whimsical, cynically absurd tale of a middle-aged Englishman's search for an elusive, adventuresome, supernatural woman. The object of the Englishman's search appears in various guises at critical periods in European history. Of his few short stories, most notable are "Entropy" (1960), a neatly structured tale in which Pynchon first used extensive technical language and scientific metaphors, and "The Secret Integration" (1964), a story in which Pynchon explored small-town bigotry and racism.

His second novel, *The Crying of Lot 49* (1966), won the Richard and Hilda Rosenthal Foundation Award of the National Institute of Arts and Letters. In the book, Pynchon described a woman's quest to discover the mysterious, conspiratorial Tristero System in a futuristic world of closed societies. The novel served a condemnation of modern industrialization. Pynchon wrote "A Journey into the Mind of Watts" for the *New York Times Magazine* (1966). He worked on *Gravity's Rainbow* for several years and in 1974 that novel shared the National Book Award for fiction with Issac Bashevis Singer's *Crown of Feathers*. *Gravity's Rainbow* was set in an area of post-World War II Germany called "the Zone." It centered on the wanderings of a US soldier who is one of many odd characters looking for a secret V-2 rocket that will supposedly break through the Earth's gravitational barrier when launched. The narrative is filled with descriptions of obsessive and paranoid fantasies, grotesque imagery, and esoteric mathematical and scientific language. Many critics deemed *Gravity's Rainbow* a visionary apocalyptic masterpiece. Judges unanimously selected *Gravity's Rainbow* for the Pulitzer Prize in literature, but the Pulitzer advisory board overruled the selection, saying the book was "unreadable," "turgid," "overwritten," and "obscene." No prize was given that year. *Gravity's Rainbow* was also awarded the William Dean Howells Medal of the American Academy of Arts and Letters in 1975, but Pynchon declined the award, suggesting that it be given to another author. In a letter, he wrote, "The Howells Medal is a great honor, and being gold, probably a good hedge against inflation, too. But I don't want it. Please don't impose on me something I don't want. It makes the Academy look arbitrary and me look rude... I know I should behave with more class, but there appears to be only one way to say no, and that's no."

Pynchon has remained elusive to his fans—his 1953 high school yearbook still provides his most recent photographic portrait. He has done best to make himself "disappear" as a biographical persona (no mean feat in the era of mass media) in order to speak only through his art. Pynchon's only deliberate emergence into public world (aside from his publications) was his 2004 "appearance" in *The Simpsons* episode "Diatribe of a Mad Housewife", where he stood outside his house with a paper bag over his head with holes cut out for the eyes, before a flashing neon sign declaring "Thomas Pynchon's House—Come on In" (Season 15, episode 10).

Many of Pynchon's early short stories were collected in 1984 under the title *Slow Learner* (1984) with the autobiographical notes by the author. Pynchon was awarded the John D. and Catherine T. MacArthur Foundation Fellowship in 1989. His novel *Vineland* was published in 1990 and *Mason and Dixon*, another novel, appeared in 1997. In recent years, two other novels of Pynchon were published, *Against the Day* (2006), and *Inherent Vice* (2009).

His Writing Career

Pynchon has been his own fiercest critic. In an introductory essay to his early stories, *Slow Learner* (1984), he has said that his fundamental problem when he began writing was an inclination "to begin with a theme, symbol, or other unifying agent, and then try to force characters and events to conform to it." His books are this self-criticism or not, it is clear that Pynchon laid down his intellectual cards early. This very important postmodernist novelist expresses complicated and profound ideas by his language games such as black humor, outlandish puns, slapsticks, running gags, parodies, and ridiculous names. The protagonists in Pynchon's novels all live in the confusion of postmodern existence reflected by the structure of fictional fragments and they undertake vague but very conscientious quests, attempting to discover their own identities and find out meaning and order in their life.

The title of his first important short story is "Entropy" (1960). It contains specific references to Henry Adams; and it follows carefully the Adams formulation, "Chaos was the law of nature; Order was the dream of man." The use of entropy as a figure for civilization running down was to become structurally formative in his later fiction. So was his use of two kinds of characters, alternative central figures first sketched out here. The situation in "Entropy" is simply and deliberately schematic. There is a downstairs and upstairs apartment. Downstairs, a character called Meatball Mulligan is holding a lease-breaking party, which moves gradually towards chaos and consequent torpor. Upstairs, another character, an intellectual called Callisto, is trying to warm a freezing bird back to life. In his room he maintains a small hothouse jungle, referred to as a "Rousseau-like fantasy." "Hermetically sealed, it was a tiny enclave in the city's chaos," the reader is told, "alien to the vagaries of the weather, national politics, of any civil disorder." The room is a fantasy, a dream of order, in which Callisto has "perfected its ecological balance." But the room leaves him in paralysis, the dream does not work; the bird dies, and Callisto's girlfriend, realizing that he is "helpless in the past", smashes the window of their hermetically sealed retreat, breaking the shell surrounding his fantasy life. Meatball Mulligan, meanwhile, does what he can to stop his party "deteriorating into total chaos" by tidying up, calming his guests, getting things mended.

"Entropy," in this way, mediates between binary opposites: which are the opposites of modern consciousness and culture. There is the pragmatist, active to the point of excess, doing what he can with the particular scene, working inside the chaos to mitigate it. And there is the theorist, passive to the point of paralysis, trying to shape and figure the cosmic process, standing outside as much as he can, constructing patterns for the chaos to explain it. Meatball is immersed, drowning in the riotous present; Callisto is imprisoned in the hermetically sealed glasshouse of the past. The text, which here and later is the dominant presence in Pynchon's writing, is the interface between these two figures, these two systems or levels of experience. As such, it sketches out human alternatives in a multiverse where mind and matter are steadily heading for extinction. Or, it may be, the alternatives of hyperactivity and containment, the open and the closed, between which the individual consciousness constantly vacillates. The two are not, in any event, mutually exclusive. To an extent, what Pynchon does in his work is to give a decidedly postmodernist spin to perennial American preoccupations. In the tradition of the American jeremiad, he presents a culture, if not bound for heaven, then bent towards hell, its own form of apocalypse or heat death. And in the grain American writing structured around the figures of the wilderness and the clearing, he develops a sometimes bewildering series of systems, human and non-human, built around the fundamental, formative principles of spatial openness and closure, immersion and separation, the flexible and the fixed, the signified and the signifier—a world that is a totality of things, data, and a world that is totality of fact, signs.

In his first novel, *V.* Pynchon returned to two formative characters recalling Callisto and Meatball in the shape of Hubert Stencil and Benny Profane. The book confirms its author's sense of the modern world as an entropic waste land, inhabited by men and women dedicated to the annihilation of all animatedness. It is bounded by dead landscapes, urban, mechanical, underground. A populous narrative, it is also packed with characters who are ciphers: seeing others and themselves not as people but as things, objects, they lapse into roles, masquerade and cliche. Blown along the mean streets, and even meaner sewers, of this story, Benny Profane, on the one hand, is a schlemiel, the suffering absurd comedian of Jewish lore. A faded copy of a picaro, he drifts through life in such enterprises as hunting alligators underneath New York City; it is there, in fact, in the darkness and oblivion of the sewers, that he finds his greatest comfort and peace. Hubert Stencil, on the other hand, searches the world for V., the mysterious female spy and anarchist who is by turns Venus, Virgin, and Void and seems to be everywhere and nowhere. Stencil appears to be on a significant quest. Described as "a century's child" and born in 1901, he is pursuing the remnants of the Virgin in the world of the Dynamo. His father, a former British spy, has left behind enigmatic clues pointing to a vast conspiracy in modern history. So, whereas Profane lives in a world of sightlessness without signs or discernible patters, Stencil enters a world of elusive signs and apparent patterns, all gravitating towards an absent presence, the lady V. His quest is for a fulcrum identity. In a sense, he is given an outline identity by his search, since he thinks of himself as "quite purely He who looks for V. (and whatever impersonations that might involve)." It is also for the identity of modern times. Using the oblique strategy of "attack and avoid," Stencil moves through many of the major events of the twentieth century, seeking to recover the master plot, the meanings of modern history and this book. The only meaning found, however, is the erasure of meaning: the emptying of a significant human history and its sacrifice to mechanism and mass. The purposiveness of Stencil, it turns out, and the purposelessness of Profane are both forms of "yo-yoing" movement, often violent oscillation, bereft of all significance except the elemental one of postponing inanimatedness.

Almost the last reported words of V. are "How pleasant to watch nothing." In his subsequent fiction, Pynchon has continued this watching, and searching, the boundlessness of "nothing" in a variety of fictional guises. In his second novel, *The Crying of Lot 49* (1966), the main character, Oedipa Mass, learns that her onetime lover, Pierce Inverarity, has made her an executor of his estate. Now he is dead, she sets out to investigate Inverarity's property: an investigation that leads to the discovery of what she takes to be a conspiratorial underground communications system dating back to the sixteenth century. Following the clues, she finally believes she will solve the enigma through a mysterious bidder keen to buy Inverarity's stamp collection. But the novel ends with the enigma unsolved, the plot and its meaning unresolved, as Oedipa awaits the crying out at the auction of the relevant lot number 49. The subject and its significance still wait to be located. So do they in *Gravity's Rainbow* (1973), Pynchon's third novel. Set in the closing years of the Second World War, the story here, a complex web of plots and counterplots, involves a Nazi Lieutenant Weissman, disguised as a mysterious Captain Blicero, and an American sleuth, Lieutenant Tyrone Slothrop, while V-2 rockets rain down London. Weissman, it appears, was once the lover of V.: in this elaborately intertextual world, Pynchon's texts echo his own as well as the texts of others. The gravitations of mood are characteristic: from black humor to lyricism to science fiction to fantasy. So is the feeling the reader experiences, while reading this book, that he or she is encountering not so much different levels of meaning or reality as different planes in fictive space, with each plane in its shadow box proving to be a false bottom, in an evidently infinite regression. So also, finally, is the suspicion of conspiracy: *Gravity's Rainbow* explores the possibility that, as one character puts it, "war was never political at all, the politics was all theater, all just to keep the people distracted."

Since *Gravity's Rainbow*, Pynchon has moved forwards to the landscape of the 1980s and, through ample reminiscence, the 1960s in *Vineland* (1990). Then, he has moved back to the early republic in *Mason and Dixon* (1997), to the days when men like the two famous surveyors mentioned in the title were trying to establish boundaries in the boundlessness of America, in order to appropriate it. America is memorably described in this novel as "a very Rubbish-Tip for subjunctive hopes, for all that may yet be true." It is the realm, the landscape that inhabits all Pynchon's fiction: the realm of measurelessness and dream, the indicative and the subjunctive, the closed and appropriated and the open. And it is typical of the author that he should weave his speculations on legends, the rich "Rubbish-Tip" of dreams ("Does Britannia when she sleeps, dream?" one character asks, "Is America her dream?"), into a densely populated social fabric and a meditation on historical decline. The fictive energy of Pynchon seems inexhaustible, not least because it careers with tireless energy between contraries. But to an extent, what drives it is summed up in one simple question one central character asks the other in his novel: "Good Christ, Dixon. What are we about?"

Analysis of and Comment on His Representative Novel

Gravity's Rainbow (1973)

 Plot Summary

Gravity's Rainbow is a novel of such vastness and range that it defies—with a determination unusual even in this age of "difficult" books—any inclusive summary. There are over 400 characters—we should perhaps say "names," since the ontological status of the figures that drift and stream across the pages is radically uncertain. There are many discernible, or half-discernible plots. These plots touch and intersect, or diverge and separate, involving characters who don't appear until the closing pages of the novel or who are introduced into the plot and then don't appear again at all. The following is only a very brief, elliptical summary trying to get the gist of the book.

Gravity's Rainbow is composed of four parts: "Beyond the Zero," "Un Perm' au Casino Hermann Goering," " In the Zone," and "The Counterforce."

In "Beyond the Zero," the opening pages of the novel follow Pirate Prentice, first in his dreams, and later around his house in wartime London. Pirate then goes to work at ACHTUNG, a top-secret military branch, with Roger Mexico and Pointsman, who both worked there at the time. It is here the reader is introduced to the possibly promiscuous US Army lieutenant named Tyrone Slothrop, whose erratic story becomes the main plot throughout most of the novel. It is noted that each of Slothrop's sexual encounters in London precedes a V-2 rocket hit in the same place by several days. Both Slothrop's encounters and the rocket sites match the Poisson Distributions calculated by Roger Mexico, leading into reflections on topics as broad as determinism, the reverse flow of time, and the sexuality of the rocket itself. Slothrop meets a woman named Katje, and they fall in love, maintaining a relationship until Slothrop's sudden removal to Germany in Part Three.

In Part Two, "Un Perm' au Casino Hermann Goering," Slothrop is studied covertly and sent away by superiors in mysterious circumstances to the Hermann Göring casino in recently liberated France, in which almost the entirety of Part Two takes place. There he learns of a rocket, with the irregular serial number 00000, and a component called the S-Gerät (short for Schwarzgerät, which translates to black device) which is made out of the hitherto unknown plastic Imipolex G. Early in Part Two, the octopus attacks Katje on the beach, and Slothrop is "conveniently" at hand to rescue her. Their romance begins here, extending into Part Three and the events that follow. It is hinted at that Slothrop's prescience of rocket hits is due to being conditioned as an infant by the creator of Imipolex G, Laszlo Jamf. Later, the reality of this story is called into question in a similar fashion as the existence of Slothrop's original sexual exploits was. After getting this information, Slothrop escapes from the casino into the coalescing post-war waste land of Europe, "the Zone," searching for the 00000 and S-Gerät. In the closing of Part Two, Katje is revealed to be safe in England, enjoying a day at the beach with Roger Mexico and Jessica, as well as Pointsman, who is in charge of Slothrop's furtive supervision. While unable to contact Slothrop (or prohibited from contacting him), Katje continues to follow his actions through Pointsman.

In Part Three "In the Zone," Slothrop's quest continues for some time as he is chased by other characters. Slothrop meets and has an extended relationship with Margherita Erdman, a pornographic film actress and masochist. Originally meeting her in an abandoned studio in the Zone, it is she who leads him on to the Anubis, a ferry on which many different characters travel at various times. Here, Slothrop later also has extended encounters with her twelve-year-old daughter Bianca, though it is unclear whether or not he has stopped his casual relationship with Margherita by this time. Towards the end of this section, several characters not seen since early in the novel make a return, including Pirate Prentice, in his first appearance since the novel's very start. "In the Zone" also contains the longest episode of the book, a lengthy tale of Franz Pökler, a rocket engineer unwittingly set to assist on the S-Gerät's production. The story details Pökler's annual meetings with his daughter Ilse, and his growing paranoia that Ilse is really a series of impostors sent each year to mollify him. The story ultimately reveals that the 00000 was fired in the spring of 1945, close to the end of the war. Slothrop spends much of the time as his invented alter-ego Rocketman, wearing an operatic Viking costume with the horns removed from the helmet, making it look like a rocket nose-cone. Rocketman completes various tasks for his own and others' purposes, including retrieving a large stash of hashish from the centre of the Potsdam Conference. This continues until he leaves the region for northern Germany, continuing his quest for the 00000, as well as answers to his past. It becomes steadily apparent that Slothrop is somehow connected to Dr. Laszlo Jamf, and a series of experiments performed on him as a child.

Slothrop later returns to the Anubis to find Bianca dead, a possible trigger for his impending decline. He continues his pilgrimage through northern Germany, at various stages donning the identities of a Russian colonel and mythical Pig Hero in turn, in search of more information on his childhood and the 00000. Unfortunately, he is repeatedly sidetracked until his persona fragments totally in Part Four, despite the efforts of some to save him. Throughout "The Counterforce," there are several brief, hallucinatory stories, of superheroes, silly Kamikaze pilots, and immortal sentient light bulbs. These are presumed to be the product of Slothrop's finally collapsed mind.

At the same time, other characters' narratives begin to collapse as well, with some characters taking a bizarre trip through Hell, and others flying into nothingness on Zeppelins. Slothrop's narrative ends a surprisingly long time before the novel's end, which focuses more on the 00000, and the people associated with its construction and launch.

Towards the end of "The Counterforce," it transpires that the S-Gerät is actually a capsule crafted by Blicero to contain a human. The story of the 00000's launch is largely told in flashbacks by the narrator, while in the present Enzian is constructing and preparing its successor, the 00001 (which isn't fired within the scope of the novel), though it is unknown who is intended to be sacrificed in this model. In the flashbacks, the maniacal Captain Blicero prepares to assemble and fire the 00000, and asks Gottfried to sacrifice himself inside the rocket. He launches the rocket in a pseudo sexual act of sacrifice with his bound adolescent sex slave Gottfried, captive within its S-Gerät. At the end of a final episode, told partially in second person, the rocket descends upon Britain. The text halts, in the middle of a song composed by Slothrop's ancestor, with a complete obliteration of narrative as the 00000 lands (or is about to land) on a cinema. Thus the novel opens and closes in wartime Britain, and opens and closes with the landing of a V-2 rocket.

 ## Themes

An Expanded Thinking About Death   One theme of the novel is considered to be an expanded thinking about death. Pynchon mixes up true details and fantastic events, contains comic and cruel scenes, evolves extensive and symbolic deducibilities and offers several perspectives about historical events. Pynchon implies that the western society, by perfecting destructive weapons like the German rocket bomb V-2, actively accelerates the death culture. He also hints that the progress of science and technology is wrongly used in historical patterns, politics, economy, social values, and especially the war effort in human world.

Continual Returns to Ideas Related to Metaphysics   Another theme is his continual returns to ideas related to metaphysics, a branch of philosophy that studies fundamental questions of reality and existence. The novel questions what is real, how one is able to discern reality, and whether there actually is any reality at all. Its complex plot can be seen as a search for causes of death and a quest to discover who or what it is (if anything) that controls the world.

Paranoia   Paranoia, "the onset, the leading edge, of the discovery that everything is connected," is also emphasized in *Gravity's Rainbow*. Slothrop's paranoia appears in various guises, ranging from his suspicion that the rock-bombs falling on London have his name written on them to his fantasy that he is the intended victim of a Father Conspiracy. According to Richard Locke, megalomaniac paranoia is the "operative emotion" behind the novel, and an increasingly central motivator for the many main characters. In many cases, this paranoia proves to be vindicated, as the many plots of the novel become increasingly interconnected, revolving around the identity and purpose of the elusive 00000 rocket and Schwarzgerät.

 Literary Techniques

Symbolism　Symbolism is richer in *Gravity's Rainbow* than in Pynchon's other novels, all of it coming together around the image of the V-2 rocket, which was the German weapon against which there was no defense, just as the American apocalyptic threat was the atomic bomb. All of the themes, characters, and episodes of the novel coalesce around the frightening missile which is a symbol simultaneously of science and technology triumphant even while reason has utterly fled, since the device has no purpose but mass destruction. At the end of the book, Pynchon tightens the screw by not merely giving the reader a questing main character to identify with, but also by placing the reader in the novel as part of an audience in a theater waiting while the rocket descends on their helpless heads.

Encyclopedic Fantasy　Pynchon's encyclopedic fantasy operates through mixed styles and breaks the boundaries between high culture and pop culture by utilizing brilliant improvisations, tall talks, obscene parables, and burlesque stage routines, all of which work together into a story of supersonic capabilities and annihilative retributions. As the four main and the countless subsidiary plots take shape, characters—and the reader as well—attempt to "read" the messages flickering, the dumb intent to communicate, in the most casual as well as the most portentous sign. Pynchon's knowingness and fascination with popular culture are overwhelmingly evident in *Gravity's Rainbow* as is his preoccupation with the lore of theoretical science, of obscure historical tales, and of contemporary comic books. No one denies the formidably encyclopedic nature of this astonishing effort.

Actual Events and Locations　Additionally, the novel uses many actual events and locations as backdrops to establish chronological order and setting within the complex structure of the book. Examples include the appearance of a photograph of Wernher Von Braun in which his arm is in a cast. Historical documents indicate the time and place of an accident which broke Von Braun's arm, thereby providing crucial structural details around which the reader can reconstruct Slothrop's journey.

Parable　The novel's title is a reference to the parabolic trajectory of a V-2 rocket: the "rainbow-shaped" path created by the missile as it moves under the influence of gravity, subsequent to the engine's deactivation; it is also thought to refer to the "shape" of the plot, which many critics such as Weisenburger have found to be cyclical or circular, like the true shape of a rainbow.

Flashbacks　The story of the rocket is told in flashbacks, along with the revelation that it was fired in 1945. The Schwarzgerät is revealed to have been a capsule designed to contain a human being. The novel ends mid-sentence as the rocket is about to hit its target, raising the possibility that the readers themselves are killed in the blast. The novel also opens with the striking of a V-2 rocket, forming a narrative circle of "rainbow" that mimics the arc of the V-2 rocket in flight.

An Omniscient Narrator Pynchon employs an omniscient narrator as a consciousness that interprets and recreates experiential reality. The consciousness of the narrator of *Gravity's Rainbow* is the screen on which the action of the novel is flashed as he tries to comprehend the apparent chaos of his time and to create an interpretive historical and cultural overview of it. *Gravity's Rainbow* revels in the juxtaposition of different voices. Steven Weisenburger's *A Gravity's Rainbow Companion* lists the "formal discourses" we encounter in the book: Hebrew, German, Kazkh, Russian, Spanish, French, Japanese, and Herero, mixed with "informal discourses" as "popular slang" (jokes, song lyrics, street speech), "ethnica usage" (black English) and "folk usage" (folktales, children's games) etc. Reading Pynchon, then is a matter of being immersed in a constant stream of different voices, an impression deepened by his characteristic long, rhythmical, parenthetical sentences.

Gravity's Rainbow is engaged with Europe at the end of the Second World War and just after. In choosing to situate his novel at this point in time, Pynchon is concentrating on a crucial moment when a new transpolitical order began to merge out of the ruins of old orders that could no longer maintain themselves. At one point he describes the movements of displaced people at the end of the war, "a great frontierless streaming." The sentences that follow mime out this "frontierless" condition in an extraordinary flow of objects and people, and conclude: "so the populations move, across the open meadow, limping, marching, shuffling, carried, hauling along the detritus of an order, a European and bourgeois order they don't yet know is destroyed forever." A later passage suggests what is taking the place of this vanished order. "Oh, a State begins to take form in the stateless German night, a State that spans oceans and surface politics, sovereign as the International or the Church of Rome, and the Rocket is its soul."

Bibliography

Baym, Nina, ed. *The Norton Anthology of American Literature, Shorter Fifth Edition*. New York & London: W. W. Norton & Company, 1999. 2476–2478.

Chambers, Judith. *Thomas Pynchon*. New York: Twayne Publishers, 1992. 2–13, 123–183.

Chen, Shidan. *A Study of American Postmodernist Fiction*. Tianjin: Nankai University Press, 2010. 153–181.

Geyh, Paula, et al. ed. *Postmodern American Fiction: A Norton Anthology*. New York and London: W. W. Norton & Company, 1997. 4.

Gray, Richard. *A History of American Literature*. Cornwall: Blackwell Publishing Ltd., 2004. 728–733.

Newman, Robert D. *Understanding Thomas Pynchon*. Columbia, S.C.: University of South Carolina Press, 1986. 1–11, 89–137.

Nicol, Bran. *The Cambridge Introduction of Postmodern Fiction*. Cambridge U.K. and New York: Cambridge University Press, 2009. 89–98.

Oakes, Elizabeth H. *American Writers*. New York: Facts on File, Inc., 2004. 284–286.

Sanders, Scott. "Pynchon's Paranoid History." *Twentieth Century Literature, Vol. 21*. New York: Hofstra University, 1975. 177–192.

Siegel, Mark R. "Creative Paranoia: Understanding the System of *Gravity's Rainbow*." *Critique, Vol. 18*. London: Glasgow University, 1977. 39–54.

Tanner, Tony. *Thomas Pynchon*. London and New York: Methuen, 1982. 11–19, 74–91.

http://en.wikipedia.org/wiki/Gravity%27s_rainbow 2013-02-15

http://en.wikipedia.org/wiki/Gravity%27s_rainbow 2013-02-15

http://www.bookrags.com/shortguide-gravitys-rainbow/techniques.html 2013-02-15

http://www.bookdrum.com/books/gravitys-rainbow/9780099533214/summary.html 2013-02-15

Vladimir Nabokov

His Life and Writing Career

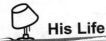

His Life

Best known as the author of *Lolita* (1955), one of the most controversial novels of the 20th century, Vladimir Nabokov (1899—1977) wrote dozens of novels, as well as several collections of poetry, which were highly praised for their eloquence and stylistic innovations. Also revered as the preeminent postmodern writer due to his metafiction *Pale Fire* (1962), his work influenced the development of postmodernism in American literature.

Vladimir Nabokov was born in St. Petersburg, Russia, on (or about) April 23, 1899, into a prominent and well-to-do, educated family. He was the oldest of five children born to his father, a distinguished liberal aristocratic jurist and member of Kerensky's government, and his mother, Elena Ivanovna, a wealthy member of the Russian nobility whose family was noted for its artistic achievements. He is said to have inherited his sensitive and artistic nature from his mother and his work ethic and love of butterflies from his father.

Nabokov's family routinely spoke French, Russian, and English around the house, which had a great effect on the development of Nabokov's linguistic talents. The tutors who assisted with his education at home instructed him and his siblings in all three languages. In 1911, he began attending the highly respected Tenishev School.

When the Bolshevik revolution broke out, the Nabokov children and their mother left St. Petersburg for Yalta, in the Crimea, where a friend had an estate. Nabokov's father remained in St. Petersburg and accepted a position in the provisional government following Czar Nicholas II's abdication, but after his imprisonment by the Bolsheviks, the senior Nabokov fled to Crimea, as well, where the family remained for approximately 18 months, at which time they went into exile in Europe.

Nabokov went to school in England, attending Trinity College, Cambridge, from 1919 to 1922. He originally studied zoology but eventually switched to Romance and Slavic languages. He wrote two volumes of poetry in Russian during these years, which were published in 1923. In 1922, he moved to Berlin, Germany, where his family now resided. That same year, his father was murdered by a reactionary White Russian who later became a Nazi official. Nabokov married Vera Slonim in 1925 and lived in Berlin with her and their son, Dimitri, who was born in 1934, until 1937, writing for the Russian newspaper his father had founded under the pseudonym of Vladimir Sirin. He also coached tennis and boxing and composed chess problems and crosswords. Many of his early Russian novels were published during these years in Berlin including *Mashen'ka* (1926; *Mary*, 1970), *Korol', dama, valet* (1928; *King, Queen, Knave*, 1968), *Zashchita* (1930; *The Defense*, 1964), *Podvig* (1933; *Glory*, 1972), and *Camera obscura* (1933; revised and translated as *Laughter in the Dark*, 1938). Other Russian works were *Otchayaniye* (1936; *Despair*, 1937), *Dar* (1937; *The Gift*, 1963), and *Priglashenie na kazn* (1938; *Invitation to a Beheading*, 1959).

With the Nazi regime's rise to power, Nabokov became disgusted with Germany and fearful due to his wife's Jewish heritage. The family moved to Paris, where Nabokov met the Irish writer James Joyce, wrote several books in French, and wrote his first novel in English, *The Real Life of Sebastian Knight*, which was published 1941. It concerns a young Russian in Paris, the narrator, who discovers the true nature of his half-brother, an English novelist, while writing his biography. Nabokov decided at around this time that English was the language in which he should write in order to have the best prospects in publishing, but when he was unable to secure a position teaching in an English university, the Nabokov family moved once again, this time to the United States.

Nabokov settled with his family in 1940 in Boston and worked as a professor of English literature at Wellesley College from 1941 to 1948. In 1948, he took a position as a professor of Russian literature at Cornell University, where he remained until 1959, and became a research fellow in entomology at Harvard, pursuing his lifelong interest in butterflies. In all, Nabokov wrote 18 papers on entomology, some of which deal with his discovery and description of new species.

In 1945, Nabokov became a US citizen. His novel, *Bend Sinister*, was published in 1947, about a politically uncommitted professor in a totalitarian state who tries to maintain personal integrity. Many of his short stories and poems appeared in the *New Yorker* during this period. His next novel, *Lolita*, which established his fortune, his reputation for some and his notoriety for others, was originally denied publication in the United States and Britain and so was first published in Paris in 1955. After censorship problems were resolved, the American publication appeared in 1958, which brought Nabokov instant fame and wealth. A film version (the first of two) was made of *Lolita* in 1962, directed by Stanley Kubrick. Within a few years, Nabokov gave up his teaching position at Cornell to focus entirely on his writing. He moved to Montreux, Switzerland, and lived the rest of his life at the Montreux Palace Hotel.

Nabokov's other novels written in English include *Pnin* (1957), *Pale Fire* (1962), *Ada, or Ardor: a Family Chronicle* (1969), *Transparent Things* (1972), and *Look at the Harlequins* (1974). His books of short stores include *Nabokov's Dozen* (1958), *Tyrants Destroyed* (1975), and *The Stories of Vladimir Nabokov* (1955), a posthumous collection that includes 13 previously unpublished stories. In addition to the two books of poetry he published in Russian, Nabokov wrote one book of poems in English, entitled simply *Poems*. It appeared in 1959. He also wrote several scholarly works of nonfiction—*Nikolai Gogol* (1944), a critical study of the 19th-century Russian writer; *Strong Opinions* (1973), a collection of his answers to questions about himself, art and public issues; *Lectures on Literature* (1980); and *Lectures on Russian Literature* (1981). He translated the novel *Eugene Onegin* by Alexander Pushkin and published the four-volume work with commentaries in 1964. He also wrote two autobiographical works. *Speak, Memory* (1966) is a compelling account of his childhood in Russia. It originally appeared under the title *Conclusive Evidence* in a shorter form in 1951.

Nabokov received the American National Medal for literature in 1977, but enjoyed few other awards during his lifetime. He declined election to the National Institute of Arts and Letters, preferring a quiet life of writing and studying butterflies. Vladimir Nabokov died on July 2, 1977, in Montreux of a mysterious lung ailment.

His Writing Career

Nabokov first treaded into the literary field with the aid of his native language, Russian. Critics generally consider that his early novels written in Russian are more autobiographical but less significant compared with his later ones written in English, which brought him international distinction. *Lolita* was controversial for its explicit portrayal of a sexual relationship between a pathetic middle-aged professor Humbert Humbert and his 12-year-old step-daughter. It became a classic postmodern novel because it expertly weaves numerous well-known literary devices in creating a parody of the romance novel. Critics have generally read the book as a satire, though Nabokov himself rejected the label. In *Lolita*, Nabokov exhibits the love of intricate word play and synaesthetic detail that characterized all his works. The novel was ranked at No. 4 in the list of the Modern Library 100 Best Novels. *Pale Fire* (1962) was ranked at No. 53 on the same list. His memoir, *Speak, Memory,* was listed No. 8 on the Modern Library nonfiction list.

As a novelist of formidable erudition, Nabokov's fictions are informed by clever wordplay, descriptive detail, multilingual puns, anagrams, and coinages of terms. He combined satire and social commentary with complex explorations of time and memory.

Nabokov embraced the view that would become increasingly popular in twentieth-century art and fiction, namely the self-referential nature of the literary text, its "extract of personal reality," and the inherently collaborative role of the reader. Writing in *Lectures on Literature*, Nabokov said that "the good reader is one who has imagination, memory, a dictionary, and some artistic sense—which sense I propose to develop in myself and in others whenever I have the chance."

All of the works by Nabokov reflects, in some way, his aesthetic of subjective idealism. All of it plays variations on the observation made by the academic commentator Kinbote in *Pale Fire*: "'reality' is neither the subject nor the object of true art," he observes, "which creates its own special reality having nothing to do with the average 'reality' perceived by the communal eye." "To be sure, there is an average reality, perceived by all of us," Nabokov admits in *Strong Opinion*. "But that is not true reality: it is only the reality of general ideas, conventional forms of humdrum, current editorials." "Average reality," Nabokov insists, "begins to rot and stink as soon as the act of individual creation ceases to animate a subjectively perceived texture." Any book he makes, any art anyone makes that is worth reading, is "a subjective and specific affair," Nabokov suggests. It is the creative act that effectively maintains reality just as—and the analogy is his—electricity binds the earth together. As a writer, a creator, he has "no purpose at all when composing the stuff except to compose it." "I work long, on a body of words," as Nabokov puts it, "until it grants me complete possession and pleasure." According to this subjective idealist creed, there can be no totalizing, totalitarian reading of experience, no monolithic entity entitled "life." There is only the "manifold shimmer" of separate, specific lives, *my* life, *your* life, *his* life or *her* life. As Nabokov has it, "life does not exist without a possessive epithet." Nor is there some kind of absolute truth or absolute morality disclose. "Reality is an infinite succession of stops, levels of perception, false bottoms, and hence unquenchable, unattainable," Nabokov argues. "You can never get near enough"; and so "whatever the mind grasps it does so with the assistance of creative fancy, that drop of water on a glass slide which gives distinction and relief to the observed organism." There is no place here for naturalism or didacticism. "I am neither a reader nor a writer of didactic fiction," Nabokov confesses. "Why do I write books, after all? For the sake of pleasure, for the sake of the difficulty." "*Lolita* has no moral in tow," he adds. "For me a work of fiction exists only insofar as it affords me what I bluntly call aesthetic bliss." That bliss is the triumph of art, for Nabokov. Its tragedy is suggested by an anecdote Nabokov tells about the original inspiration for *Lolita*, which is a story about an ape who, after months of coaxing, produced the first ever drawing by an animal. "This sketch showed the bars of the poor creature's cage."

In *Lolita*, Humbert, the narrator, is constantly teasing and eluding his audience by using a style both outrageously lyrical and outrageously jokey. He tells his reader "I shall not exist if you do not imagine me." Undercutting what might seem predictably valid responses, he plays on the whole literary history of dubious anti-heroes and duplicitous first-person protagonist from Diderot to Dostovesky. "I am writing this under observation," Humbert admits. Within the narrative, this is literal, since he is in the psychiatric ward of the prison waiting for his trial for murdering Lolita's new lover. But Humbert is, additionally acutely aware of being under our observation as well. That helps to make his story slippery, his character protean, and his language radically, magically self-referential. Like all Nabokov's novels, but even more than most, *Lolita* is a verbal game, a maze: what one character in *Pale Fire* christens a "lexical playfield."

Analysis of and Comment on His Representative Novel

Pale Fire (1962)

 ## Plot Summary

Pale Fire is written in very strange form. It consists of four parts: an allegedly posthumous autobiographical poem "Pale Fire" in heroic couplets of 999 lines by a fictional professor and poet John Shade and Foreword, Commentary and Index by another fictional figure, the self-appointed editor, Charles Kinbote.

Shade's poem consists of four cantos full of reminiscences in which the prominent 61-year-old poet and professor tells in detail his trivial matters in his life: his parents who were both ornithologists, brought him up and lived in the house in New Wye where he has lived all his life; his special sensitivity that he has had from his childhood and accompanies him even when he is in a fitful state of unconsciousness; his gentle and soft emotions to his wife who was his high school sweetheart; his deep love for his fat but intelligent daughter who committed suicide; his methods of writing poems and his philosophical thinking of life, death, and afterlife.

Charles Kinbote, the refugee professor who is a neighbor of Shade, is given permission by Shade's wife Sybil to be in charge of annotating and editing the poem. He adds foreword, commentary, and index to the poem. In Kinbote's editorial contributions, he tells three stories intermixed with each other. One is his own story, notably including what he thinks of as his friendship with Shade. After Shade was murdered, Kinbote acquired the manuscript, including some variants, and has taken it upon himself to oversee the poem's publication, telling readers that it lacks only line 1,000. Kinbote's second story deals with King Charles II, "The Beloved," the deposed king of Zembla. King Charles escaped imprisonment by Soviet-backed revolutionaries, making use of a secret passage and brave adherents in disguise. Kinbote repeatedly claims that he inspired Shade to write the poem by recounting King Charles' escape to him and that possible allusions to the king, and to Zembla, appear in Shade's poem, especially in rejected drafts. However, no explicit reference to King Charles is to be found in the poem. Kinbote's third story is that of Gradus, an assassin dispatched by the new rulers of Zembla to kill the exiled King Charles. Gradus makes his way from Zembla through Europe and America to New Wye, suffering comic mishaps. In the last note, to the missing line 1,000, Kinbote narrates how Gradus killed Shade by mistake.

The reader soon realizes that Kinbote is King Charles, living incognito—or, though Kinbote builds an elaborate picture of Zembla complete with samples of a constructed language, that he is insane and that his identification with King Charles is a delusion, as perhaps all of Zembla is.

 Themes

Artist, Art, and Criticism Perhaps even more dynamic than the conflict between Gradus and King Charles is the inherent conflict between John Shade, the author of the poem "Pale Fire," and Charles Kinbote, the expert who writes extensive commentary on the poem. In terms of volume, it is immediately obvious to the reader that the critic's commentary is far longer and far more involved than the actual poem. Kinbote really ceases to be a critic and he creates his own work of creative literature, presenting a romantic portrait of an exiled king and a crystal land. The question remains as to which work of art is true; this is complicated because both the poem and the commentary follow the conventions of their respective genre. The poem "Pale Fire" is "art about art." We find that the artist John Shade primarily defines himself in terms of his artistic and aesthetic experiences. Likewise, the use of the written text in Kinbote's hands is much like Humbert in Nabokov's *Lolita*, who writes as a means of immortalizing himself and his love.

Reality, Disguise, and Delusion Charles Kinbote is really at the center of this theme, as one of the novel's plot elements forces the question of whether or not Charles Kinbote is really King Charles the Beloved of Zembla. Either reality has been seriously disrupted and Kinbote is the exiled king of Zembla or else Kinbote is dangerously delusional. Kinbote's descriptions of his rival critics and professors have a way of making him seem less honest and less professional. For that matter, Sybil explicitly states that Kinbote is deranged. The difference between the poem and the biography that Kinbote produces also suggests that reality is difficult to understand in a comprehensive, satisfying way.

Besides the disguise of Charles the Beloved as Charles Kinbote of New Wye, there is the red-clad escape from the Zemblan palace and the one hundred look-alike Royalists. Gradus, the incompetent assassin is nonetheless, a man full of disguises and pseudonyms. D'Argus, Gradus, Degre becomes disguises that also refer to the meaning of disguise. Not mere pseudonyms, D'Argus and Gradus are anagrams. Gradus and Degre refer to gradations of change, from one identity to another. Gradus' disguises meet with varying degrees of success in New Wye. The irony of all of the efforts to disguise oneself is the fact that Gradus makes his way to New Wye quite by accident. When Gradus has the opportunity to kill Charles Kinbote (who may or may not be the exiled king of Zembla), he accidentally kills John Shade (who is definitely not the exiled king of Zembla). In the end, none of Kinbote's commentary can be assumed to be "true."

Exile and Memory Exile is one of the autobiographical themes that dominate the body of Nabokov's major work. There is, of course, a major parallel between Nabokov who left Russia and Charles the Beloved/Charles Kinbote, who flees Zembla (a Russia-like place, whose name is, in fact, derived from that of a Russian island Novaya Zemlya). There is generally a combination of nostalgia and memory-loss in addressing one's homeland. Kinbote remains full of nostalgia to the point that he sees Zembla, his "crystal land" in John Shade's descriptions of the wintry New England landscape. It is also worth noting that Kinbote is double-exiled, for after leaving Zembla, he moves to New Wye only to be ostracized after the events surrounding John Shade's death. He is literally writing the commentary from some hideout among the desolate caves of the American West.

Fate and Destiny The idea of fate and destiny is challenged throughout Nabokov's novel. The underlying argument that Nabokov essentially makes is that there are so many accidents (so much chaos) that it is difficult to thread a direct connection between "act" and "consequence." The most dramatic example of this is the murder of John Shade by Gradus, an assassin who intended to kill the disguised exiled king of Zembla. If fate does exist, Nabokov shows that it is not determined by intention, but can be foiled by disguises and by human error. The idea of destiny is related to "purpose." On the one hand, the exiled king represents the idea of destiny (dynasty) gone awry; on the other hand, Gradus, the assassin, is described as a man who is inept but full of purpose. His trajectory goes from Zembla, through Europe, across the Atlantic and deep into New England, and it is described as the workings of fate to bring murderer to victim. Logically, the concept of "fate" cannot really be proven or denied.

Literary Techniques

In *Pale Fire*, Nabokov constructs a complicated and labyrinthine narrative by using a game of words including multilingual puns, anagrams, wordplay (containing palindrome, the alphabetic games, and word golf), and language games. His purpose is to invite the reader to perform and participate in his games and make the reader feel pleased in the course of trying to go out of the labyrinth. The following are two notable techniques he utilized as a preeminent postmodernist.

Intertextuality In writing *Pale Fire*, Nabokov blows up the previous unification of poetry and fiction, turns his fictional world inside out, pours out all the fragmented contents in it on the table top, leaving the work of integrating poetry and narration to the reader to do as well as possible. The intertextual characteristics are very obvious in the correlative relationship between Shade poem and Kinbote's commentary, which are basically not related to each other in contents, forming a juxtaposition of two texts of different genres and embodying hybridization, one of the characteristics of the reconstructive tendency of postmodernism. Kinbote annotates the poem in such a way that he just extends a word or a phrase mentioned in Shade's poem to narrate his own story. By unfolding the three stories such as the escape of Charles the Second, the friendship of Kinbote and Shade, and Gradus' hunting down the disguised king in the sequence of time, Nabokov invites even the most conservative reader to find the comic nature of the novel produced by the inconsistency between the poem and the commentary. The special aesthetic effect produced by the poem and the commentary lies where they associate each other: they intertextualize and intercross each other from the beginning to the end, expressing a common theme: the awful solitude of the self and the attempt to crush it; it is just from these two texts that are seemingly unrelated to each other but actually interdependent in existence that the reader spells over the moral of the pale fire: between different lonely people, between a poet and a critic, between a realist and a romanticist, between people living in different conditions or working in different fields, even if they speak different languages, they may still interplay and communicate with each other.

Parody Nabokov creates not only the "correlated pattern in the game" but also "pleasure" for the reader by cleverly and fully using parody and many kinds of implications in *Pale Fire*. By reading Kinbote's "Commentary," the reader gradually becomes aware that he is in the face of an unreliable, stupid, pedantic, demure, especially infinitely arrogant editor. The image of Kinbote seems to embody all the worst shortcomings that an editor may have.

Shade's poem is also an obvious parody of Pope's poem "An Essay on Man" (1734). There are quotations from Pope's poem and similar to Pope's poem, Shake's "Pale Fire" is also written in heroic couplets and discusses the meaning of life. The difference between them lies in that Pope enters the general philosophical discussion about the meaning of life while Shade as a pot-romantic poet would rather solve the problem in the subjective way of looking back on his personal life and the things that he has experienced in his life. However, Shade's systematic thinking does not lead him to penetrate the essence and the aim of life but on the contrary the essence and aim of life are exposed to him through his accidental discovery of the similarity between the structure of life and that of art, which is "…not text, but texture; not the dream / But topsy-turvial coincidence, / Not flimsy nonsense, but a web of sense." Even like Pope, Shade also ironically and satirically discusses the attempt to have a more precise picture of the otherworldliness in his poem. With the method of parody, Nabokov denies the philosophical discussion about the meaning of life that is considered meaningless in the postmodern times.

Metafiction As a typical metafiction, *Pale Fire* focuses more on the fictionality rather on following a clear plot and the usual development of traditional novels. To initial appearances, *Pale Fire* is the final, unfinished poem by renowned poet John Shade, with a forward and commentary by fellow university instructor Charles Kinbote. The poem is clear and simple and orderly from its form to its contents but it is only a small part of the whole book. Kinbote's "Commentary," however, is a peritext which explicates the poem surprisingly little. Focusing instead on his own concerns about the "distant northern land" Zembla, he divulges what proves to be the plot piece by piece, some of which can be connected by following the many cross-references, and the reader must attempt to discern the layers of illusive truth behind the tale. Thus the novel is a mixture of poetry and commentary, fiction and facts, reality and history with fragments and collages.

Unreliable Narrator *Pale Fire* magnifies vastly the effects of *Lolita*'s unreliable narrator. The convention of the "unreliable narrator" is when an account is demonstrably erroneous or biased, not necessarily because the narrator is lying but because something—such as age, vanity, spite, questionable sanity—causes his or her presentation of "the facts" to be distorted. While modernist fictionists can determine in what ways and the degree to which a narrator is being unreliable, the unreliable narration in *Pale Fire*, by contrast, is much more destabilizing. In the end, the reader's option is to accept that a number of possibilities have equal validity.

The first impression on encountering the novel is not of being immersed in a fully realized world, but that the reader must come to this world through a collection of different texts. The main text, the poem "Pale Fire" is framed by texts written by the critic, Charles Kinbote. The structure of book can be illuminated by Gérard Genette's theory of "paratexts," his term for the various kinds of texts which supplement a "main" text, such as the dedication, the preface or postscripts in the work, or an interview with the author, letters or diaries by the author. The function of Kinbote's paratexts conforms to Genette's theory, only more obviously so—their explicitness about their purpose expressing what most "real" paratext keep implicit. Kinbote is trying deliberately to steer the reader towards a particular reading of the poem. In his foreword he writes: "Let me state that without my notes Shade's text simply has no reality at all since the human reality of such a poem as his…has to depend entirely on the reality of its author and his surroundings, attachments and so forth, a reality that only my notes can provide." "For better or worse," the "Foreword" concludes, "it is the commentator who has the last word." He insists that the poem is a meditation on the land of Zembla and that his own friendship with Shade and his tales of the exiled king of Zembla "Charles the Beloved" have inspired the poet to write this veiled tribute to the King. Given that Zembla nor Charles are never mentioned directly in the poem, swallowing this reading takes some persuasion. In his efforts to persuade, Kinbote's reading of specific images and lines stretch credibility. The words "that crystal land," for example, are interpreted by Kinbote as being "Perhaps as allusion to Zembla, my fair country."

Nabokov does not provide linear and hierarchical narrative for one single truth of the story, instead, he gives the reader many plausible texts—each story, each reading of the text is potentially as valid as the other. Not even the "real, real story," "the plane of ordinary sanity and common sense" can be considered final. This means that even Kinbote's "Zemblan" reading of the poem does have certain validity, even though it appears untenable because these are no direct references to the country anywhere. The interpretive gymnastics *Pale Fire* invites is a way of asking readers not to solve the mysteries of the text so much as to consider what a legitimate reading of the text is. Kinbote's narration is undoubtedly partial, even delusive, but just in this way, Nabokov exposes the partiality of all narration.

Bibliography

Chen, Shidan. *A Study of American Postmodernist Fiction*. Tianjin: Nankai University Press, 2010. 227–264.

Gray, Richard. *A History of American Literature*. Cornwall: Blackwell Publishing Ltd., 2004. 768–771.

Nicol, Bran. *The Cambridge Introduction of Postmodern Fiction*. Cambridge U.K. and New York: Cambridge University Press, 2009. 83–86.

Oakes, Elizabeth H. *American Writers*. New York: Facts on File, Inc., 2004. 252–253.

Yang, Renjing & Chen Shidan, eds. *Selected Readings in American Postmodernist Fiction*. Beijing: Foreign Languages Teaching and Research Press, 2009. 49–51.

http://en.wikipedia.org/wiki/Vladimir_Nabokov 2013-02-15

http://en.wikipedia.org/wiki/Pale_Fire 2013-02-15

http://www.newworldencyclopedia.org/entry/Vladimir_Nabokov 2013-02-16

http://www.novelguide.com/PaleFire/index.html 2013-02-16

http://www.gradesaver.com/pale-fire/study-guide/major-themes/ 2013-02-16

434

A History of American Literature
美国文学史

Toni Morrison

Her Life and Writing Career

Her Life

Considered one of the foremost figures in contemporary American fiction, Toni Morrison (1931—) has won international acclaim for works in which she examines the role of race in American society. Her novels are known for their epic themes, vivid dialogue, and richly detailed characters. Her novels explore issues of African-American female identity in stories that integrate elements of the oral tradition, postmodern literary techniques, and magical realism to give voice to the experiences of women living on the margins of white American society. Among her best-known novels are *The Bluest Eye* (1970), *Sula* (1974), *Song of Solomon* (1977), and *Beloved* (1987). As a best-selling African-American female author, Morrison represented a breakthrough for other black women novelists to succeed in the mainstream publishing industry. But Morrison's work does not only focus on black experience of white racism. There is a recurring interest in black people who have acquired social status through accommodating themselves to white society and by approaching white values. Of course, Morrison herself has been very successful as a writer and as a university teacher.

Morrison once received the Pulitzer Prize, the National Book Critics Circle Award and in 1993, she became the first African-American writer to receive the Nobel Prize in Literature. The citation for the award reads: "Toni Morrison, who in novels characterizes by visionary force and poetic import, gives life to an essential aspect of American reality." In 1996, she received National Book Foundation Medal for Distinguished Contribution to American Letters. In April 2012, it was announced she would be awarded the Presidential Medal of Freedom, and on May 29, 2012, she received the award.

Toni Morrison was born Chloe Anthony Wofford in Lorain, Ohio. Her parents had moved to the North to escape the problems of southern racism and she grew up relatively unscarred by racial prejudices. Hers was a family of migrants, sharecroppers on both sides. She spent her childhood in the midwest and read voraciously, from Jane Austen to Tolstoy.

From her farther, Chloe gained a Marcus-Garvey-like perspective on whites, one that left her with distrust for them all. In 1949 she entered Howard University in Washington, D.C., America's most distinguished black college. There she changed her name from "Chloe" to "Toni," explaining once that people found "Chloe" too difficult to pronounce. After obtaining a degree in English and in the classics, Morrison enrolled in graduate school at Cornell University where she wrote her master's thesis on the works of William Faulkner and Virginia Woolf, and received her MA in 1955.

In 1955, Morrison began her teaching career at the Texas Southern University. She returned to Howard in 1957 as an English instructor and began working on her own writing. It was there that she met and married Harold Morrison, a Jamaican architect. They divorced in 1964, and Morrison moved to Syracuse, New York to become an editor for Random House. There she edited books by such black authors as Toni Cade Bambara and Gayl Jones. She also continued to teach at two branches of the State University of New York. In 1984 she was appointed to an Albert Schweitzer chair at the University of New York at Albany, where she nurtured young writers through two-year fellowships.

 ## Her Writing Career

While teaching at Howard University and caring for her two children, Morrison wrote her first novel, *The Bluest Eye* (1970). With the publication of the book, Morrison also established her new identity, which she later in 1992 rejected: "I am really Chloe Anthony Wofford. That's who I am. I have been writing under this other person's name. I write some things now as Chloe Wofford, private things. I regret having called myself Toni Morrison when I published my first novel, *The Bluest Eye*." The story is set in the community of a small, midwestern town. Its characters are all black. The book was partly based on a story Morrison wrote for a writers' group in 1966, which she had joined after the break-up of her six-year marriage with the Jamaican architect Harold Morrison. Pecola Breedlove, the central character, is a black girl, who prays each night for the blue-eyed beauty of Shirley Temple. She believes everything would be all right if only she had beautiful blue eyes. The narrator, Claudia MacTeer, tries to understand the destruction of Pecola. Although *The Bluest Eye* received scant notice at first, Morrison's career as a nationally recognized author was launched with the success of *Sula* (1974), her second novel, after which *The Bluest Eye* was retrospectively given renewed consideration as an important work of fiction. *Sula* depicts two black women friends and their community of Medallion, Ohio. It follows the lives of Sula, considered a threat against the community, and her cherished friend Nel, from their childhood to maturity and to death. The novel won the National Book Critics Award.

With the publication of *Song of Solomon* (1977), a family chronicle comparable to Alex Haley's *Roots*, Morrison gained international attention. *Song of Solomon* won the National book Critics Circle Award. It was the main selection of the Book-of-the-Month Club, the first novel by a black writer to be chosen since Richard Wright's *Native Son* in 1949. Morrison wrote the book from a male point of view. The story dealt with Milkman Dead's efforts to recover his "ancient properties," a cache of gold. After the success of *Song of Solomon* Morrison bought a four-story house near Nyack, N.Y. Since 1989, she has maintained a post as professor of Humanities at Princeton University.

Morrison published her next novel, *Beloved*, in 1987. A central incident in the work involves a fugitive slave who murders her infant daughter to spare her a life in bondage. Morrison based this scenario on an article she read in a nineteenth-century magazine while editing *The Black Book* (1974), and unconventional history of blacks in America, for Random House. Like Sethe, the protagonist of *Beloved*, Margaret Garner was a runaway slave who was tracked by her owner to Cincinnati, where she sought refuge with her freed mother-in-law. Faced with imminent capture, Garner attempted to murder her four children, succeeding in killing one. "I just imagined the life of a dead girl which was the girl that Margaret Garner killed," Morrison explained. "And I call her *Beloved* so that I can filter all these confrontations and questions that she has…and then to extend her life…her search, her quest." In *Beloved*, Sethe's daughter returns from the grave after twenty years, seeking revenge for her death. The highly acclaimed novel became a source of controversy several months after publication. When *Beloved* failed to win National Book Award in 1987, forty-eight prominent black writers and critics signed a tribute to Morrison's career and published it in the January 24, 1988, edition of the *New York Times Book Review*. The writers' statement promoted heated debate within the New York literary community, and some critics charged Morrison's supporters with racist manipulation. In 1988, *Beloved* received the Pulitzer Prize.

Beloved was adapted into the 1998 film of the same name starring Oprah Winfrey and Danny Glover. Morrison later used Margaret Garner's life story again in the libretto for a new opera, *Margaret Garner*, with music by Richard Danielpour. In May 2006, *The New York Times Book Review* named *Beloved* the best American novel published in the previous twenty-five years.

Although her novels typically concentrate on black women, Morrison does not identify her works as feminist. She has stated that she thinks "it's off-putting to some readers, who may feel that I'm involved in writing some kind of feminist tract. I don't subscribe to patriarchy, and I don't think it should be substituted with matriarchy. I think it's a question of equitable access, and opening doors to all sorts of things."

Morrison's overarching thematic concern throughout her oeuvre is with issues of African-American female identity in the contemporary world. Her novels offer complex examinations of problems within the African-American community, power dynamics between men and women, and issues of racism in relations between black and white America. Morrison's primary interest lies with the experiences of African-American women, whose quests for individual identity are integrally intertwined with their community and their cultural history.

Toni Morrison has published 10 main masterpieces as follows: *The Bluest Eye* (1970), *Sula* (1974), *Song of Solomon* (1977), *Beloved* (1987), *Tar Baby* (1981), *Jazz* (1992), *Paradise* (1997), *Love* (2003), *A Mercy* (2008), and *Home* (2012).

Analysis of and Comment on Her Representative Novel

Song of Solomon (1977)

Plot Summary

Song of Solomon is based around the search of a young black man, Milkman Dead, for his legacy. He has been brought up in a family where his father has shunned his own community whilst striving to become a small businessman represented by white people. His mother has been ostracized by her husband because he believed he had discovered her in a Negrophile relationship with her father. Milkman's adolescence and early adulthood are years of irresponsibility and of indifference to the emerging civil rights movement of the time. But he quests for the lost, family gold eventually a search for spiritual values and for the black ancestry in which he had previously shown no interest and which had also been denied by his father. His spiritual mentor in this search and the guardian of the lore he hopes to find is his aunt, Pilate, another member of the family disowned by his father because she is not respectable enough for him.

Macon Dead Jr. is the only father in the novel who is physically present with his children, but his presence is so overpowering that it appears to do more harm than good. Cold, controlling, and domineering, Macon rules his household like a tyrant. With a wife who is "stunned into silence" by his rejection, two "half-grown" daughters, and a son who refuses to accept responsibility for his life, Macon exemplifies the western patriarch whose penchant for order and discipline provides him with the illusion of being in control.

Milkman's mother (Ruth Foster Dead) is the daughter of the town's only black doctor; she makes her husband feel inadequate, and it is clear she idolized her father, Doctor Foster, to the point of obsession. After her father dies, her husband claims to have found her in bed with the dead body, sucking his fingers. Ruth later tells Milkman that she was kneeling at her father's bedside kissing the only part of him that remained unaffected by the illness from which he died. These conflicting stories expose the problems between his parents and show Milkman that "truth" is difficult or impossible to obtain. Macon (Jr.) is often violently aggressive towards Ruth because he believes that she was involved sexually with her father and loved her father more than her own husband. On one occasion, Milkman punches his father after he strikes Ruth, exposing the growing rift between father and son.

In contrast, Macon Dead Jr.'s sister, Pilate, is seen as nurturing—an Earth Mother character. Born without a navel, she is a somewhat mystical character. It is strongly implied that she is Divine—a female Christ—in spite of her name. Macon Jr. has not spoken to his sister for years and does not think highly of her. She, like Macon, has had to fend for herself from an early age after their father's murder, but she has dealt with her past in a different way than Macon, who has embraced money as the way to show his love for his father. Pilate has a daughter, Reba, and a granddaughter named Hagar. Hagar falls desperately and obsessively in love with Milkman, and is unable to cope with his rejection, attempting to kill him at least six times.

Hagar is not the only character who attempts to kill Milkman. Guitar, Milkman's erstwhile best friend, tries to kill Milkman more than once after incorrectly suspecting that Milkman has cheated him out of hidden gold, a fortune he planned to use to help his Seven Days group fund their revenge killings in response to killings of blacks.

Searching for the gold near the old family farm in Pennsylvania, Milkman stops at the rotting Butler Mansion, former home of the people who killed his ancestor to claim the farm. Here he meets Circe, an almost supernaturally old ex-slave of the Butlers. She tells Milkman of his family history and this leads him to the town of Shalimar. There he learns his great-grandfather Solomon was said to have escaped slavery by flying back to Africa, leaving behind twenty-one children and his wife Ryna, who goes crazy with loss. Returning home, he learns that Hagar has died of a broken heart. He accompanies Pilate back to Shalimar, where she is accidentally shot and killed by Guitar, who had intended to kill Milkman.

Themes

Acceptance and Return to African American Culture In *Song of Solomon*, Macon Dead is the epitome of the black man who has acquiesced to the white capitalist system. Estranged from his family, his community, and his African heritage, Macon is hated and feared by blacks, who detest his arrogance, and ignored and ostracized by whites, who use him primarily to keep black tenants in their place. A fervent believer in the mythological American dream, Macon prizes his ring of keys, which distinguishes him as a man of property. Convinced that his wealth will compensate for his race, Macon has no time for lower-class blacks, whom he considers beneath him socially and economically. As a result, he finds himself spiritually and psychologically estranged from himself and others, desperately clinging to the illusion that material success is all he needs to make his life worthwhile.

Pilate is the ancestor who, as the critic Stelamaris Coser notes, represents "the only sign of a vital black tradition surviving in the urban industrial environment." Milkman's "pilot" on his "flight" home, she defies virtually every stereotype of a black woman and exemplifies Morrison's rejection of binary thinking. Just as Milkman fails to recognize Pilate's innate beauty and dignity until he sees it reflected in the women of Shalimar, readers may fail to recognize her courage and power until they place it within the context of African history and classical mythology. Viewed from these perspectives, readers find that Pilate is both a storyteller and village elder, charged with preserving the cultural memory of her people, and a wise, moral teacher who offers a new vision of the future. A conjurer and root woman skilled in the art of voodoo, she is a healer and peacemaker who has no qualms about resorting to any means necessary to protect those she loves.

Even according to conventional Eurocentric standards, Pilate is the true hero: Odysseus wanders for ten years; Pilate wanders for twenty years and experiences a series of adventures that shape her character and free her to make hard choices concerning her role in society. From the moment she emerges from her mother's womb, she creates herself, improving her situation by working her way up from washerwoman to entrepreneur. Unlike her brother, Macon, who inherits his wealth from Ruth, Pilate creates her own way. And unlike Odysseus, whose journey is aided by gods and goddesses with supernatural powers, Pilate herself is endowed with supernatural powers; she completes her journey without the help of others' magic or divine intervention. She is a courageous woman who assumes full responsibility for her life and meets life head on, but because she is neither white and male nor young and beautiful, her accomplishments are discounted and her wisdom discredited—even by the black community.

Song of Solomon explores the quest for cultural identity. Based on the African-American folktale about enslaved Africans who escape slavery by flying back to Africa, it tells the story of Macon "Milkman" Dead, a young man alienated from himself and estranged from his family, his community, and his historical and cultural roots. Milkman is mentally enslaved and spiritually dead, but with the help of his eccentric aunt, Pilate, and his best friend, Guitar Bains, he embarks on a physical and spiritual journey that enables him to reconnect with his past and realize his self-worth.

Through Milkman's quest, this novel introduces an important theme: the acceptance and return to African American culture. It is the return that helps Milkman find his root and acquire his maturity and identity. The novel also depicts the alienating effects of racism. Racism is the central cause of suffering in the novel. It has long-lasting damaging effects on the community, the knowledge that his father died because of his white employers' negligence made Guitar especially sensitive to the injustices perpetrated against African-American, and transformed him into a ruthless, vengeful murder. Guitar's story shows that racism alienates its victims from their native communities and causes them to lose touch with their own humanity.

With the help of Pilate and Guitar, Milkman eventually discovers the secret of Solomon's song once he recognizes the vital link between the past and the future. His mission to find Pilate's gold takes him back to his ancestral roots, enabling him to learn the origin of his name and to reconnect with the black community—his "tribe."

Flight   The concept of flight is clearly addressed in the beginning of the novel with Mr. Smith's jump—his attempt to fly. Although flight may have positive attributes of the possibility of escape, it also contains negative connotations. Escape suggests leaving behind one's old world and thus pain for those left behind. Solomon, who flew back to Africa, leaves behind his wife Ryna and their twenty-one children. Solomon's departure, although happy in the face of his struggle with slavery, is disastrous for Ryna, who goes mad with grief. Milkman's escape from Not Doctor Street, a relief from his daily unhappiness, is devastating for Hagar, who eventually dies from heartbreak. The overall theme of flight, therefore, is associated with abandonment. Although it is an impossible feat, flight is regarded as natural in the novel. It is believed that Milkman's great-grandfather, Solomon, literally flew away by simply spinning around with his arms spread out until he elevated. Milkman, at the beginning of the novel, spiritually dead and mentally enslaved by apathy and materialism, embarks on a quest for his inheritance, which he initially believes to be Pilate's gold. Instead, through a series of mishaps and coincidences, he finds himself on a spiritual quest for his identity. Eventually he learns the meaning of grace and mercy, and he inherits the gift of flight.

The community's acceptance of flight as normal highlights Morrison's use of magical realism in her writing. Even the novel's epigraph, "The fathers may soar and the children may know their names," references the theme of flight.

Allusions in Characters' Names   Names hold a special significance in regards to each character. Pilate, a biblical reference to the Roman governor who allowed the execution of Jesus Christ, shares some similar traits with her namesake, such as strength and power. Although she is not cruel in her authority, Pilate is a male name suggesting that she bears the stereotypical characteristics of a man, at least as perceived by society at the time. Circe's name bears homage to the enchantress in Homer's *Odyssey*, who provides Odysseus with crucial information on how to end his voyage. In *Song of Solomon*, Circe supplies Milkman with segments of his family history, so that he may end his search for his family heritage. Hagar, a biblical name, is a direct explanation of her strained and desperate relationship with Milkman, who abandons her, as can be predicted through the Bible.

The family surname of Dead is a spiritual wordplay. Milkman's family accidentally received the name from white oppressors, thus suggesting that their real name died, and at that point, so did their family history. The importance of names relates to a sense of belonging, to being able to trace one's roots through the ages. Throughout the entire novel, there are continuous references to Milkman being Dead, both in terms of name and character. Upon Milkman's rebirth, he no longer can be called Dead, neither by name nor by personality.

Singing   The theme of singing and songs is a reference not only to the African oral tradition but also to the days of slavery. Slaves, as means of getting through their work on the plantation, sang spirituals. Such songs talked of faith and hope, and how to live with the spirit of God. Singing was a way in which slaves could express their personal feelings, and it was also a means of cheering one another up. Many songs also contained "secret messages," for instance making indirect references to the Underground Railroad.

The act of singing communicates the importance of the oral tradition, demonstrated through Pilate's "Oh Sugarman done fly away..." The song, originally a reference to Solomon, tells the tale of Milkman's great-grandfather. It is this song that transmits Milkman's family history, and steers him towards his spiritual rebirth. Overall, songs underline the rebuilding of a spiritual and emotional bond. In the novel, Pilate, Hagar, and Reba all bond through the act of singing. And, after Hagar's death, Reba and Pilate comfort one another through a song.

Racial Injustice As a black man, Macon's lack of compassion is illustrated in his treatment of Porter and Mrs. Bains, both tenants of his, but it is especially evident in his treatment of his sister, Pilate, whom he despises for refusing to conform to his rigidly defined standards of correct behavior. His disdain and lack of respect for other blacks are also evident in his speech, which echoes the beliefs and stereotypes of racist whites—he is the first one in the novel to use the word "nigger" to refer to Porter, Pilate, and Guitar.

Toni Morrison emphasizes the country's state of racial injustice. Chapter One mentions racial uplift groups and makes note of segregated hospitals to create a focus on race. Further emphasis is placed on white oppression in regards to race as Guitar remembers that his mother received four ten dollar bills for his father's body. The reasons for Guitar's anger towards whites are reemphasized in his unfair treatment by a white nurse. His hatred grows to transform him into a revengeful fiend who loses his humanity. The Seven Days society, of which Guitar is a member of, takes justice into their own hands.

Wealth The pursuit of money and property is a struggle for which Macon Dead II has sacrificed his humanity. Macon inherited his initial wealth through Ruth. Not satisfied with his wife's inheritance, his insatiable greed prompts him to try to steal his sister's inheritance—gold—as well. The gold further accents his greed, and his desire for monetary objects consumes Milkman as well. Although Macon's longing to accumulate worldly goods is a sign of bereavement for his father, his manner of mourning soon turns against him. Milkman's search for the gold becomes a search for his identity, his real inheritance.

The Color White Throughout the novel, black and white colors are used to differentiate between good and evil. Stereotypically, on the one hand, society associates white with good and black with evil. *Song of Solomon*, on the other hand, presents the color white as a symbol of malevolence. All the white characters as well as white symbols represent wrongdoing and/or violence. Guitar's father's employer, who is white, gives his mother forty dollars for his father's dead body, a suggestion of how much a black man is thought to be worth. Corinthian's employer, white as well, also does not regard her employee as an equal, although she claims her views are liberal. Freddie's description of his mother's death involves a white bull. And the white peacock that Milkman and Guitar chase represents greed.

Literary Techniques

Quality of Speech Morrison's prose has the quality of speech. She deliberately strives for this effect, which she calls "aural literature." She hears her prose as she writes, and during the revision process she cuts phrasing which sounds literary or written rather than spoken. She rejects critics' assertions that her prose is rich; to those who say her prose is poetic, she responds that metaphors are natural in black speech. Morrison wants readers to participate in her novels, to be involved actively. Readers are encouraged to create the novel with her and to help construct meaning.

Postmodern Meta-Narratives Morrison's fictions are self-consciously concerned with myth, legend, storytelling, and the oral tradition, as well as with memory, history, and historiography, and have thus been recognized as postmodern meta-narratives. Morrison's stories are conscious of African cultural heritage as well as Africa-American history, thus demonstrating the importance of the past to the struggles of contemporary African-Americans. She employs strong elements of Black English in her dialogue and narration to express the importance of language in the formation of identity.

One of the most important concerns in her writing is the "use value" of narrative. Storytelling is historiography in Morrison's fiction, and in most novels she carefully examines the role of narrative in the reconstitution of both the individual self and society at large.

Magical Realism Morrison uses fantasy, folktales, supernatural and mythic elements along with realistic depiction of racial, gender, and class conflict. Her style combines these unrealistic elements with a realistic presentation of life and characters. This mixture has been called "magical realism."

Bibliography

常耀信. 美国文学简史.（第二版修订本）. 天津：南开大学出版社，2006. 541–545.

Bouson, J. Brooks. *Quiet As It's Kept*. Albany: State University of New York Press, 1999. 75–98.

Gunton, Sharon R. & Jean C. Stine, eds. *Contemporary Literary Criticism, Vol. 22*. Detroit,

Michigan: Gale Research Company, 1982. 314–320.

Hunter, Jeffrey W. ed. *Contemporary Literary Criticism, Vol.194.* Farmington Hills: Thomson Gale, 2005. 150–160.

Peach, Linden. *Toni Morrison.* New York: St. Martin's Press, 2000. 65–101.

Samuels, W. D. & Celnora Hudson-Weems. *Toni Morrison.* Boston: Twayne Publishers, 1990. 58–78.

http://en.wikipedia.org/wiki/Toni_Morrison 2013-02-15

http://www.newworldencyclopedia.org/entry/Toni_Morrison 2013-02-15

后　记

　　《美国文学史》（上、下）作为高等学校英语专业本科生美国文学课程使用的教学用书，是中国人民大学外国语学院院长何其莘教授与杨孝明教授担任总主编的高校本科英语专业"超越概念"系列教材的一部分。其内容、规模和体例的设计等均在总主编何其莘教授与杨孝明教授的指导和大力支持下进行。中国人民大学出版社领导高度重视本书的编写工作，对本书编写内容、规模、体例等提出了宝贵的指导意见，负责该书的编辑同志们为本书的出版做了大量深入细致的工作。在此，本书编写组特向何其莘教授与杨孝明教授以及中国人民大学出版社领导和外语分社的编辑表示衷心的感谢！

　　《美国文学史》（上、下）的编写分工如下：陈世丹、屈晓丽担任主编，负责全书内容、规模、体例设计，陈世丹负责第一、第二、第三、第六部分的统稿工作，屈晓丽负责第四、第五部分的统稿工作，最后由陈世丹统合成书、修改、定稿。

　　全书各章节编写分工如下：

PART I　AMERICAN LITERATURE IN THE COLONIAL PERIOD (1607—1700)

　　　　史岩林：Historical Introduction

　　　　　　　　American Puritanism

　　　　　　　　Early New England Literature

　　　　　　　　John Smith

　　　　　　　　John Cotton

　　　　　　　　Roger Williams

　　　　　　　　Anne Bradstreet

　　　　　　　　Edward Taylor

PART II　AMERICAN LITERATURE IN THE AGE OF REASON AND REVOLUTION (1700—1800)

　　　　张东芹：Historical Introduction

Modernism

Terms of Modernist Literature

吴银燕：Ezra Pound

Robert Frost

Wallace Stevens

T. S. Eliot

尹　宇：F. Scott Fitzgerald

屈晓丽：Ernest Hemingway

William Faulkner

王阿芳：Eugene O'Neill

Arthur Miller

PART VI　AMERICAN LITERATURE IN THE POSTMODERN PERIOD (1945—　)

陈世丹：Historical Introduction

Postmodernism

Postmodernist Fiction

Metafiction

吴泽庆：Robert Lowell

Charles Olson

张丽秀：Joseph Heller

陈世丹：Kurt Vonnegut

张丽秀：John Barth

Donald Barthelme

尹　宇：Thomas Pynchon

Vladimir Nabokov

王阿芳：Toni Morrison

主　编

2013 年 7 月 20 日

图书在版编目（CIP）数据

美国文学史 / 陈世丹，屈晓丽主编 . —北京：中国人民大学出版社，2013.9
（超越概念）
高等院校英语专业系列教材
ISBN 978-7-300-17976-6

Ⅰ.①美…　Ⅱ.①陈…　②屈…　Ⅲ.①英语-阅读教学-高等学校-教材　②文学史-美国-高等学校-教材
Ⅳ.①H319.4：I

中国版本图书馆 CIP 数据核字（2013）第 202939 号

超越概念——高等院校英语专业系列教材
总主编　何其莘　［美］杨孝明
美国文学史
主　编　陈世丹　屈晓丽
编　者　（以姓名拼音首字母为序）
　　　　陈世丹　李金云　屈晓丽　史岩林　苏　凤
　　　　王阿芳　王桃花　吴银燕　吴泽庆　尹　宇
　　　　张东芹　张丽秀　赵　丽
Meiguo Wenxue Shi

出版发行	中国人民大学出版社			
社　　址	北京中关村大街 31 号		**邮政编码**	100080
电　　话	010-62511242（总编室）		010-62511398（质管部）	
	010-82501766（邮购部）		010-62514148（门市部）	
	010-62515195（发行公司）		010-62515275（盗版举报）	
网　　址	http:// www. crup. com. cn			
	http:// www. ttrnet. com（人大教研网）			
经　　销	新华书店			
印　　刷	北京东君印刷有限公司			
规　　格	200 mm×252 mm　16 开本		**版　次**	2013 年 10 月第 1 版
印　　张	29		**印　次**	2013 年 10 月第 1 次印刷
字　　数	720 000		**定　价**	56.00 元

中国人民大学出版社外语出版分社读者信息反馈表

尊敬的读者：

感谢您购买和使用中国人民大学出版社外语出版分社的 ＿＿＿＿＿＿＿ 一书，我们希望通过这张小小的反馈卡来获得您更多的建议和意见，以改进我们的工作，加强我们双方的沟通和联系。我们期待着能为更多的读者提供更多的好书。

请您填妥下表后，寄回或传真回复我们，对您的支持我们不胜感激！

1. 您是从何种途径得知本书的：
   □书店　　　　□网上　　　　□报纸杂志　　　　□朋友推荐

2. 您为什么决定购买本书：
   □工作需要　　□学习参考　　□对本书主题感兴趣　　□随便翻翻

3. 您对本书内容的评价是：
   □很好　　　　□好　　　　□一般　　　　□差　　　　□很差

4. 您在阅读本书的过程中有没有发现明显的专业及编校错误，如果有，它们是：

   ＿＿＿

   ＿＿＿

   ＿＿＿

5. 您对哪些专业的图书信息比较感兴趣：

   ＿＿＿

   ＿＿＿

   ＿＿＿

6. 如果方便，请提供您的个人信息，以便于我们和您联系（您的个人资料我们将严格保密）：

   您供职的单位：＿＿＿＿＿＿＿＿＿＿＿＿＿＿＿＿＿＿＿＿＿＿＿＿＿＿＿＿＿＿＿＿＿

   您教授的课程（教师填写）：＿＿＿＿＿＿＿＿＿＿＿＿＿＿＿＿＿＿＿＿＿＿＿＿＿＿＿

   您的通信地址：＿＿＿＿＿＿＿＿＿＿＿＿＿＿＿＿＿＿＿＿＿＿＿＿＿＿＿＿＿＿＿＿＿

   您的电子邮箱：＿＿＿＿＿＿＿＿＿＿＿＿＿＿＿＿＿＿＿＿＿＿＿＿＿＿＿＿＿＿＿＿＿

请联系我们：黄婷　程子殊　于真妮　鞠方安

电话：010-62512737，62513265，62515037，62515576

传真：010-62514961

E-mail：huangt@crup.com.cn　　chengzsh@crup.com.cn　　yuzn@crup.com.cn
　　　　jufa@crup.com.cn

通信地址：北京市海淀区中关村大街甲 59 号文化大厦 15 层　　邮编：100872

中国人民大学出版社外语出版分社